EGYPT'S HOUSING CRISIS

EGYPT'S HOUSING CRISIS

The Shaping of Urban Space

Yahia Shawkat

Foreword by
David Sims

The American University in Cairo Press
Cairo New York

First published in 2020 by
The American University in Cairo Press
113 Sharia Kasr el Aini, Cairo, Egypt
One Rockefeller Plaza, New York, NY 10020
www.aucpress.com

Dar el Kutub No. 10611/19
ISBN 978 977 416 957 1

Dar el Kutub Cataloging-in-Publication Data

Shawkat, Yahia
Egypt's Housing Crisis: The Shaping of Urban Space / Yahia Shawkat.—Cairo: The American University in Cairo Press, 2020.
p. cm.
ISBN 978 977 416 957 1
1. Housing
2. Political Science
3. Public Administration
363.5

1 2 3 4 5 24 23 22 21 20

Designed by Adam el-Sehemy
Printed in the United States of America

In memory of my father, Ezzeldin Shawkat
To my wife, Alia Mossallam
To my children, Taya, Rawi, and Nura

CONTENTS

FIGURES

TABLES

TABLES

[illegible]

FOREWORD
David Sims

Housing in developing countries is a huge subject. It is a field that has produced conflicting narratives and is not a pretty story, especially in terms of housing production and exchange that is affordable to the majority and is socially equitable. This is not to say that housing markets in advanced countries are anywhere near perfect, but in poor and emerging economies—with increasing populations and rampant urbanization—it could be said there is a perfect storm, where government institutions and legislation plus the formal private sector seem congenitally unable to deliver housing that is anywhere near the needs and capacities of the majority of today's households, let alone future families under formation. Lack of access to serviced land and finance by the majority have been recognized by observers and policy makers for decades, but all of this angst about 'housing crises' has had little effect, and today the situation seems to have deteriorated, condemning more and more modest families to seek housing solutions that are outside formal structures and outside what is supposed to be the rule of law, whether by crowding into densifying urban slums, building extra-legally on the urban fringes, or encroaching on public land.

How did this situation become so intractable? Although one has recourse to a vast and growing literature about housing in particular developing countries and even across them, produced by housing specialists, academics, international development agencies, and government bodies, much of this is either contradictory, single-lensed, or downright self-serving. Wading through all of this noise is discouraging—to say the least—and thus it is extremely welcome that Yahia Shawkat has come out with his book *Egypt's Housing Crisis: The Shaping of Urban Space*. Shawkat makes a definitive contribution to the issues surrounding housing in Egypt, one that is long overdue. He manages to unpack decades of narratives about the country's 'housing problems' and 'housing crisis' by looking at how housing is really produced and financed, analyzing such elements as rural housing, informal (or self-built) housing, public housing, and various types of private sector (corporate) housing. He also weaves into his analysis the shifts in government policies toward housing, urban development, and real estate, and puts his finger on the reasons why, after so many years of increasingly irrelevant government posturing, housing solutions that are equitable and socially acceptable remain so unattainable.

The unique value of Shawkat's book, not to be found elsewhere in the various commentaries on Egypt's housing sector (whether in English or Arabic), rests on a number of angles of attack. First, he delves into early efforts by both government and visionary professionals in improving both rural and social housing in the late 19th and 20th centuries, and how this thinking was grounded in, and formulated through, the succession of ruling regimes of different political stripes, the increasing preoccupation with modernization, and the realities of overwhelming population growth, rapid urbanization, and rising elite classes. Second, he zeroes in on various subsidized government housing programs, how they were conceived and how they evolved, including the recent obsession with settling excess population in Egypt's very extensive desert. Third, he correctly identifies self-built (mainly informal) housing as the main and most suitable means of production for the majority, and he spends considerable effort at analyzing the equivocal and sometimes knee-jerk postures of government toward it, unable as it is to understand such an in-your-face reality and preoccupied with modernist, 'scientific,' and *dirigiste* principles toward the economy and toward an obsession with top-down, engineered urban development. Fourth, Shawkat reviews in detail how rental markets—including the particular distortions of rent control—have evolved from the early 20th century, and how government has been unable to provide a simple regulatory environment that would enable rental tenure to thrive, instead creating more conditions of uncertainty, insecurity and a resulting additional layer of informality. Fifth, the book looks at the recent rise of powerful real estate developers, their cozy relationships with government agencies, and the resulting accelerated commodification of housing (especially high-end luxury units) that seems increasingly to define what formal housing in Egypt is all about, with the concomitant shrinking of the concept of housing as a social good. Sixth, the book tracks how the government deals with slums and has used the objective of ridding its cities of dilapidated housing to justify neighborhood clearances and wholesale resettlement, as yet another tool to create the 'City Beautiful.' Finally, Shawkat shifts through statistics to illuminate and explain the huge phenomenon of unoccupied housing throughout Egypt—a vacancy rate which, on a per capita basis, is, by far, the highest in the world—and one that is perplexing in a country where so many families cannot find anything like suitable accommodation.

Because of the author's architectural and housing rights background, he is able to enliven and deepen the comprehension of these subjects by adding a number of concrete examples and personal stories about how people struggle to acquire, maintain, and protect their homes, further fleshed out by popular films that take up the subject. It is exceptionally rare for books on housing—about whatever country—to have this kind of tactile, human, and cultural grounding, and this helps illustrate the complex ways that personal and community relations work in the face of often times confusing and contradictory government regulations related to land, construction, and rights related to shelter.

The book benefits greatly from an omnivorous approach towards sources of data and information. In particular, the scouring of Egyptian libraries and archives yields a rich treasure of useful material, as does a combing of local newspapers, websites, government publications and statistics, most of which is only found in Arabic. Of particular value is the author's diligent reading of the copious amounts of government laws, decrees, and explanatory notes related to housing.

In the concluding chapter, Shawkat brings the various threads of the book together and posits that the Egyptian government's arbitrary policies and programs have over time created a chronic state of informality that exists in all forms of tenure—owner-built, government-built, or rented homes—and in all steps of housing production. The results are confusion and insecurity, reinforced by contradictory, almost paradoxical rules and legislation that give huge space for abuse, selective application, and not a little corruption. This state of informality, in which any clear 'rule of law' is constantly in recession, is the result of both the *dirigiste* idea of an all-powerful regime, combined with what appears to be an intentional ignorance of the reality of housing markets. It is a state of informality in which special interests and regime allies seem to be the main benefactors, something that Shawkat describes as "manufactured informality."

Even though the author deals with housing in a single country, his meticulous approach to the subject, his recourse to sources that are ignored by most, and his conclusions about 'manufactured informality' that blanket Egypt's housing sector today, all provide a methodology that could well contribute to a better understanding of and approach to housing issues in other developing countries. In fact, *Egypt's Housing Crisis* represents a fresh analytical approach to housing that those in other countries could well learn from.

ACKNOWLEDGMENTS

Like all the behind-the-scenes work on a film, the book you hold in your hands was only possible to write with the support of a great many people. Writing has been very much a part of my family, which goes some way to explaining why I have strayed from my chosen profession of architecture. I saw my grandmother, Safa Nour, tirelessly type out and edit drafts of my grandfather's memoirs, while my mother, Laila Hafez, has hundreds of news reports to her credit. My sister, Amna Shawkat, has always been the creative one. I am indebted to them for nurturing endless possibilities. The concern with data and facts you may find in this book I owe to my late father, Ezzeldin Shawkat, whose degree in library sciences and penchant for accuracy meant I could never get anything past him unless I could prove it worked. Even though he never knew about this book, he has been my main critic throughout its writing. Since I have known my wife, Alia Mossallam, she has scripted her PhD, numerous articles, and a play, most of this while taking care of three children and an adult. I would like to thank her for an endless list of giving, familial as well as professional. All I know about studying history I owe to her.

I am grateful to David Sims, who not only wrote the foreword, and encouraged me to write the book during its humble beginnings as a draft chapter, but has been an informal supervisor since I read his first book in 2010, and later when I got to know him personally. Much of the book, especially chapters 6 and 7, is based on my work as an urban researcher and housing rights officer. Therefore, I would like to thank Hossam Bahgat for inviting me to work at the Egyptian Initiative for Personal Rights in 2013 and teaching me to read laws. Until then, I don't think I had even read the traffic law. Amr Gharbeia gave me the keys to the archive, and Tarek Abdelal helped me decipher the jargon. I would also like to thank Samuel Tharwat,

Mohamed al-Kashef, Marwa Barakat, Hala Makhlouf, Ahmed Saleh, Gasser Abdel-Razek, and Khaled Mansour. Working at 10 Tooba over the last five years has meant that much information here is based on projects I have worked on there, in particular with Shaimaa Atef, Abdelrahman Hegazy and Safa Youssef, and fellow co-founders Omnia Khalil and Ahmed Zaazaa.

For their patience with my questions, I would like to thank all my anonymized interviewees who opened my eyes to happenings that ranged from the amazing to the horrific, all of which enriched my research. My father-in-law Ahmed Mossallam's encyclopedic knowledge of Egypt's political history revealed many key events I was unaware of. Ralph Bodenstein and Eric Denis generously donated sources, as did Mohamed Ezzeldin and Ali al-Adawi. I would also like to thank Lucia Carminati and Aya Nassar, who went out of their way to track down archival material, as well as Asef Bayat, Reem Saad, Mohamed Abdel Gawad, Pascale Ghazaleh, Mona Abaza, Najat Abdulhaq, Yazan Doughan, Salma Khamis, and Mohamed Wafiq for their time discussing different aspects of the book. In writing, I have been inspired by the critical investigative works of the late Milad Hanna, Timothy Mitchell, and Gehan Selim.

I am greatly indebted to my friends Karim Malak and Heba Mostafa, who made the time to review draft chapters and helped nudge them into more cohesive writing. I would like to thank Roman Stadnicki and Graham Cairns for reviewing and publishing papers that make up parts of chapters 6 and 7, as well as Nora Lafi and ZMO in Berlin for hosting talks that included sections of the book. My friend Naira Antoun did a fantastic job copy-editing a carcass of writing into a legible manuscript, and once at AUC Press, Laura Gribbon's dedication over months ensured it transformed into this book. Tarek Ghanem, formerly with the Press, and Nadia Naqib's enthusiasm egged me on; without them the words on the following pages would still be in my head.

The unthanked people behind the effort required to keep archival material and to collect data need to be mentioned here, for without them, much of the analysis would have been impossible. I'd like to thank the foot soldiers at CAPMAS, Egypt's statistics agency, for doing their monotonous job, especially with the knowledge that it might never be read. Also, the people that take care of the archives at the Bibliotheca Alexandrina, al-Arshif li-l-majallat al-adabiya wal-thaqafiya CEDEJ, the Fine Arts Library of the Harvard College Library, and the Internet Archive, especially the anonymous person(s) who uploaded al-Ahram's back catalog.

ABBREVIATIONS AND ACRONYMS

ARA	Agrarian Reform Agency
ASU	Arab Socialist Union
CAC	Central Agency for Construction
CAPMAS	Central Agency for Public Mobilization and Statistics
CEDEJ	Centre d'Études et de Documentation Économiques, Juridiques et Sociales
CRSL	Committee to Recover State Land
EARIS	Egyptian American Rural Improvement Service
EBA	Egyptian Businessmen's Association
EHF	Economic Housing Fund
EIPR	Egyptian Initiative for Personal Rights
FJP	Freedom and Justice Party
GARPAD	General Authority for Reconstruction Projects and Agricultural Development
GOHBC	General Organization for Housing and Building Cooperatives
GOPP	General Organization for Physical Planning
GSF	Guarantee and Subsidy Fund
IDSC	Information and Decision Support Center
IMF	International Monetary Fund
ISDF	Informal Settlements Development Facility
MFA	Mortgage Finance Authority
MoH	Ministry of Housing*

MoMVA	Ministry of Municipal and Village Affairs
MoRNC	Ministry of Reconstruction and New Communities
MSWC	Mahalla Spinning and Weaving Company
NDP	National Democratic Party
NHP	National Housing Program
NUCA	New Urban Communities Authority
SHF	Social Houisng Fund
SHMFF	Social Housing and Mortgage Finance Fund
SHP	Social Housing Project
UNESCO	United Nations Educational, Scientific, and Cultural Organization
WFP	World Food Program

* A number of longer names exist for the Ministry of Housing, which has witnessed many changes. However this is a general abbreviation.

TIMELINE

<table>
<tr><th></th><th>Key Events</th><th colspan="4">Official Discourse</th></tr>
<tr><td>1940s</td><td>1939–1945: Second World War, rent control imposed
1947: First serious government housing breaks ground in Imbaba
1948: Arab–Israeli War</td><td rowspan="2">mushkilat al-masakin (homes problem)</td><td></td><td></td><td></td></tr>
<tr><td>1950s</td><td>1950: Department of Popular Homes, first official office established
1952: July revolution, rent reductions, government housing expands
1953: Egyptian Republic, Muhammad Naguib becomes president
1956: Nasser elected, Suez Crisis/Tripartite Aggression, first amnesty for illegal buildings
1958: Second amnesty</td><td rowspan="2">azmit al-masakin (homes crisis)</td><td></td><td></td></tr>
<tr><td>1960s</td><td>1961: Ministry of Housing and Utilities, rent control expanded
1962: Arab Socialist Union
1966: Third amnesty
1967: Fourth amnesty
1967: Six Day War
1968: Fifth amnesty for illegal buildings</td><td></td><td rowspan="2">azmit al-iskan (housing crisis)</td><td></td></tr>
<tr><td>1970s</td><td>1970: Sadat sworn in after Nasser dies
1973: October/Yom Kippur War
1974: Infitah (Open Door Policy)
Reconstruction of Suez Canal cities
1977: Bread riots, rent control revised, new desert city program breaks ground</td><td></td><td></td><td>mushkilat al-iskan (housing problem)</td></tr>
</table>

<table>
<tr><th></th><th>Key Events</th><th colspan="4">Official Discourse</th></tr>
<tr><td>1980s</td><td>1981: Mubarak sworn in after Sadat assassinated, sixth amnesty for illegal buildings
1984: Seventh amensty
1986: Central Security conscripts riot, eighth amnesty for illegal buildings
1987: Mubarak presidential referrendum (second term)</td><td></td><td></td><td></td><td rowspan="4">mushkilat al-iskan
(housing problem)</td></tr>
<tr><td>1990s</td><td>1991: IMF/World Bank Economic Reform and Structural Adjustment Program, public spending on housing curbed
1992: October earthquake
1993: Mubarak presidential referrendum (third term), national project to upgrade slums
1996: Rents liberalized
1999: Mubarak presidential referrendum (fourth term)</td><td></td><td></td><td></td></tr>
<tr><td>2000s</td><td>2005: Mubarak elected (fifth term), 500,000-unit National Housing Project
2008: Duweiqa rockslide, national project to upgrade unsafe areas</td><td></td><td></td><td></td></tr>
<tr><td>2010s</td><td>2011: January revolution, Mubarak deposed, military council rules, million-unit Social Housing Project announced
2012: Muhammad Mursi elected
2013: June revolution, Mursi deposed, interim president rules
2014: Abd al-Fattah al-Sisi elected, Social Housing Project relaunched
2018: al-Sisi reelected (second term)
2019: Ninth amnesty for illegal buildings</td><td></td><td></td><td></td></tr>
</table>

INTRODUCTION: THE POLITICS OF SHELTER IN EGYPT

Housing is a fundamental cornerstone of Egyptian life: It can make or break marriage proposals, boom or bust the economy, and popularize or embarrass a ruler. It is debated as much as football and religion. Egypt's airwaves regularly beam footage of neat government housing and chaotic self-built settlements. Facebook is chock-full of people seeking buying advice, complaining about delayed housing projects, and protesting eviction, rent control, or a new development.

Housing is social. It is the cradle that shelters people's lives, with an entire spectrum of responses having evolved to suit the means of millions of households. Communities have mobilized to self-build, with construction completely managed by the owner down to the last detail. Other people buy their own homes, while only one-quarter of urban Egyptians rent. Those who cannot afford to build, buy, or rent are compelled to squat, some in cemetery courtyards and vacant government-built housing.

Housing is money. Buying is seen as the most effective way to invest your hard-earned cash, where local and foreign investors, as well as speculators, have taken advantage of a deregulated property market to make what they believe is a guaranteed return. The construction sector is one of the largest industries in Egypt today, employing millions. However, this deregulation by the government has also resulted in an inexorable erosion of affordability, with over half of Egyptians unable to afford median-priced homes, and millions forced to live in inadequate shelter.[1]

Housing is political. Almost every Egyptian ruler over the last nine decades, from King Fouad to President Abd al-Fattah al-Sisi, has directly associated himself with at least one large-scale housing project. In other words, housing has transcended a whole range of political ideologies—from colonial, through socialist, and then neoliberal regimes. Publicly owned housing agencies invest billions every year to build subsidized and for-profit housing. In many instances, government housing has been used as a tool to rally political support or demobilize social unrest—Advertisements for social housing would spontaneously appear in the newspapers during elections, or whenever the streets would tremble with protest.

Housing is also contentious. While most people associate a home with stability, it is only so for some people, some of the time. Millions of mostly poor, but also middle-income families, live in a state of legal or physical precarity. Those seen by the government as living in informal housing face a constant threat of eviction, and tens of thousands of families have been evicted to make way for urban development projects, or because their buildings were deemed illegal and demolished. Almost one million families live with the threat of imminent disaster, with hundreds of buildings collapsing every year[2]—many of which are damaged, left to decay, or even tampered with on purpose to allow landlords to evict rent control tenants, while the rest are shoddily constructed by unscrupulous developers.

Egypt's Housing Crisis delves into this multilayered world, tracing an almost perpetual housing crisis in Egypt. It explores the shift in official discourse over the last eight decades, from an issue of 'homes' to 'housing,' and from a 'problem' to a 'crisis' and back to a 'problem' again. While this shift in language may have happened quietly, it belies how officials in Egypt changed their view of dwellings over the last century.

An Overview

Egypt's Housing Crisis provides an urban history of housing in Egypt over the course of eighty years. It does so through a reading of the main policy elements the government has used to shape housing supply during this time: regulation and provision. Chapters 2 and 3 trace how laws have been enacted to regulate the use of private property—through the self-build process (chapter 2) and through the rental market and, briefly, the sales market (chapter 3). Chapters 4, 5, and 6 cover provision in both rural and urban settings. The final chapter shows how all forms of housing have simply unravelled, weighed down by decades of regressive policies that have only been propped up to serve particular interests. *Egypt's Housing Crisis* need not be read in any particular order, as each chapter is a standalone essay.

Chapter 1 (Etymology of a Crisis) provides a brief politico-statistical history of housing in Egypt, tracing official discourse from the 1940s to the present, providing the book's backbone, from which the reader can then branch off directly to the chapters that provide more detail. It starts by outlining the history of the discourse around housing, and then adds statistical background on housing production from the 1960s, as well as tenure patterns from the 1970s onward.

Chapter 2 (Self-builders) looks at the most popular avenue to housing. While most owners do not do the actual building themselves, this chapter details how they acquire the land, design their homes, and manage the entire building process. Chapter 2 also discusses how, despite a raft of laws outlawing many of the self-built homes, along with squatting on state-owned land, the government has de facto tolerated the practice since 1956. This was through a host of amnesties with the goal of helping to ease the homes crisis and even the extension of formal infrastructure to most settlements, but in exchange for what?

Chapter 3 (Old to New Rent) chronicles changes in rent legislation from the 1940s through the 1990s, and the major effects this has had on housing. Old Rent, which is Egypt's special blend of rent control—introduced under a colonial regime, bolstered during a socialist one, and maintained through neoliberal times—has been especially contentious. Many landlords have sought to evict tenants by condemning buildings and sometimes fatal actions that include deliberately knocking them down. Its ambiguity has also led to cases of massive fraud. The chapter then details the introduction of New Rent (market rent) in the neoliberal 1990s, with its promise to liberate vacant property and solve the housing problem. Initially it may have helped, but today, almost half of Egyptians cannot afford median rents. Meanwhile, over a million homes are still under Old Rent with growing, anxious demands from landlords to get their properties back.

Erving Goffman's concept of a 'total institution' helps explain some of chapter 4 ('Model' Villages for 'Model' Citizens). This chapter investigates how the government sought to control the rural population between the mid-nineteenth century and the end of the twentieth century. The first section of the chapter looks at *'izba*s, private hamlets that were located on large landowners' estates, which came to house a considerable portion of the population who were ruled by proxy between the 1840s and 1952. The chapter goes on to chronicle the 'model village' movement of the 1930s and 1940s, whereby the government, as well as private enterprise, aimed to reconstruct rural housing and remold people into 'model citizens.' The movement would also set the stage for later forms of mass rural housing, the

New Villages, popularized during the Arab socialist era (1952–70), resettling tens of thousands of people on desert land reclamation schemes in 'model societies.' The chapter concludes with the demise of rural population control through government villages by the end of the millennium, to be replaced by a resurgence of private agricultural workers' camps—a rebirth of the *'izba*.

The story of chapter 5 (Government Housing, a Brief History) is the evolution of urban mass housing over the last century—tracing its origins from the *musta'marat* (workers' colonies) and company towns built by private industry from the 1920s, through their popularization in the 1940s, and their transformation into government housing estates in the 1950s to solve the housing crisis. Egypt's rulers have associated themselves with mass housing, something that has made it more political than pragmatic, where the uniformity of the housing blocks belies myriad tenure options, and application regimes that changed as the politics did. The chapter concludes with the final major transformation of mass government housing in the late 1970s, from renting to ownership, or from a political social provision to a political commodity, a policy that has remained in place until today.

Chapter 6 (Government Housing Today) takes an in-depth look at current mass urban housing through two of the largest schemes in its history—Mubarak's National Housing Project, initiated as part of his election campaign in 2005, and the million-unit Social Housing Project, born amid the 2011 uprising that toppled him.

The seventh and final chapter (Housing Unravels) delves into the spectrum of informality that pervades not just self-build, but all other housing in Egypt. It examines a number of cases, some that converge from previous chapters on self-build, rent, and government housing, and others that are about state-led gentrification. All are about one form of informal tenure or another, in a climate that looks increasingly like a manufactured informality, and a bureaucratic regime that is structured so that dwellers across the income spectrum rarely have secure and stable tenure.

A Note on Sources

I have relied on a wide array of sources to cover the many facets such a fundamental issue presents. Reams of primary official documents have given the government's view on housing. Archives for both presidents Gamal Abd al-Nasser and Anwar Sadat have been compiled by the Bibliotheca Alexandrina, offering their speeches, but more importantly for Nasser, minutes of cabinet and Arab Socialist Union (ASU) meetings, a rare source of frank government material. For President Hosni Mubarak, the government's State Information Service (SIS) has published books and keeps an online archive of speeches, though these need to be accessed through the Internet Archive. SIS has been less consistent with later presidents, Muhammad Mursi and Abd al-Fattah al-Sisi, but has still provided some material.

Legislation has provided a wealth of official material, where besides the articles of the laws themselves, attached Explanatory Notes usually written by the ministers submitting the laws to parliament, are available from the 1950s through the 1990s. Attached Parliamentary Reports, generally available from the 1970s to the 1990s, have summarized the parliamentary committees' main arguments for the laws, giving a candid insight into that institution's workings. While printed volumes of the laws are available at government outlets, I have relied on a searchable subscription-based database of Egyptian legislation provided by Eastlaws.

Countless tables of statistics have enabled the matching of policy shifts to repercussions in brick and mortar. For this, I relied on the Central Agency for Public Mobilization and Statistics, known as CAPMAS, which is the main official government body in Egypt that collects statistics and produces the census. Estimations, correlations, and triangulations I made to plug gaps, smooth out inconsistencies, or address errors, are explained in chapter 1, which provides an overview of most of the statistical information used in the book. Other material has come from government reports, primarily from the Ministry of Housing. Some unpublished or historic material that has not been properly archived has been found in foreign financial agency reports, produced jointly with ministry teams or through official government support.

Additionally, vignettes of first-hand experiences of over fifteen individuals I interviewed over several years have given the on-the-ground dimension of the shift from 'homes' to 'housing,' providing nuance and detail. While a portion have been conducted for this book, the rest are based on my work on urban and housing policy that started with the Shadow Ministry of Housing blog, back in 2008, during which I wrote a number of articles and produced ten short documentaries on housing issues. Chapter 6 is based in part on previous work on government housing projects, and chapter 7 is based in part on my work on eviction cases during a stint as housing rights officer at the Egyptian Initiative for Personal Rights (EIPR). Work from 10 Tooba and the Built Environment Observatory, which I cofounded and manage, has also contributed to the book.

In addition to the primary material, a wealth of academic research written by architects, planners, geographers, sociologists, anthropologists, historians, political scientists, and economists has been invaluable in smoothing out gaps between official texts and oral accounts, especially for historic events or detailed case studies. The Egyptian architecture and planning magazine *Majallat al-'imara* has been an important resource for information from the 1940s, and the digital archive prepared by the Special Collections at the Fine Arts Library of Harvard University has been invaluable. Newspaper reports have also been consulted in reporting both official discourse and popular views. For historic coverage, an online archive of the semiofficial daily *al-Ahram* hosted on the Internet Archive covering the 1960s through the 1990s has been used, as well as the Egyptian Press Archive compiled by CEDEJ that covers the 1980s through the 2000s and is hosted online by the Bibliotheca Alexandrina.

1

ETYMOLOGY OF A CRISIS

Over the last century, literature and film have portrayed a series of housing crises in Egypt of one sort or another. Images of overcrowded rooms, crumbling housing, and unpainted redbrick and concrete towers carpeting once fertile land match regular news reports capturing a housing problem.

In the famous 1950s film *Yasmin*, when the orphaned child entertainer played by Fayruz asks Anwar Wagdi's character Wahid how he managed to get his rooftop shack from the chickens and pigeons who had lived there, he simply replies, "I paid them *khiliw* (key money) and then they left." Two decades later, a film around the problem of finding a home to rent, *Shaqqa mafrusha* (Furnished Apartment),[1] follows Zaynab, played by movie star Magda al-Khatib, as she steps off a train in Cairo and spends an entire day (the first fifteen minutes of the film) being driven around the city in a taxi looking for an apartment to rent. All are apparently taken, and her only option is to pay double rent for an already rented home. The scheme is comically cooked up by the broker, where the current tenant, who works nights, hopes he would not bump into Zaynab.

In 1972, *Azmit sakan* (Homes Crisis) was released. It opens with actress Mervat Amin as Afaf, an employee in her twenties, whose broker tells her in a crowded elevator that he has found her an empty apartment, to which all the elevator's occupants react in surprise unison. Afaf is eager to sign the contract, but the broker reassures her the apartment is not going anywhere because the building's foundations have not yet been built. She finally finds a place to rent, but the landlord refuses to lease it to a single woman. She returns disguised as her brother who would be living with her and manages to rent the apartment. The screenwriter, Faisal Nada, went on to pen other works focusing on the housing crisis: *Shaqqa wa 'arusa ya Rab* (Please God,

Give Me an Apartment and a Bride) in 1978, and a televison series in 1984 titled *Ahlan ahlan bi-l-sukkan* (Welcome Residents!).

The silver screen continued to grapple with the housing crisis in the 1980s. *Sha'ban taht al-sifr* (Sha'ban below Zero) follows a young man, played by movie star Adel Imam in 1980, who lives in a rented room, as he tries to find a suitable home that would allow him to marry his fiancée. Affordable rents are nonexistent, and his future father-in-law refuses to let the couple move in with them. Buying a home is out of the question on his government salary, which if he saved would "pay for the key money by the time I reach pension age, and then we can give the home to our kids." *Gharib fi bayti* (A Stranger in My Home), released in 1982, parodies serious incidents of property fraud. In the film, a single property is sold to two different buyers—a rising football player and a widow juggling a son and a job as a medical doctor. Leading disparate lives, they must tolerate living with each other for the foreseeable future or risk losing their home.

The 1986 film *Karakun fi al-shari'* (Prison in the Street), starring Adel Imam, presented the full spectrum of the housing crisis. The protagonist and his family lose their original rented home in a building collapse, after which they live in a government emergency camp with the promise of a government housing unit that would be given to them 'soon.' An impossibly long waiting list and less than desirable conditions in the camp force them to move in with his sister-in-law. However, the family is not made to feel welcome, and they decide to move into their own mausoleum in the City of the Dead, which to their surprise is already occupied by a squatter. They share the mausoleum with the squatter, a drug dealer, while Imam loses his life savings to a fraudulent developer, leading him to build a caravan that he parks in the upscale Zamalek neighborhood in Cairo. This triggers a series of misfortunes with the police, who find multiple reasons to arrest him. In an attempt to escape all this harassment, and by now the leader of a caravan dwellers' movement, Imam takes to the desert to establish a community. A television crew films the invasion with Imam's charcter declaring that they don't need anything from the government (except the land for a nominal fee). The police show up and attempt to evict the squatters, only to be interrupted by a last-minute order to stop, supposedly from the president, who has just seen their plight on the news.

This dramatized official response to the housing crisis is rare, with films generally shying away from finger pointing, especially at the government. The crisis is in fact highly normalized, with greedy and unscrupulous landlords or developers understood as being behind the problem. When films do lay some official blame, it is usually aimed at bureaucratic procedures or low-level government corruption. Almost all of Egypt's presidents from the 1950s until today have publicly admitted to there being a housing crisis or a housing problem, but usually in the same breath they have proudly presented their advances to solve it. The language officials used was also prone to subtle etymological shifts. In the 1940s officials talked of *mushkilat al-masakin* (the homes problem), before becoming *azmit al-masakin* (the homes crisis) in the 1950s. Why the 'homes problem' and not the 'housing problem,' as English readers are more accustomed to seeing? Initially, the Arabic word for homes or dwellings, *masakin*, was used, and not *iskan* (housing), which in English is both noun and verb, although in Arabic it is only a verb. But by the 1960s, it transformed into *azmit al-iskan* (the housing crisis), possibly reflecting the government's more hands-on role in housing. In the late 1970s, it would be demoted back to a problem, but as *mushkilat al-iskan* (the housing problem), remaining so until today.

This chapter also digs below the surface of official discourse, down to the policy papers and legislation that leaders and their ministers of housing have written and passed seeking to solve this mysterious problem, which they have not been able to do for eight decades. Housing production data, dating back to the 1960s and describing 91 percent of all urban housing existing today, helps us map the effects of these policies, and what the big three players were doing: the formal private sector, from one-man-show developers to large urban development companies; the (mostly) self-build informal sector, and the government. Statistics on tenure, available from 1976, show us the changes in the most popular avenues that people have taken to acquire their homes—as builders, owners, or tenants—and again, how these changes were affected by policies. The unsightly matters of methodology and sources used are covered in a special note at the end of this chapter.

1940s: The Second World War and the Homes Problem

By the mid-twentieth century, a significant percentage of Egypt's rural population lived in homes built by the private sector in hamlets on large agricultural estates known as *'izba*s, as we see in chapter 4. The urban cousins to the rural *'izba*s, *musta'marat* (workers' colonies) began housing increasing numbers of both blue- and white-collar employees in the 1940s within factory complexes, adjacent to remote public services such as railways or waterworks, or on construction sites dotted all over Egypt, as detailed in chapter 5. Some of these compounds were big enough to become their own company towns—new settlements built in remote areas where corporations would not only provide housing to employees, but have almost total control over residents, segregating neighborhoods between foreigners/executives and natives/workers and providing public services.

Actors, who today we would describe as private developers, started operating in the late nineteenth century, building new districts from scratch next to historic districts. In Cairo, real estate corporations rode a speculative land boom, building Dokki, Zamalek, Maadi, Garden City, Kobba Gardens, and Heliopolis,[2] and in Alexandria, they built the Eastern Harbor corniche, as well as its eastern suburbs all along the new Raml tramline.

Much like the private sector, the government provided housing for some of its much smaller workforce. Many administrative housing units were built for engineers and inspectors of its ministries in remote locations. In Cairo, the private Heliopolis Company assigned housing for high-level civil servants through an agreement with the government.

However, if you wanted to live in the city and were not a regularly employed worker or government employee, or affluent enough to buy or even rent in the new districts, your only option was to self-build, as explained in chapter 2. The *huwsh* (courtyard house) and *'isha* (shack) sheltered a considerable proportion of urban dwellers in Egypt's major cities in the late nineteenth century, while the majority of rural residents that were not housed in *'izba*s built their own homes, mostly out of mudbrick and stone.

Despite all these forms of housing, many of them were inadequate. Homes were overcrowded. Worker's accommodation on rural and industrial estates came with surveillance and coercion, and proper accommodation was simply out of reach for many. The Second World War exacerbated these underlying tensions, as there were associated building material shortages—with Egypt heavily reliant on imports for construction—along with influxes of Commonwealth, and later American, troops who crowded the market. Writing just as the war was ending in 1945, the architect Mahmud Riad gave a sobering account of *mushkilat al-masakin* (the homes problem), one which he considered a "major national problem that should urgently garner the lion's share of attention to ensure the peoples' development."[3]

Riad's essay methodically analyzed housing policy in a number of western European countries, singling out Austria's interwar socialist democratic policies for being the most successful in providing affordable housing, and recommending similar policies in Egypt. Some of these were applied in the first government housing estate in Imbaba, which broke ground in 1947. One could argue that the rent control measures codified that year drew on some of his concepts, though the more progressive of his proposals fell on deaf ears. With these policies, the 1940s became the decade that would shape housing in Egypt until this day, and in 1950, Riad would become the head of the Department of Popular Homes—Egypt's first high office for housing.

1950s: Revolution and the Homes Crisis

The 1950s would witness an explosion in government-built housing, as a socialist republic replaced the colonial monarchy in 1952. The republic's president, Gamal Abd al-Nasser, clearly saw that "building popular homes" would "relieve" what he described as "*azmit al-masakin*" (the homes crisis), which was elevated from a problem to a crisis during a speech in 1955 that described in detail the efforts made to address the issue.[4] Nasser's lawmakers duly followed suit, as their Explanatory Notes for laws that expanded rent control and extended amnesty to informally built homes show they were also written to "relieve the homes crisis."[5]

Decolonization along with mass migration in the 1950s and 1960s—planned, forced, and voluntary—fundamentally reshaped housing in Egypt. The newly founded socialist republic dismantled most of the large agricultural estates within months of the 1952 revolution, and with it ended the practice of private sector housing in rural areas, at least for the ensuing half century. At the same time, government-sponsored new villages would get a boost, and tens of thousands of fellahin would relocate to the large-scale desert land reclamation schemes. However, this was a far cry from the envisioned millions leaving the crowded Nile Valley for the open desert, who continued to rely on community self-building for their housing.

Hundreds of thousands of mostly urban Egyptians, as well as non-Egyptians, were forced to move. The Tripartite Aggression by Britain, France, and Israel in 1956 saw almost fourteen hundred civilians killed in Port Said and twenty-five thousand made homeless after their homes were bombed. This invasion in part led to the expulsion, and compelled migration of thousands of *mutamassirun* (Egyptianized) people from foreign ancestry, including European and Egyptian Jews, but particularly British, Australian, and French citizens.[6] In 1961, fifty thousand or so Cairenes were to have their homes demolished in a grand replanning scheme gentrifying Cairo's old districts. In 1963 and 1964, around fifty thousand Nubian–Egyptians were displaced from their ancestral homeland south of Aswan to make way for the High Dam. Over 800,000 people were forced to flee Sinai and the Suez Canal cities and villages after Israel occupied Sinai in the 1967 War. Rural–urban migration also peaked, with hundreds of thousands of people leaving their villages and mainly heading to Cairo, making up two-fifths of its population increase.[7]

This tremendous flow of people in a small amount of time inevitably left its mark on the housing landscape. While the *muhaggarin* (forced migrants) from Sinai and the Suez zone were sheltered in schools and tents at first, they later crowded in with relatives or rented apartments.[8] Vacant housing also absorbed some of the migrants, whether government-sequestered vacation homes in the Mediterranean resort towns of Ras al-Bar and Gamasa,[9] or squatted private and government housing in Cairo.[10] In Zagazig, a sleepy provincial capital in the Delta, *muhaggarin* made up almost two-fifths of its population in 1969.[11] Most farmers chose to be relocated to the new villages being built in the desert land reclamation schemes.

1960s: Socialism and the Housing Crisis

Existing housing was no match for the increase in urban residents, and thus much of the expansion in government housing sheltered tens of thousands of the displaced. Even with *al-iskan al-sha'bi* (popular housing) blocks making up 12 percent of urban housing production in 1966, up from almost zero a decade earlier (figure 1.1), Nasser became defensive during a debate on housing with his party in 1965, and his irritation was palpable:

> Each one of us wants to do everything in a year, but can we do everything in a year? Each one of us wants to solve the housing crisis. . . . Each one of you wants to solve the housing crisis, but can we really solve the housing crisis in one year, or three, or four, or five? Did England, which is an advanced and developed country, solve the housing crisis? . . . Can anyone here in parliament stand up and ask the housing minister why this is so? I want to build popular housing and affordable housing and so on . . . but can we in a short time change this situation that is a result of exploitation and colonialism of hundreds of years?[12]

Nasser went on to explain how he could not spend as much as he would like on services, including housing, without compromising public investments in industry, which were necessary to "build the economic base." What Nasser's speech also belied was the second etymological change. The 'homes crisis' had now become the 'housing crisis,' possibly reflecting the government's active involvement in shelter provision, or at least what it saw itself as doing. Besides already building housing, it was heavily regulating the private sector through rent control, construction committees, and amnesties from demolitions of illegal buildings.

After the abolition of the *'izbas* and the sequestration of large landholders' estates and later the nationalization of industries, the private sector shifted its investments to real estate.[13] This new speculative building spree saw a high incidence of the demolition of buildings in good condition to build ones that were larger and more profitable. It was met head-on primarily through rent control, which was strengthened and expanded under Nasser's socialist regime. Another less elaborate set of legislation also controlled private production, through high building permit costs[14] and the Committee Regulating Construction and Demolition Works.[15] This committee would approve any building, modification, repair, or demolition valued over LE500 only if it was in line with what it saw as the public good or national policy that prioritized industrialization projects rather than real estate speculation. This 'temporary' provision no doubt slowed construction work, as it lasted well into the 1980s, with only a brief hiatus between 1961 and 1964.

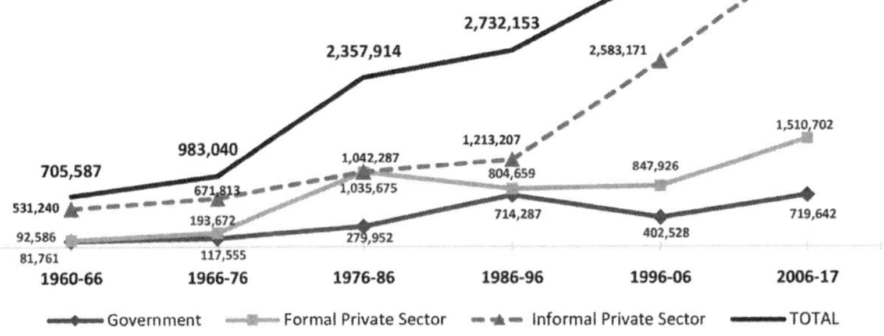

1.1: Share of urban housing production by provider, 1960–2017. (See section on methodology page 25.)

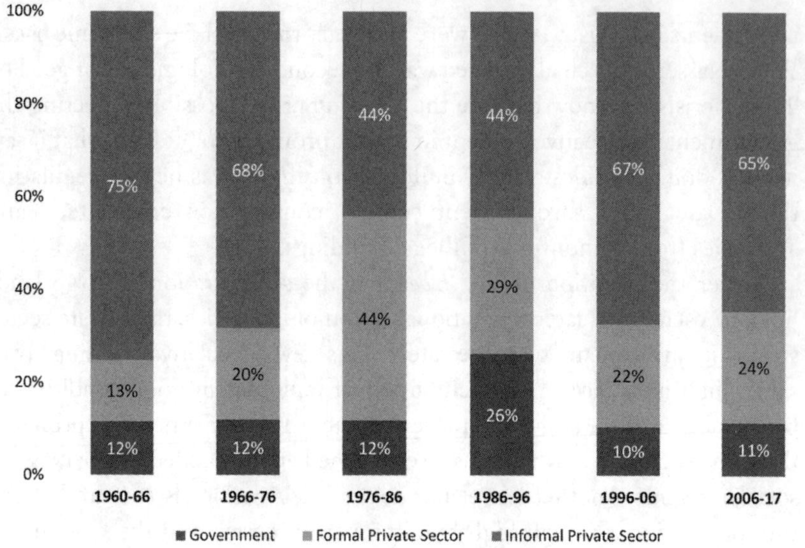

1.2: Number of urban housing units produced by provider, 1960–2017. (See section on methodology page 25.)

Despite these regulations, the private sector was able to produce fifteen thousand homes a year between 1960 and 1966. This rose to nineteen thousand a year during the decade of the Egyptian–Israeli war, 1966–76 (figure 1.2), to capture almost a quarter of housing production (figure 1.1). Did this represent a new class of 'war-rich' citizens?

However, government and private sector housing covered only a third of urban housing provision in that time, leaving two-thirds to be built through community self-build. An astonishing 1.6 million homes were self-built between 1960 and 1976, their builder-owners seemingly unfazed by the cement shortages and the war (figure 1.2). They were no doubt encouraged by a string of amnesties from demolitions—as well as an end to fines and jail terms for builders—passed between 1956 and 1967, all framed as the government's "contribution to relieving the homes crisis."[16]

1970s: Infitah and the Housing Crisis, or Was It the Housing Problem?

Much would change in the 1970s under Nasser's successor Anwar Sadat after he took apart the socialist state and initiated the Infitah 'open door' policy in light of political success of the October War of 1973 and warming relations with the West. His policies were so unpopular however, and the housing crisis so dire, that protesters in the 1977 Bread Riots chanted, *"Howa beyilbis akher moda, wehna benuskun 'ashara fi owda!"* (He [Sadat] wears the latest fashion, while we live ten to a room!).

Even parliamentarians admitted that housing conditions had been bad for a long time. Muhib Ramzi Stino, parliamentary housing committee head, conceded in 1981 that the housing crisis had continued uninterrupted for two decades from "1960 until today."[17] But Sadat was having none of that. In 1976, when he addressed an audience of international dignitaries at the first Habitat Conference held in Vancouver, Canada, he saw only a problem, not a crisis:

> The prevailing circumstances in most of the human settlements in the Third World call for serious international procedure that would help reach a suitable solution for the grave problems of housing, services, water, energy and communications . . . problems [that] are the final outcome of a long period of colonialism, and frequent armed aggressions directed against the unity of Egyptian territories.[18]

Sadat would not be found saying the words "housing crisis" even if he was blaming it on colonialism and Egypt's wars with Israel. In fact, it seems the only time he did use the term, it was inadvertently. On the day he laid the cornerstone of the first new desert city in May 1977, Sadat proclaimed that it would "eliminate the housing crisis, and relieve it from the widest of doors."[19] But, in the same speech, he stated how the "two most important problems ahead of us are food and housing." Sadat would repeat that statement three years later, before detailing the progress made in "solving the housing problem."[20] His ministers were also careful to talk about a 'housing problem,' as we see in the Explanatory Notes of the laws they drafted. In these very laws, Sadat's parliamentarians still held to their old habits and spoke of a 'housing crisis,' but not for long.

In explaining the need for a national housing fund in 1976, Minister of Housing and Reconstruction Osman Ahmed Osman wrote that "the housing problem is one of the main public problems that touches the lives of all people . . . [and] requires a great deal of investments to remedy."[21] On the other hand, parliamentary housing committee head Ahmad Hilmi Badr saw that establishing the housing fund would be "a step toward solving the housing crisis."[22] When the time came in 1977 to pen a new rent control law, Minister of Housing Ahmad Muhammad Hasan argued for change, citing how "the current laws showed that they were unable to confront some aspects of the housing problem," whereas committee head Abbas Safi al-Din's argument for a "renewed need for a complete and comprehensive law" was about how it would help the "country exit the currently pertinent housing crisis that burns the Egyptian citizen."[23] Safi al-Din also used the phrase 'housing problem' in his report, a sign that the new discourse was steadily gaining ground.

By 1979, this discourse was finally cast with the founding of a cabinet-level committee to "draft a national policy that aimed to solve the housing problem."[24] When a law was published that year to regulate the new cities the government was building, the parliamentary housing committee head Adli Abd al-Shahid had got the message. It was the 'housing problem' that was "one of the most important problems [in] the Arab Republic of Egypt," and not the 'housing crisis.'[25] Demoting housing from a 'crisis' to a 'problem' transformed it from a limitless drama into a definable question that could potentially be solved.

Reconstruction in the Suez Canal cities and the building of the so-called new cities in the desert boosted government housing production to twenty-seven thousand units a year (figure 1.2). This was all aided by a new policy to sell the homes rather than rent them out, creating a lucrative business for the battalion of government agencies that were now in the business of housing.

Controversially, this increase in production only kept the government's share of urban housing the same as that of the 1960s. The Infitah's unshackling of the private sector from rent control (through de facto circumvention, as we see in chapter 3), and a relaxing of the building permit regime, saw private sector housing boom, doubling its share of urban housing to 43 percent—its highest in the last half century (figure 1.1).[26] Most of the one million homes built by the private sector between 1976 and 1986 were bought or funded by the almost two million expatriate Egyptians who had moved to the Arab Gulf states in the 1970s. As nonnatives were not allowed to own property in the Gulf or become citizens, billions of their earnings found their way back home.

This inflow of private cash gave the economic migrants newfound leverage over their stay-at-home cousins; they were able to buy them out of their rent-controlled homes through *khiliw rigl* (key money), as well as elbow out locals with the ability to pay higher upfront deposits to landlords of newly built units. The cash of absentee owners also produced a new market for *tamlik* (owned units), while up until the mid-1970s it had been unheard of to have the means to buy ready-built homes, and cooperative housing had been the only avenue to ownership for the salaried class through subsidized government loans. A plethora of mostly small-scale private developers sprouted in the major cities, filling the long-abandoned subdivisions of new districts plotted out in the 1960s with housing. And when those were exhausted, owners started adding floors to existing buildings, in many cases breaching zoning regulations by paying bribes, creating a staircase skyline of short and tall buildings. When they maxed out the rooftops, older buildings, especially villas, were torn down and replaced with high-rises.

With government housing expensive and being built in remote areas—and private housing out of reach—the marginalized poor would largely rely on self-build, though moving their construction out of the cities. Less than half of the 2.5 million homes they built from 1976 to 1986 were in urban areas, and the rest were extensions of villages. This looks to have signaled a paradigm shift, from adding rooms and shacks to existing dwellings in old, inner-city neighborhoods, to building good-quality housing on the fields at the fringes of the city. Indeed, statistics show that older neighborhoods in Cairo, Alexandria, and other cities were depopulating, even though the cities as a whole were growing.[27] The rural or periurban areas around them, such as Matariya and Bulaq al-Dakrur in Greater Cairo, and al-Amiriya in Alexandria, were growing faster than average. Like Abd al-Nasser, Sadat would acknowledge informal housing during his rule, but unlike his predecessor, he extended amnesty to those who built on squatted state-owned land.

The 1970s saw the first collection of tenure data. The 1976 census shows that rent—Old Rent (rent control), furnished, and in-kind use—was the most popular form of tenure in urban Egypt, comprising 60 percent of households. The rest lived in owned homes—bought, built/inherited, and gifted. Rather than a snapshot of the 1970s, this dataset shows us what earlier policies from the 1960s achieved, with renting households living in both private and social housing.

Taking a closer look, trailing Old Rent were two far less popular options, which comprised less than 1 percent each of households—furnished rent, which is expensive property in choice city and vacation locations; and in-kind use, which are homes provided by employers to their employees. These may be on factory compounds, so-called administrative housing for government employees in remote locations, or the porters' rooms for *bawwabin* and servants in the entrances, basements, or rooftops of big-city buildings.

Moving to ownership, the 40 percent of urban Egyptians who did own their homes in 1976 owned them mostly through building,[28] whether formally through housing cooperatives or informally. Housing cooperatives were not an option except for professionals and government officials, as cooperatives could only be set up based on a common denominator, which more often than not meant the union or office of employment. Engineers, doctors, journalists, judges, police, and the military formed cooperatives. But they still represented a minority of owner-built homes, possibly in the low thousands, compared to mostly informal self-build, which as we saw previously was the primary urban housing provider between 1960 and 1976. Buying property was virtually unheard of, representing less than 2 percent of urban tenure, a testament to how the housing market was a recent invention in Egypt.

Egypt's patrimonial roots are evident in another ownership subcategory: gifted, which made up less than 2 percent in 1976. This commonly means that current owners received their homes entirely as a gift from their parents, usually from a father to his son. The census, however, does not tell us whether the unit was originally self-built by the family or bought on the market.

Of course, ownership is not without contestation. Street-side and rooftop shacks are very possibly enumerated as owned, even though the land they occupy is squatted on. The same goes for more substantial buildings on the desert fringes of the cities, or on the part of seminomadic tribes in the desert proper. Squatting on state-owned land was legal up to 1958, though judging by a constant flow of decrees regularizing squatting from the late 1970s, as we see in chapters 2 and 7, the practice did not stop. The same goes for ownership through squatting in abandoned properties, which takes place in older dilapidated districts but is not picked up as such by the census.[29]

The census does not identify other types of ownership. Government-built homes are not differentiated from privately built homes, and neither are homes owned outright differentiated from those being paid for by installments. Indefinite long-term leases, which are homes acquired through sale contracts minus *hissa fi al-ard* (share of the land), are also not identified. But overall, the 1976 census still gives us a picture to work with.

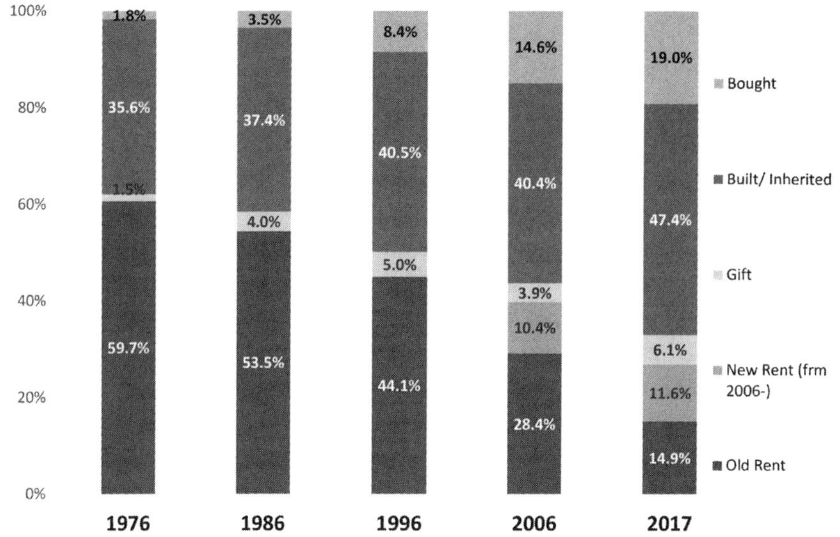

1.3: Change of household tenure for urban Egypt, 1976–2017.
(Sources: CAPMAS Census for Population and Housing Conditions 1976, 1986, 1996, 2006, and 2017. Also see section on methodology below.)

1980s to 1990s: Mubarak and the Housing Problem

In November 1981, less than a month into what would be his thirty-year rule, President Hosni Mubarak announced to both upper and lower houses of parliament during their inaugural session how "he sought the opinions and ideas of the largest number of economic experts [on] finding a radical solution for the housing problem, so that every citizen can plan his future, and ensure he can acquire an adequate home at a set date."[30] A few months later, Mubarak demanded from his minister of reconstruction and new communities, Hassaballah al-Kafrawi, a "radical and urgent solution for the housing problem," a problem that he saw had "reached an acute level."[31] Two years later, al-Kafrawi had not solved the acute housing problem, radically or otherwise, leading Mubarak to redirect his demand to "universities and research centers" during a conference in 1984 titled *Egypt in the Year 2000*, hoping to receive "studies, scientific visions, and case studies that would radically confront the problem."[32] But by 1986, it seems the experts had not done their job. This time, it was Prime Minister Ali Lutfi who, during a National Democratic Party (NDP) meeting, promised that "this year would be the start of solving the housing problem through the provision of construction material."[33] This was not exactly what one would call a radical solution. Al-Kafrawi would come around in 1987 and promise to solve the said housing problem within three years. In 1990, it remained stubbornly unsolved, and he would renew exactly the same promise, garnering a sarcastic caricature in leading state-owned *al-Ahram* in the process.[34]

But why was the government seeking to solve the housing problem? Egypt was producing a record number of homes during that time, putting out 2.7 million urban units between 1986 and 1996 (figure 1.2), up by about 12 percent over the previous decade. Government housing production would surge to an all-time high of almost one-third of urban housing (figure 1.1), producing an unprecedented seventy thousand units a year. Formal private housing production shrunk by one-fifth though, compared to the previous decade, almost matching government housing. Informal housing production remained supremely popular, gaining a fifth on the previous decade to produce 1.2 million homes. Overall, there was a surplus of housing, but limited access to it.

Tenure-wise, things were slowly changing. The 1986 census would show the beginning of what would be the inexorable erosion of renters, seeing their share drop 10 percent since 1976, and by 1996 dropping by 20 percent compared to the 1986 census (figure 1.3). Even though rent control laws were still in force, it appears they were not enforced. While the number of renters was growing modestly, most were actually entering into a form of leasing, with tenants paying large amounts of illegal *khiliw rigl* (key money) to acquire rental contracts, as we see in chapter 3. Ownership, on the other hand, was skyrocketing.

Inevitably, the proportion of homeowners grew, not least because *tamlik* became the official government banner, and everyone followed. From 1978 onward, all tenants in government housing were allowed to buy their homes, beating Margaret Thatcher's Right to Buy scheme in the United Kingdom by two years. But where Thatcher was not able to completely liberalize social housing, Sadat was, and all new 'public' housing from that point onward would be sold, the effects of which were now starting to appear.

Both the government and the private sector were now capitalizing on billions of Arab Gulf petrodollars, which were being remitted by around two million expatriate Egyptians. Alternative forms of investment were risky or hard to come by, and interest rates remained lower than inflation. So-called Islamic investment companies flourished for a few years, promising returns that both outpaced inflation and were non-bank investments, as interest is generally frowned upon in the Muslim-majority world. However, it was too good to be true, and they all went belly up by the end of the 1980s. State media portrayed these companies as Ponzi schemes, which many might have been, but it was ultimately the commercial banks—largely state-owned—that pressured the government to 'eliminate' them because they had diverted much cash, especially hard currency, away from them.[35] Thousands of people lost their life savings overnight, and bricks and mortar proved itself yet again to be a sound investment.

In urban Egypt, home purchases almost doubled in the 1976–86 period to nearly 4 percent of households, and doubled again to 8 percent by 1996, showing how caps on home sales introduced through the rent control law from 1977 were barely effective. Ownership through building also continued to grow steadily, reaching two-fifths of households by 1996, almost equaling rentals. Up to half of them were informally built homes, as we can tell from the dataset on housing production. The other half that was formally built mostly exploited a rent control loophole that allowed individuals to group together in an *ittihad mullak* (owners' union) to build condominiums, as we see in chapter 3. Housing cooperatives were built in the same way, giving members a share of the venture equal to one or more units. While production figures enumerate cooperative production, it most likely does not include independent cooperatives, and is limited to endeavors by the government-owned General Organization for Building and Housing Cooperatives (GOHBC).

For those that could not afford to build, buy, or rent, there was a housing problem.

1990s–2010s: Neoliberalism and the Housing Problem

Much started unraveling in the 1990s, beginning with the first significant legislation related to housing during Mubarak's rule. During an interview in 1995, Minister of Housing and Utilities Salah Hassaballah made yet another three-year promise to "solve the housing problem" based on a projection that the proposed liberalization of rent control would put two million vacant apartments on the market.[36] Rents were indeed liberalized in January 1996, in what the housing committee head stated was but "a step toward solving the housing problem."[37] Bringing in the laws of supply and demand was just part of the neoliberal structural adjustment package led by the World Bank and International Monetary Fund, and Mubarak seemed to have finally found the solution to the housing problem, almost two decades after he had first demanded it.

Continuing on the path of market liberalization, in 1998 Mubarak stressed "the importance of the role of the private sector in solving the housing problem," whereby real estate developers would build and the government would regulate.[38] Two years later, he would follow through with an address to parliament, in which he argued for enshrining the 'right to debt' by passing a mortgage law which he hoped would "help solve the housing problem . . . through long-term loans that would allow [newly formed families] to buy available housing."[39]

Indeed, the 1996–2006 decade would see yet another set of tectonic shifts in the housing landscape. First to go was government housing production, which would drop by almost half, to forty thousand units a year (figure 1.2). More pertinently, its share would drop to only 10 percent of urban housing (figure 1.1), its lowest since housing production statistics have been available. Ironically, even with all the promarket concessions, the formal private sector did not step up, maintaining the numbers of the previous decade, but in the process, dropping to just over a fifth of urban housing production. Informal housing, on the other hand, saw its share jump to two-thirds of urban housing in the 1996–2006 period, with a phenomenal 2.6 million units built. It seems that the side effect of all this liberalization was not the solution to the housing problem that its proponents had in mind.

This tectonic shift would also ripple through tenure patterns. There was a surge of new renters by almost a million households between 1996 and 2006, almost all of them urban. But since the law liberalizing rents only applied to new buildings, or those officially vacated, Old Rent tenants continued on and held fast throughout the decade. Even with the considerable increase in renters, by 2006 the combined share of New and Old Rent households actually fell to less than 40 percent of urban households (figure 1.3). Another type of rent was also liberalized: agricultural land rent—leading to an expulsion of around one million families in 1997, from both their land and their *'izba* homes, as we see in chapters 4 and 7.

Ownership of course continued to grow, with those who bought again doubling, reaching 14 percent of households, while self-builds remained stable at two-fifths of households. With shrinking formal production from both the government and the private sector, this could only mean that much buying was now moving to the informal sector, and its mainstay as an owner-built category was eroding.

2010s: Revolution and the Housing Problem

Mortgages were still thin on the ground in 2005 when Mubarak decided to "confront the housing problem" yet again, but by dusting off an old and trusted method: "building eighty thousand new homes a year . . . subsidized by the state to facilitate ownership through reasonable installments."[40] This was Mubarak's electoral housing promise, as he pledged to build half a million homes in six years—his fifth presidential term. But it would prove to be his last when in January 2011 a popular uprising managed to unseat him.

The military council that filled the vacuum fell into step, and its Engineering Authority started building housing units. The project was described by the department's head, Major General Kamel al-Wazir, as "the Armed Forces' contribution toward solving the housing problem."[41] By mid-2012, Egypt had a new president and a new regime. The Muslim Brotherhood candidate Muhammad Mursi won the elections and their Freedom and Justice Party (FJP) filled the cabinet. But the new housing minister, urban planner Tarek Wafiq, did not stray from the playbook. Egypt's first housing strategy in some time, scripted under his watch, observed that "the housing laws that were enacted over the second half of the twentieth century . . . produced side effects such as social, economic, and urban distortion, which led to an exacerbated housing problem, and the urban disfigurement of Egyptian cities."[42]

The new strategy did not see the light of day, however, as the third regime change in as many years saw Mursi deposed by the military, and an interim government installed in July 2013. Mursi's minister of defense Abd al-Fattah al-Sisi led the ouster and continued on in his post, in addition to becoming deputy prime minister. In March 2014, three months before presidential elections, al-Sisi produced an "initiative to build one million housing units" as "a serious step to start solving the housing problem for low-income households in Egypt."[43] The project fizzled out, but its patron won, and the 'housing problem' continued. In 2017, in a roundtable interview by the state-owned daily *al-Ahram*, Housing Minister Mustafa Madbuli would echo the ministerial pledge of yore, promising:

> Within four years there will be a major breakthrough for the housing problem in Egypt, as the state will have been able to achieve a balance between demand and supply through the different housing projects, and also by finding alternative [sites] for the places that suffer from land shortage.[44]

That same year, the census indicated that government housing production saw the biggest decade-on-decade increase out of the three sectors, growing by almost 80 percent, and building 720,000 units (figure 1.2). This of course was not only down to a post-2014 government housing boom, but to one started during Mubarak's last hurrah in 2005, as we see in chapter 6. The years between 2006 and 2017 also marked a phenomenal three-quarter increase in production for the formal private sector, with the building of 1.5 million units, a little more than double the government's production. While a large part of the globe was starting to feel the pinch of the 2008 subprime mortgage crisis, which would lead to more government regulation and intervention, Egypt was doing the exact opposite, letting the stops out of most market plugs, the excessive deregulation leading to a boom in construction and inflated prices.[45]

The informal sector, which until this point had been largely self-built, owner-occupied housing, was also affected by the housing commodification bug, morphing into full-on real estate development, boosting production by 57 percent with the building of a record four million housing units—more than all housing produced during the preceding decade by the three sectors combined. This phenomenal surge in production was no doubt helped by exploiting the history of government amnesties toward informal housing that continued under Mubarak, as well as the police vacuum and multiple regime changes that followed the January 2011 revolution that toppled him (see chapter 2). Despite the big changes in numbers across all three sectors, their relative shares remained largely the same, with government housing rising slightly to 11 percent of overall production, the formal private sector nudging closer to one-quarter of production, and the informal private sector falling slightly to 65 percent of all urban housing production (figure 1.1).

If we add both urban and rural housing together, then this period of 2006–17 saw an average of 1. 27 million homes built a year. That makes Egypt one of the largest producers of housing worldwide. In a group of countries that includes the bigger producers in the Americas, Europe, and Asia, Egypt comes only third, behind India and China, which respectively build five and eight times more homes a year than Egypt does.[46] But with its population less than one-tenth of the Asian countries, Egypt comes first in the amount of housing produced in relation to its population at fourteen homes per thousand citizens (figure 1.4). Turkey's significantly high 10.7 homes per thousand citizens makes it a distant second, and China comes third at almost half of Egypt's rate. Developed markets, such as the United

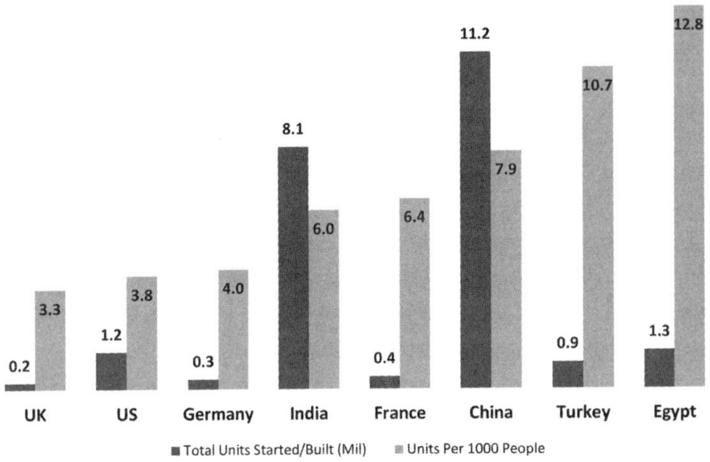

1.4: Comparing housing production to population (units per 1,000) in selected countries. (Sources: National Bureau of Statistics of China, "National Real Estate Development and Sales in the First Nine Months of 2018"; US Census Bureau, "Building Permits Survey—United States (2017)"; MoHCLG, "Housing Supply: Net Additional Dwellings, England: 2017 to 2018"; Trading Economics, "Building Permits: Countries—List"; Kaul, "Why Are More than 10 Million Homes Vacant in India?")

States, the United Kingdom, and Germany, are only producing three to four homes per thousand people.

Moving on to tenure, 2006–17 saw relatively modest increases in the addition of New Rent tenants, while Old Rent tenancy started to freefall, losing one hundred thousand tenants a year. By the end of this period, all renters made up a little over a quarter of urban households, their lowest share ever, down from a high of 60 percent only four decades earlier. The slack was of course picked up by ownership, which now dominates in urban Egypt. Where buying a home was close to nonexistent forty years ago, in 2017 it was running a close second to renting, representing 19 percent of households.[47] Even with the proliferation of real estate developers and a big boost in government housing, ownership through building remains king, growing to 47 percent of urban households by 2017.

A Note on Methodology

This chapter is a patchwork of statistical data that has been put together and analyzed from a number of sources, with some data inferred. First off is formal housing production, collated in CAPMAS Statistical Yearbooks since at least the 1960s. However, these did not differentiate between government and private sector production until the 1996–97 edition, and so three secondary, semiofficial sources all quoting the Ministry of Housing have been used to plug the gap for both sectors on an annual basis between 1960–61 and 1995–96.[48] For the rest of the data, figures from the chapter on housing of the CAPMAS Statistical Yearbooks of 1996 to 2017 have been used, which in turn cite the Ministry of Housing as the source.

But a word of warning is in order. Yearbooks from 2003 until 2008 had numerical errors for the financial years 1994/95 to 1999/2000 in their tables, showing erroneous subtotals that were only observed when the figures were added to a program for spreadsheets. It is a good idea to always consult more than one source for the data, and to manually enter disaggregations. Some later versions of the yearbooks are published in both Arabic and English, with inconsistencies between the two languages. Here, Arabic was the language consulted.

The only pre-1960 statistics found were for government housing production during the 1952–60 period, and in the 1973 Statistical Yearbook, which quoted a total of thirty-two thousand government-built housing units during the period.[49] It is important to note that the yearbooks from 1980 to 1997 quote an entirely different figure of fifty-six thousand units *annually* for the same period,[50] which is an outlandish error, and one that has been quoted in a number of studies to detrimental effect.[51]

But the official statistics on private production are only enumerated through building permits, which leaves out all buildings constructed without a permit. So how can we count them? As early as 1980, housing experts identified large discrepancies between official statistics on formal housing production and figures of the total existing housing units enumerated in the official censuses,[52] which only happen every ten years. Using what they described as the "residual method," to infer informal housing production, they deducted the total amount of formal housing (government and formal private sector) produced in an intercensal period from the net amount of added housing units recorded between the census years.

This chapter applies the same methodology for the period 1960 to 2017, using the seven censuses conducted in that period, and subtracting the 'formal' production for the intervening ten years—eleven for the 2006–17 period—starting with the financial year the census falls in (table 1.3). So for the period 1986–96, for example, the financial years used are 1986/87 to 1995/96, and so on.

However, gathering the census data has itself been far from straightforward. The 1960 public census documents do not enumerate buildings, so an official secondary source quoting the Ministry of Housing and Reconstruction was used, but this only referred to urban housing stock.[53] Rural and total housing stock figures are inferred by using the rural–urban ratio of households as the 1960 census, but do not feature in the figures presented in this chapter. The 1966 census only enumerated total housing units, as detailed in the 1973 Statistical Yearbook.[54] This time the rural–urban ratio was used the other way around to infer urban units.

The 1976 census was a completely different beast altogether. While it did enumerate urban residential stock, the total of 3.9 million residential buildings was just implausible, since when subtracted from the total housing units enumerated in the same census, it would have left *fewer* rural housing units than there were rural buildings (table 1.1). Since the 1976 census enumerated housing as either apartments or rooms, this may have been cause for extreme overcounting. Therefore, assuming that all rural buildings were single-unit homes, subtracting them from the total housing units enumerated in the census gives us 3.4 million urban units, which is the figure used in the final calculations (table 1.2).

From 1986 on, the censuses would enumerate both rural and urban residential units using much the same methodology, and their figures for 'normal residential units' have been used, omitting the vague or utilitarian 'marginal

	Calculation A			**Calculation B**		
	Residential Buildings	**Units**	**Unit/ Building**	**Buildings**	**Units**	**Unit/ Building**
Urban	1,405,911	3,940,827	2.8	1,405,911	3,363,627	2.4
Rural	3,947,512	3,370,312	0.9	3,947,512	3,947,512	1.0
Total	**5,353,423**	**7,311,139**	1.4	**5,353,423**	**7,311,139**	1.4

Notes: Calculation A: 'Urban' figures from Census for Buildings, 'Total' from overall census, 'Rural' inferred. Calculation B: 'Urban' units inferred from subtraction of 'Rural' from 'Total,' where 'Rural' units equal 'Rural' buildings.
Sources: CAPMAS, "al-Ta'dad al-'am li-l-mabani 1976: al-natai'j al-tafsiliya li-ijmali al-jumhuriya," 11 and 59. (Only those labelled 'Residential' and 'Residential & work'), and 1976 Census in CAPMAS, "al-Kitab al-ihsa'i al-sanawi li-jumhuriyat Misr al-'arabiya 1952–1980," 152.

1.1: Sorting contradictory figures in the 1976 census.

residential units'—which included tens of thousands of kiosks and shops, or those used for work (table 1.2).[55] Again the results in this format for 1986 were only available from a secondary source.[56] Given all this patchworking, the proportions of the different providers presented here may differ from those found in other literature. Ultimately, these numbers only serve as an indication of the scale of activity of the different housing providers, rather than an absolute reality, as many other factors play into their not being totally accurate, from the changing methodology used by CAPMAS in defining units in the census, to the reclassifying of 'rural' areas as 'urban,' to the deliberate inflation of some figures.[57] There is also the fact that thousands of units are lost to collapse or demolition between the censuses that are not accounted for, while not all building permits have resulted in actual buildings, thereby contributing toward the undercounting of informal production.

Census	**Place**	**Whole Building (Includes houses & villas)**	**Whole Floor or More**	**Apartment**	**Stand-alone Room or More**	**Total**
1960	Urban					1,675,000
	Rural					2,670,410
	Total					**4,345,410**
1966	Urban					2,380,587
	Rural					3,441,840
	Total					**5,822,427**
1976	Urban					3,363,627
	Rural					3,947,512
	Total					**7,311,139**
1986	Urban					5,721,541
	Rural					5,424,362
	Total					**11,145,903**
1996	Urban	871,498	202,611	6,846,049	533,536	8,453,694
	Rural	4,653,579	231,171	2,702,184	169,677	7,756,611
	Total	**5,525,077**	**433,782**	**9,548,233**	**703,213**	**16,210,305**

Census	Place	Whole Building (Includes houses & villas)	Whole Floor or More	Apartment	Stand-alone Room or More	Total
2006	Urban	613,538	492,575	10,692,056	489,150	12,287,319
	Rural	3,528,914	865,149	7,071,391	378,998	11,844,452
	Total	**4,142,452**	**1,357,724**	**17,763,447**	**868,148**	**24,131,771**
2017	Urban	817,993	316,372	16,746,757	703,321	18,584,443
	Rural	3,714,506	923,051	12,633,259	2,229,658	19,500,474
	Total	**4,532,499**	**1,239,423**	**29,380,016**	**2,932,979**	**38,084,917**

Sources: CAPMAS censuses.

1.2: Residential housing stock in the census years 1960–2017.

Intercensal Period	Area	Govern-ment	Formal Private Sector	Informal Private Sector	TOTAL	For-mal	Infor-mal
1960-66	Urban	81,761	92,586	531,240	**705,587**	25%	75%
	Rural			771,430	**771,430**	0%	100%
	Total	**81,761**	**92,586**	**1,302,670**	**1,477,017**	**12%**	**88%**
1966-76	Urban	117,555	193,672	671,813	**983,040**	32%	68%
	Rural	28,650		477,022	**505,672**	6%	94%
	Total	**146,205**	**193,672**	**1,148,835**	**1,488,712**	**23%**	**77%**
1976-86	Urban	279,952	1,035,675	1,042,287	**2,357,914**	56%	44%
	Rural			1,476,850	**1,476,850**	0%	100%
	Total	**279,952**	**1,035,675**	**2,519,137**	**3,834,764**	**34%**	**66%**
1986-96	Urban	714,287	804,659	1,213,207	**2,732,153**	56%	44%
	Rural			2,332,249	**2,332,249**	0%	100%
	Total	**714,287**	**804,659**	**3,545,456**	**5,064,402**	**30%**	**70%**
1996-06	Urban	402,528	847,926	2,583,171	**3,833,625**	33%	67%
	Rural			4,087,841	**4,087,841**	0%	100%
	Total	**402,528**	**847,926**	**6,671,012**	**7,921,466**	**16%**	**84%**

Intercensal Period	Area	Government	Formal Private Sector	Informal Private Sector	TOTAL	Formal	Informal
2006-17	Urban	719,642	1,510,702	4,066,780	**6,297,124**	35%	65%
	Rural			7,656,022	**7,656,022**	0%	100%
	Total	**719,642**	**1,510,702**	**11,722,802**	**13,953,146**	**16%**	**84%**

Sources: 'Total' is difference between two consecutive censuses from Table 1.2. 'Informal Private Sector' is 'Government' and 'Formal Private Sector' subtracted from 'Total.' For 'Government' and 'Formal Private Sector,' see text.

1.3: Housing production in Egypt by provider in units, 1960–2017.

2

SELF-BUILDERS

Self-build, popularly known as *buna ahali* (community-build) and *al-maghudat al-zatiya* (self-help), is how most Egyptians acquire their homes. Self-build has been the most popular form of housing provision for centuries, perhaps even millennia, and this continues to be the case, even with the proliferation of private real estate companies, public housing schemes, and the development of a rental market over the past half century. While most owners do not do the actual building themselves, they acquire the land, design their homes, and manage the entire construction process.

The government designates a very small proportion of self-build as formal—on land divisions plotted out by government agencies, planned by 'experts,' and where a building permit has been acquired. The overwhelming majority of self-builds are considered *'ashwa'iyat*—literally randomly built settlements that contravene planning and building laws. Both forms of self-build have been marginalized by government policy over the last few decades, especially informal self-building, which has been demonized.

Over the past 130 years, successive authoritarian regimes have attempted to control and regulate construction in both urban and rural settlements. These attempts were met with resistance throughout the almost century-and-a-half of building legislation. There is also a history of exceptional rule, where government has, for the most part, tolerated informal housing through amnesty from the law, stopping short of labeling self-build as outright illegal, and instead using a wide array of terms such as *taqsim mukhalif* (informal subdivisions), *manatiq ghayr rasmiya* (informal areas), *manatiq ghayr mukhattata* (unplanned areas), or *manatiq ghayr amina* (structurally unsafe areas). Over time, although most buildings have not been legalized through the amnesties, many settlements have been incorporated into 'formal' cities through the extension of infrastructure and even some upgrading of services. This is a de facto tolerance, whereby communities have been coerced by the government into breaking the law by building informally until granted amnesty—at choice moments and for a price. These communities have thus been made dependent on the government and demobilized from protesting against its injustices.[1]

What follows is an analysis of six decades (1956–2018) of the disincentivization of entire communities that have built their own homes, through an exploration of the relationship between legislation, statistics, and political events. It focuses particularly on the coerced clientelism on the part of the government, in which it threatens force, fines, and jail terms to those that have built informally, but paradoxically issues laws offering amnesty under the pretext of protecting the public good, and hailing the self-builders for playing their part in alleviating the housing crisis. Stopping short of full legalization, the government extends formal infrastructure to buildings and entire neighborhoods it has labeled as informal, usually when doing so has been critical to preserving or building up a regime's popularity.

Why Self-build?

There is much written on why people self-build, especially in the Global South, with reasons varying widely, even within the same country.[2] Each factor would require its own book, let alone chapter; therefore this section will simply summarize those that are key. While this chapter addresses both formal and informal self-builds, for a wider discussion of informality and housing, see chapter 7.

One main driver of self-building has been the sheer accessibility and autonomy garnered by building one's own home. The housing market is a modern invention in Egypt, beginning in earnest in the late 1970s, and today barely supplying a fifth of Egypt's urban housing needs. While rental housing predates the housing market, chapter 3 shows just how limited it remains to particular social groups—those who live in cities and are salaried working- or middle-class employees. As recently as 2017, almost two-thirds of the Egyptian workforce was not formally employed with a contract, and half of those people did not have a regular job.[3] These conditions are not exactly suited to practices of formal credit or the payment of regular monthly installments or rent.

This of course does not necessarily mean that those working informally are poor—as anyone who has visited Cairo or any other Egyptian city, town, or village can attest. Self-built housing is predominantly made up of well-built concrete and brick structures (figure 2.1). A smaller portion has also been formally built, meaning that these dwellings were designed by architects and engineers, and had a construction permit. Since the 1950s, access to formal serviced land has been mostly limited to the salaried middle class through profession-based housing cooperatives, as we see in chapter 5. The poor generally cannot afford to build anything besides shacks, which represent a small yet structurally and legally precarious portion of self-builds (figure 2.2). The most affordable option for them is to rent rooms or shacks from slumlords or squat in abandoned properties.

Irregular income means that incremental building is the most adequate way to acquire a home—one builds as conditions allow. The initial money earned goes toward buying a plot, then over the years, family heads are able to finance and oversee construction. This proceeds in an almost seasonal manner after a period of saving, usually coinciding with the religious Eid festivals, when local migrants return home for the holidays,[4] or during the summer break when expatriate Egyptians return. Self-employed owner-builders in trade or crafts are able to use their seasonal downtime, and thus can put in the time at will, something the regularly employed would find harder to do. Foundations are dug, concrete skeletons for one or two floors go up, or are added onto existing structures, bricks are built into walls, and interiors are finished.[5] Some of the more entrepreneurial buy building materials whenever their cash flow allows, storing it until everything is in place, which could be months or years away.[6] As such, building incrementally is also a way to beat inflation, where bank interest has generally lagged behind the inexorable deterioration of the value of the Egyptian pound, as prices continue to rise, sometimes on a monthly basis.

Ultimately, it is also much cheaper to self-build than to buy. On the one hand, all that developer, contractor, and middleman profit is saved. Building rather than buying may save about 20 percent of costs—a small-scale informal developer's typical profit margin—while informal construction costs can be up to 10 percent cheaper than formal housing, even taking into account bribes and fines.[7] Indeed, one owner-builder paid two-thirds of the price of a ready-built apartment in the same building, after buying the roof and—informally—adding a floor.[8] If someone already owns the land on which they will build, say a cultivated plot that may be informally subdivided, they save a fortune over buying the land, which increases in price exponentially as more homes and utilities appear.[9]

2.1: Extended family home in a mature part of the informally self-built 'Izbit al-Haggana, Cairo, December 2011. (Photograph by Yahia Shawkat.)

2.2: A row of shacks built under high-voltage cables in a more precarious part of 'Izbit al-Haggana. Cairo, March 2012. (Photograph by Yahia Shawkat.)

A self-built home also affords a socioeconomic flexibility not found in many ready-built structures. Most notably, owner-builders often include work or commercial space in their homes. Ground floor shops or workshops dominate informally built neighborhoods, which are used by owners or rented out. Offices for professionals exist in homes in both informal and formally built neighborhoods, and even if the workspace is not inside the home, it is usually within walking distance.[10] The 'air rights' over a shack, house, or villa provide futureproofing for offspring, as owner-builders add floors for sons and daughters to move into when they get married (figure 2.3). Indeed, the uniformity of mass government housing has been punctuated by residents building horizontal as well as vertical additions to accommodate their needs.[11]

Perils of Self-build

As extended families live in one building or adjacent structures—and in some areas, tribal, geographical, or religious ties extend through streets and even zones—social cohesion and support becomes strong.[12] This brings us to some of the perils of self-built communities, where social cohesion can "give the best and worst kinds of support,"[13] especially for minorities or the marginalized. Many women aspire to leave the neighborhoods they grew up in or those they moved into after marriage because they want to escape social surveillance and control of their families and neighbors.[14] They are also well aware of bullying, violence, and drugs on the streets and in the schools of rougher parts of some neighborhoods, and naturally seek better areas within the same neighborhood or elsewhere.[15]

In popular neighborhoods, power lies with particular individuals or families, who orchestrate the invasion of state-owned land and facilitate informal construction[16]—all for a fee of course.[17] Their power may linger on after a neighborhood is built, extorting residents and enforcing vigilante justice.[18]

Coptic Christian individuals and families were evicted from their homes in at least ten sectarian incidents in Egypt between 2011 and 2014.[19] In two of the incidents, Muslim families implicated in the sectarian acts were also evicted by fellow Muslims under the *'urfi* (customary) reconciliation agreements sanctioned by the government. A majority of incidents happened in villages in provincial governorates, although two occurred in periurban villages around Cairo, and Alexandria, and one in a self-built neighborhood in Cairo.

It may be that customary law is more present in rural Egypt, but it is by no means absent from urban areas, both formal or informal. In fact, the rule of law, or the lack of it, is a major issue across Egypt.[20] In the 'formal' new cities, which are hailed as the government's pride and joy, organized criminal groups—described as Bedouin or *'Arab* (Arabs), with no factual evidence to support they are indeed nomads—control the construction process. This ranges from collecting protection money for 'guarding' building materials, to forcing self-builders to buy materials from them or to contract them for work. Such a situation proved to be a huge scandal in the Ibni Baytak (Build Your Home) project that was part of deposed president Hosni Mubarak's National Housing Program of the mid-2000s, leading residents to set up a Facebook page dedicated to publicizing cases of robbery and extortion (figure 2.4).[21] Thousands of homes built through the program also remain without utilities—almost a decade after they were built.[22] In an ironic twist, President al-Sisi derided these government planned self-built neighborhoods in 2016 saying, "Take the youth to see the *'ashwa'iy Ibni Baytak*! We don't do that! Our work is skillful, perfect, and respectable."[23] But even his showcase projects, such as the New Administrative Capital, are not immune from thuggery: one member of the Egyptian

2.3: Three stages of development in the formally planned self-built neighborhood of Muqattam, Cairo: From single-story homes, through an ongoing vertical extension (foreground), to a multistory low-rise (background). November 2016. (Photograph by Yahia Shawkat.)

2.4: A row of Ibni Baytak (Build Your Home) houses in various stages of development in Badr New City. This is a rare example of a formally planned self-build project for low-income households. February 2013. (Photograph by Yahia Shawkat.)

Federation for Construction and Building Contractors estimated that protection money has raised construction prices by up to one-fifth.[24]

Origins of Control: 1889–1956

Since the late nineteenth century, legislation has fluctuated between criminalizing the unsanctioned production of homes, providing amnesty, and extending formal infrastructure.

In the late nineteenth century, large numbers of the urban poor lived in substandard *ahwash* (courtyard houses) and *'ishash* (shacks), which sheltered a quarter of Cairenes[25] and two-thirds of Port Saidis.[26] The ruling elite was so irked by them that the first *tanzim* law, literally a law 'ordering' urban space, was passed in 1889. It was applied only to the major cities, conceived of simply as streets with set widths bound by invisible *tanzim* lines that should not be transgressed by any building.[27] The law also stipulated the issuance of building permits for new construction, as well as the demolition of any existing protrusions on *tanzim* lines or new transgressions.[28]

Villages also saw some regulation from as early as 1885, where legislation regulated—albeit lightly—the construction of *'izbas* (hamlets) built by large landowners on their estates. In 1909, this legislation became more detailed as to how *'izba*s should be built, but more importantly, it decreed the demolition of *'izba*s built without a permit or not according to regulations.[29] This would become the mainstay of official government response to illegal construction in general.

Government grew in size and scope throughout the first half of the twentieth century. Ministries, departments, and agencies were added to oversee the built environment in a hurried quest to control the spread of epidemics, which infected over a million people in the early 1940s, and to quell growing social unrest. The suffering was blamed on squalid rural living conditions, rather than the social inequities of living as bonded labor in the *'izbas*,[30] and before the end of the first half of the twentieth century, both the *tanzim* and *'izba* laws evolved from a handful of lines to multipage documents, elaborating in detail how both urban and rural settlements should be built.[31]

For the first half of the twentieth century, direct regulation by government of informal or illegal building continued to focus on urban areas, namely the large cities, which at the time housed a minority of the population, but where shack building and urban decay continued. This was especially so in industrial boom towns, such as al-Mahalla, where an acute housing shortage in the 1930s saw a spike in homelessness, crowding, adverse possession of land, and the informal building of homes and shacks.[32] In response, government officials and architects advocated the demolition of entire neighborhoods and building of 'model housing' on the outskirts of cities. Mahmud Sabri Mahbub, the director of the Ministry of Health's Tanzim Department, designed a number of reconstruction schemes for Cairene neighborhoods in the 1920s and 1930s, which prioritized the "replanning and reconstruction of badly planned, unhealthy, or slum areas" by cutting through them with new roads.[33] He saw one of these neighborhoods, Bulaq Abu al-'Ila, as comprising

> the vilest slums, some of the most degraded classes of the population, hordes of beggars and vagabonds intermingled with a large number of laborers, artisans, etc. The population numbers 140,000, the housing conditions are in many areas deplorably unsanitary, and the greater part of the area is densely covered with buildings of a class and value in no way commensurate with possible site values if developed as a modern commercial and good class residential area.[34]

Another engineer in the Tanzim Department described the poor district of al-Manakhein in Port Said as home to "fertile nodes for the birth of germs and insects," before proposing a plan in 1935 to demolish the area and relocate the residents.[35] However, none of these vast demolition plans were implemented, as they ultimately proved to be too expensive, and only small-scale demolitions were carried out.

Informal Subdivision Amnesties: 1956–68

As regime change swept Egypt in 1952 and the colonial monarchy was deposed and replaced by an authoritarian republic, rural–urban migration accelerated once again. This followed a severe 'homes crisis' that started with the Second World War and that the cities had yet to recover from.[36] Affordable informal housing flourished, and in 1956, one month shy of the fourth anniversary of the July revolution, a new law was passed to freeze any demolition orders issued for buildings that contravened building leglislation.[37] The 1956 freeze was exclusively for informal construction, especially that of *taqsim mukhalif* (informal subdivision) of privately owned land, usually agricultural land, and did not extend to informal construction on state-owned land, or that which contravened *tanzim* lines. It was a so-called temporary law that only froze decrees lodged against illegal building until the date the law was enacted, while it would continue to be imposed on infractions after that date. Indeed, the minister of municipal and village affairs explained that his ministry had allowed for a suspension of demolitions, due to the severe *azmit al-masakin* (homes crisis), but acknowledged that the "leniency has encouraged many individuals to contravene these [planning and building] laws, and since the homes crisis has now abated, it has been decided to put a limit to this leniency."[38] For reasons of public health, the law also allowed for the extension of formal infrastructure to the public areas in the new neighborhoods—streets, plazas, gardens—for free, as well as to private homes, though for a fee which would be paid for by the owners.

It is not entirely clear whether this law freezing demolitions was a formal admission that the new government did not have the resources to fight informal construction during a tumultuous period of regime change, or if it was a tactic to shore up popular support. Judging by the spike in informal housing construction in the wake of the January 2011 revolution, it is not inconceivable that the government apparatus was so tied up in regime change that it simply did not prioritize regulating construction. Moreover, we cannot ignore the political significance of such a law granting thousands of people amnesty. Indeed, Law 259/1956 was published three days before the June 23 elections that would see Gamal Abd al-Nasser elected as the second president of the nascent republic, and a month before he announced the nationalization of the Suez Canal—two major political events that required popular support.

This political leniency toward the homes crisis did not dissipate however, and the temporary law would be reissued in much the same format a number of times over the next four decades. The Nasser era would see it reissued on three occasions,[39] the last of which was a few months after the Israeli invasion of Sinai in 1967, when the ensuing War of Attrition would put pressure on government spending on public housing, as well as result in the immediate need to rehouse almost one million people displaced from Sinai and the Suez Canal cities. Nasser also gravely needed to placate the population after the humiliating defeat of 1967.

One of the areas to benefit from these amnesties was Arab al-Guesr, to the east of Cairo, where 800 subdivisions were marked out and built in the 1950s and 1960s, and homes rented to waves of rural to urban migrants, as well as Suez Canal evacuees.[40] In 1966, the area received four public water taps, ostensibly through the mediation of local ASU representatives. Ultimately, this policy of temporary laws would see informal housing provision in urban areas—meaning apartment units, but also substandard single room and shack dwellings—comprising around 70 percent of urban housing production between 1960 and 1976 (figure 2.5).

Clientelism of a Ruling Elite: 1976–1990

President Anwar Sadat, famous for taking apart the Arab socialist state built by his predecessor, and ushering in the free market Infitah era, would formally encourage informal housing twice during his rule (1970–1981). The first time was in 1976, when he would issue a slightly different amnesty from his predecessor: the sale of state-owned land to squatters who had built on it.[41] Since 1957, adverse possession of state-owned land had been banned,[42] but it seems this was not entirely enforced. The second amnesty, issued in 1981, months before Sadat's assassination, was pretty much a copy of Nasser's laws. It enforced a temporary freeze on demolitions of informal construction whereby the state "voluntarily declined to exercise its right [to prosecute] in order to uphold the public good as its contribution to solve" what had now become *azmit al-iskan* (the housing crisis).[43] The new freeze also provided for the "replanning of the informal subdivisions to raise their standards," although "without the demolition of buildings that contravene the new plans until alternative housing is provided." Infrastructure would still be extended as with the previous laws.

The Sadat government pursued a contradictory path, and various amendments were made to the *tanzim* laws, while completely new and complex laws were written, stipulating longer jail terms and higher fines for offenders. A prime example is the building law passed in 1976, the same year amnesty was given for illegal housing on state land. It highlighted the failure of Law 45/1962 to "confront buildings constructed without a permit,"[44] especially in light of recent building collapses, which led to an estimated loss of 12,000 units every year due to structural failure.[45] Law 107/1976 bumped up fines to between LE10 and LE1,000, or/in addition to jail terms of up to six months for construction without a permit.[46]

As we saw with Nasser, Sadat's conflicting legislation can be best understood through a political lens. Sadat's free market policies, and later the peace treaty with Israel, were unpopular, especially among leftist opposition, resulting in waves of protests, mostly by industrial workers, which started in 1974 and culminated in the January 1977 Bread Riots.[47] Thus, the regime needed to shore up legitimacy and pacify opposition. As this was also the time of Western aid flowing back into Egypt, officials worked with their American counterparts to regularize and extend formal infrastructure to "potential hotbeds of revolution," identifying seven informal communities in the industrial district of Helwan for their new flagship project.[48] Ultimately, the upgrading of the informal areas in Helwan met with much resistance from Ministry of Housing officials, who only believed in "bulldozing and displacing people to remote areas." The upgrading process took almost a decade,[49] while much of the project money went to building government housing blocks.

Around the same time, another donor-funded project was underway in Ismailia. The al-Hikr/Hay al-Salam project approached the eponymous district, which was the largest self-built community there, both to upgrade the existing area, while planning its considerable growth through a sites and services approach on land donated by the government. What was unique here was an approach that aimed to do the most possible with minimal funding—cash from the British Overseas Development Administration as well as the aforementioned land—would be supported by a cross-subsidization model, where high value land plots on the main streets would be sold at market prices in order to cover a large part of the cost of servicing smaller, inner plots that were priced at affordable rates for poor and low income families.[50] Hay al-Salam won a couple of awards on the merits of this "critically important departure in the development of low-income housing in Egypt," benefitting 90,000 people.[51] And while it was able to initiate a new, mostly successful approach in meaningful upgrading and self-build centered planning, it stopped exactly there. Studies a few years after the project was implemented found a high proportion of higher income households living there, speculating that the poor capitalized on the land subsidies and sold their plots at market rates, moving to lower quality areas in other parts of the city.[52] The project had apparently caught the interest of the local politicians, who used it for political support by removing restrictions on who would buy the subsidized plots, while lower cost building technologies that were initially "tolerated" were later banned by the governor, making construction much more expensive.

Hay al-Salam's cross-subsidization and high—though not full—self-financing was rarely if ever repeated. When a similar sites and services project was recommended to Cairo governor Yusuf Sabri Abu Taleb in 1985, he strongly opposed it, saying, "I don't want to be known for building slums."[53] Existing self-built neighborhoods were also left to suffer, where infrastructure took between five and twelve years to reach al-Munira, Manshiyat Nasir, and al-Basatine in Cairo for example,[54] while costs for residents were high, with a number of them not being able to pay back the government, even with fifteen-year repayment plans.

After the 1977 protests, Sadat was also vengeful toward Cairo's residents, whom he called *arzal* (rude or insolent), and he quickly revived plans to demolish Bulaq neighborhood, which the government claimed sheltered protesters.[55] Images of modernity and discourses of social engineering were invoked to legitimize the forced relocation of five thousand residents of 'Ishash al-Turguman and 'Arab al-Muhammadi to the outskirts of Cairo,[56] even though the residents themselves were not politically active. This marked the first time that the narrow organic streets of informal areas were framed as a security concern because they prevented police cars from chasing protesters.[57] It was also the first time that the law allowing for the expropriation of entire neighborhoods in order to replan them was used on such a scale.[58]

If officials did not embrace upgrading informal areas, and if wholescale slum clearance projects were being planned and implemented, then who were the temporary freezes on building regulations and the amnesty from prosecution actually for?

Informal subdivisions, especially on state-owned land, were not just the preserve of the masses. In the months after Sadat was assassinated, several family members and in-laws were accused of corrupt land deals. The mega contracting company of Sadat's brother-in-law and his former Minister of Housing Osman Ahmed Osman was accused of illegally acquiring state land worth $10.3 million.[59] Sadat's half brother, Esmat Sadat, and three of his sons were found guilty of twenty-four counts of corruption, amassing a fortune of $150 million in less than a decade, including through the illegal acquisition of land.[60] One of these land deals allegedly involved a large informal area to the east of Cairo, 'Izbit al-Haggana, where subdivisions were sold between 1978 and 1981 to unwitting buyers who were promised 'good' plots on the main Cairo–Suez road, but were given land on the hill, far from the road.[61] When buyers went to complain at the local police station, they were roughed up, and ended up accepting the less desirable plots. Paperwork was all done through a *kahul*, a fall guy who signed all the sales contracts in return for a cut, or as an insurance clause lest he end up in jail, which he did.[62]

Sadat was also linked to a highly controversial project described as "the most colossal rip-off of the twentieth century," through which land around the Pyramids of Giza was to be developed into a golf resort in a joint venture between a government agency and a Western investor.[63] The project was duly canceled by Sadat some months later in response to local backlash. However, there were already some three hundred informally built cabins and weekend cottages right on the pyramid plateau in what was called Sahara City. Some cabins were owned by Western embassies, and one was used by Sadat himself. These were all demolished just two months after he was assassinated in a move by the Ministry of Culture, supported by the newly appointed president, Hosni Mubarak, to "safeguard the national interest."[64]

The first few years of Mubarak's rule appeared to signal the end of informal housing construction. Fatal building collapses continued and most notably sixty people were killed in a single disaster in 1983. This led to a raft of amendments to the Building Law 106/1976, citing the "dearth of penalties, which encouraged some in continuing to build informally . . . in contravention of construction standards."[65] As well as seeking to fight shoddy construction, the Mubarak government also wanted to limit informal urban expansion. To this end, in 1982 it separated urban planning legislation from that of construction, after reaching the implausible conclusion that a lack of "sound urban planning standards" was to blame for the "urban backwardness the cities and villages suffer from."[66] Law 3/1982 also introduced fines from LE10,000 to LE50,000 and jail terms of five to ten years for illegal subdivision of land, especially in the case of fraudulent projects,[67] which were at least ten times higher than those in the previous legislation.

Mubarak, however, would reissue the so-called temporary demolition freezes for illegal construction three times in the first decade of his rule,[68] the first time just one year after the building law was strengthened. The 'symbol of stability,' as Mubarak was nicknamed, would pass further legislation in 1984 regularizing informal construction on state-owned land in recognition that "exercising the [government's] right to remove the transgression on state land could conflict with political, economic, or social affairs, which may lead to grievous harm of the public good . . . harm of the national economy or destabilizing stable conditions, even though they were not legally sound."[69]

It is not clear how many poor communities benefited from these discretionary amnesties. The residents of 'Izbit Khayrallah, a self-built community on a rocky plateau in Cairo, were able to appeal a set of eviction orders issued in the 1980s by the Cairo governorate and the state-owned Maadi Company for Real Estate Development, the original owners of the land. In fifteen years of litigation and counter-litigation, the administrative court issued three rulings in favor of the community, in 1984, 1993, and 1999, all stating in various ways that the destruction of the residents' houses represented "a major breach of [the state's] responsibilities to maintain citizens' safety and security."[70] This overruled the law that prohibited adverse possession by citing "public interest," as with the "social use of the land," rather than its investment in profitable real estate. However, fourteen years after the ruling, only a handful of residents have completed the formalization of their tenure, as the Cairo governorate set land prices that were too high, and residents' appeals are still being heard in court.[71]

Electrifying the *'Ashwa'iyat*: 1990–1993

While the 'Izbit Khayrallah residents were in court fighting against eviction, the Cairo governor issued a decree allowing for the extension of electricity to *'ashwa'iyat* in Cairo.[72] Decree 75/1990 marked the first time the term *'ashwa'iyat*—literally meaning randomly built—was used in legislation to describe informal areas. It was also the first time that a specific form of infrastructure—electricity—would be extended to informal areas. The decree was the exemplar of targeted exceptionalism, the official surgical creation of loopholes amid increasingly tight building controls that since the late 1970s stipulated demolition and imposed fines, and jail terms that could extend to ten years for illegal construction and subdivision of land. Decree 75/1990 laid out in black and white how the provision of electricity would not "hinder the application of measures stipulated by Building Law 106/1976 or Planning Law 3/1982."[73] The law also provided for the extension of electricity to informal buildings on state-owned land, provided they were in accordance with Law 31/1984 that had been passed five years prior to regularize those transgressions, although that law only concerned buildings built before the date it was passed.

But what about water, sanitation, and secure land titles? Between 1976—the earliest year for which there are statistics on utilities—and 2017, the proportion of households with access to municipal electricity more than doubled, reaching near universal connection (figure 2.5). Access to water was more progressive, rising steadily from around a third of households in 1976 to more than 90 percent forty years later. Municipal sewers lagged far

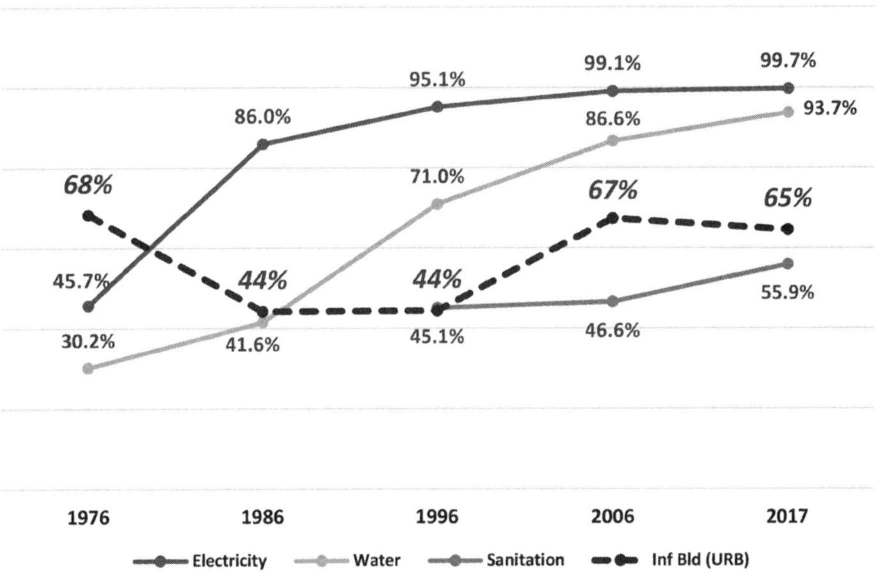

2.5: Comparison between household connection to infrastructure in Egypt and informal housing production, 1976–2017. (Note: Water refers to tap inside home, and housing production includes only the strictly urban. Sources: CAPMAS Census for Population and Living Conditions 1976, 1986, 1996, 2006, and 2017. Also see section on methodology in chapter 1.)

behind, with the earliest statistics generated in 1996, indicating that less than half of households were connected. This would not change much, and today almost half of all households remain without proper sanitation.

The doubling of households with connection to electricity happened over just one decade, 1976–86. This may be partly because the Aswan hydroelectric dam had been in use since the early 1970s, and a large-scale electrification project was implemented. But this was also the time when over half of urban dwellings were being informally built (figure 2.5). We can thereby infer that a significant portion of them were hooked up to the grid.

While the poor masses illegally tapping into electricity—described by sociologist Asef Bayat as "quiet encroachment"—may have forced the government's hand to formally extend electricity to them in exchange for paying for their consumption,[74] this does not explain why one particular service was favored over another. Is watching television, lighting rooms, and preserving food in fridges more important for people than piped drinking water or sanitary sewage collection? Informal access to services ends up being much more expensive than formal access. In one district in 2003, water bought from vendors was twenty-seven times more costly than municipal water,[75] while buying and running a generator for electricity can be prohibitively expensive. The absence of sewers means the costly emptying of septic tanks every two weeks, with failure to do so leading to toxic overflow and street flooding.

A key reason for the popular 'demand' for formal electrical connections is that government has made it a prerequisite for the issuance of official IDs and access to subsidized services that most Egyptians depend on. Proof of address is required to issue the national ID card,[76] usually in the form of a document indicating registered ownership or a rental contract in the name of the applicant. Given that most housing is informal, and so registered contracts are extremely rare, they can be supplemented with an electricity bill in the applicant's name, or the name of the landlord if renting. This is also the case for subsidy cards,[77] registering children in public schools located in the district, or applying for subsidized housing, which is governorate specific. Electricity bills have also been used as a de facto proof of ownership,[78] although by law they only prove residency, as tenants of rental units may also have meters in their name.

The government was able to manufacture a need for electricity on the part of self-builders as a move to control them through access to social services. It was thereby able to disincentivize masses of people, forcing them to illegally tap into the formal grid.[79] On top of the illegal building process itself, illegal electricity connections carry steep fines of between LE10,000 and LE100,000 and/or jail terms of between six months and two years.[80] But without taking these risks, families could not get legal electricity connections and display the sought-after *hadida* (metal plaque) outside their door (figure 2.6). Residents who want legal meters must willingly ask the police to register the offense in a *mahdar mumarsa*.[81] Inspectors from the electricity company then examine the residential unit to make sure it is occupied, usually checking for a working stove, hung laundry, and food, before (arbitrarily) calculating consumption based on current appliances, registering the unit, and issuing a flat bi- or trimonthly *mumarsa* fee that tends to be far higher than what would be paid through metered electricity.[82] These quasi-legal connections have worked wonders to generate extra revenue for the electricity companies whose tariffs were historically subsidized. It has also meant that their inspectors, along with the Electricity Police, wield significant power over entire communities, as they can impose steep fines as well as jail terms if payment is missed, or if there is a change in appliances and thus electricity consumption.[83] This has of course also meant that bribery to look the other way is rife: "*ka'anni mashuftish haga*" (as if I didn't see anything).[84]

2.6: The revered *hadida* (metal plaque) proclaiming a formal electricity connection barely hangs on a crumbling mudbrick village home in Qaranfil, Qalubiya. March 2012. (Photograph by Yahia Shawkat.)

The manufactured need for electricity also helped the government to wash its hands of any meaningful obligations toward self-built settlements, forcing people to accept—and maybe even demand—the bare minimum of recognition. Two years after it decreed the provision of electricity to informal areas in Cairo, the government moved to steepen fines and reprimands for both builders and civil servants tasked with regulating construction. Amendments to the building law were made in 1992 as "it was found out during the implementation of Law 106/1976 that its penalties were inadequate and encouraged the continuation of illegal building."[85] The law stipulated that building owners submit proof of building permits when requesting the extension of infrastructure, and mandated the creation of a specialized agency that would oversee municipalities in implementing the law.[86] However, the amendments carried over exceptions to the building code from previous legislation, whereby a governor could submit a request to the housing minister that entire portions of cities or villages be exempt from unspecified articles in the law.[87]

'Upgrading' the *'Ashwa'iyat*: 1993–2011

On October 12, 1992, a medium-force earthquake struck near Cairo. In thirty seconds, 5,000 buildings collapsed, and a further 11,500 were damaged, killing over 560 people and leaving more than 10,000 families homeless.[88] The urban tragedy itself was not enough to put informal subdivisions in the government's sights, however; it was rather the political disaster attached to it.

International news networks portrayed a working-class district in Giza as the 'republic' or 'emirate' of Imbaba, because of the clear presence of a local Jama'a al-Islamiya group in postdisaster aid effort, in contrast to the absence of official help. This "overt, visible and publicized challenge to the authority of the Egyptian state" led to the heavy-handed 'siege of Imbaba,'[89] in which thousands of paramilitary Central Security Forces surrounded the neighborhood for six weeks before violently storming it, resulting in the death of one hundred people and the arbitrary arrest of six hundred.

In line with what had become the traditional stigmatizing response of authorities to residents of impoverished neighborhoods from as far back as the 1930s, the (mostly state-run) media portrayed the *'ashwa'iyat* as a breeding ground for Islamism, which was the current form of political opposition. The brutal show of force in Imbaba could not be replicated in all the *'ashwa'iyat*, and so a carrot was needed to go with the stick. Here a leaf was taken from the pages of the limited upgrading experiments of the late 1970s, but instead of a handful of projects here and there, the country-wide National Project for Upgrading Slums was born in 1993.

Egypt's Shura Council, the upper chamber of parliament, commissioned a study that identified 1,221 *'ashwa'iyat*, detailing their population and area, slating 1,201 of them for upgrading, and twenty for demolition, as upgrading them was found to be "futile."[90] Those designated for upgrading were mainly entire districts of informal subdivisions on private agricultural land that would be incorporated into cities. They would also be provided with formal infrastructure,[91] including electricity, water, sanitation, as well as street paving, waste collection, and police and fire services.[92] Those areas slated for demolition were small pockets of the often villainized *'ishash* built on state land.[93]

Electrification was still prioritized, and so rather than putting the ministers of housing or local administration (municipalities) in charge of the project, it was the minister of electricity who would head the official committee to "coordinate between the projects to upgrade the *'ashwa'iyat* in all of Egypt's governorates."[94]

It was also an election year for Mubarak and a national project could not hurt. The number of households provided with formal electricity rose from 95 to 99 percent over the following decade (figure 2.5), which more or less coincided with the project's duration. Tellingly, the share of informal housing in urban Egypt, which had dropped to less than half of total production between 1976 and 1996, skyrocketed to 67 percent in the decade of 1996–2006 (figure 2.5). Amazingly, builders were also defying military decrees issued in 1996 prohibiting construction without a permit and the urbanization of arable land, referring anyone found guilty of doing so to the dreaded State Security courts.[95]

The fanfare around the upgrading of the *'ashwa'iyat* lasted for over a decade, and it was even invoked during Mubarak's fourth election campaign in 2005. The military decrees were repealed by Mubarak a year earlier,[96] while an editorial in the leading state-run *al-Ahram* at the time underscored how the *'ashwa'iyat* were a "priority . . . and he has put in place particular procedures to implement this goal by regularizing ownership and extending infrastructure."[97] Indeed, the annual Ministry of Electricity reports between 2007 and 2011 have reserved a few paragraphs highlighting how many units or households they provided electricity to "at the order of the President of the Republic to aid the citizens in extending infrastructure to the *'ashwa'iyat* and the *mabani al-mukhalifa* (buildings in breach of the law)."[98]

Here it is important to note the distinction made by the government between two forms of informality. The first is the *'ashwa'iyat*, referred to as households, and most likely the term refers to those covered by the national project from 1993 onward, with a specific cabinet approval,[99] issued one day *before* Mubarak was sworn in for his sixth term. The provision for the second form, the *mabani al-mukhalifa*, was approved by the Council of Governors a little over a month later, with requests by owners vetted on a case-by-case basis by the governors according to whom they decided was 'deserving.'[100] Cabinet and governor approvals it seems were built on shaky grounds, and within a year Mubarak would issue a law ordering the extension of basic infrastructure to the *mabani al-mukhalifa*, for which owners had three months to apply.[101]

The Ministry of Electricity would receive over half a million requests in those three months—423,000 of which were approved—and over the next five years, 366,000 homes would receive formal connections to electricity.[102] By comparison, 530,000 *'ashwa'iyat* households had electricity formally extended in eighteen years.[103] Overall, these numbers seem quite conservative, given the number of homes being built informally, and the number of households cited by the census as having access to electricity. This can only mean that the majority of households living in informal homes continued to do so in breach of the law under the *mumarsa* agreements. So much for Mubarak's guarantee "for our compatriots in the countryside" of "their right to appropriate housing away from legal chasing."[104]

As with Sadat, regime cronies were big beneficiaries of legal exceptionalism. A major standoff between Mustafa al-Sallab, a parliamentarian from Mubarak's National Democratic Party (NDP), and Cairo Governor 'Abd al-'Azim Wazir erupted in 2009, when Wazir issued demolition decrees for twenty-eight residential towers in 'Izbit al-Haggana.[105] Most of these buildings were empty or still under construction, with some partially occupied. Police faced off with residents, killing one, while al-Sallab protested for his constituency in parliament, temporarily freezing demolitions. These were not owner-built homes, but rather what author David Sims referred to as "one-off speculative towers."[106] By the late 2000s, these structures were not one-off any more, as well-connected informal developers rode the real estate wave in the neighborhoods within and around cities,[107] financed by those with the means to do so, from football stars to judges.[108]

The governor believed al-Sallab, also a tycoon in the ceramics industry, to be behind the informal towers, both as facilitator and developer, as the use of a *kahul* (fall guy) became more common. Months after the Haggana orders, he and his family were issued demolition orders for a number of properties, all in his district, that were either constructed without permits or had their use changed without the proper paperwork.[109] But being an important member of parliament in Mubarak's ruling NDP, Prime Minister Ahmad Nazif would overrule the governor's decrees, [110] a highly exceptional move that publicly shamed the governor, but more importantly, established parliamentarians as superior to governors.

Why Wazir had decided to move then is anybody's guess—perhaps power struggles between the two, or a piling up of unpaid bribes. Indeed, false demolitions can be arranged when nonstructural elements such as a wall are knocked out, leaving the concrete structure intact, just so a demolition could be jotted down as 'executed.' One can see this in many demolitions, leaving buildings looking like they have contracted some sort of skin disease (figure 2.7). It was also the time in which Wazir was fresh out of the Duweiqa disaster, when a rockslide in September 2008 killed over 115 people,[111] and he probably wanted to appear to be doing his job fighting informal construction. For Wazir had used yet another new law in the legal arsenal for the demolition orders, the Unified Building Law 119/2008, thus named because it cobbled together most legislation related to buildings, including urban planning, elevator installations, condominium unions, and heritage conservation. One of its many stipulations, Article 62, prohibited any amnesty or the extension of utilities to informal buildings, tactically rescinding Mubarak's election amnesty, three years after it was made in 2005.

Duweiqa was also the second time in fifteen years that an urban disaster would reshape policy toward the *'ashwa'iyat*. A new agency, the Informal Settlements Development Facility (ISDF), was set up a month after the rockslide.[112] Within a year it had prepared a National Map for Unsafe Areas, which included 404 communities with 212,201 homes.[113] Many of these communities were already identified in the older National Project to Upgrade the *'Ashwa'iyat*, but its 1,200 communities were a much more unattainable target, as barely a third were upgraded in the fifteen years since it was started, [114] and so the project was killed off, conveniently ignoring about twelve million people still living without proper infrastructure.

2.7: A new informal developer tower stands 'falsely' demolished in Maryutiya, Giza. Only the walls have been knocked out, making it easy to remedy as opposed to an actual demolition that affects the concrete structure. Notice some sections have been left as they are, and are possibly occupied apartments. December 2018. (Photograph by Yahia Shawkat.)

Despite the diminished scale of the new project, in five years only 14 percent of areas designated unsafe were 'developed.'[115] The main reason behind the slow pace was that residents resisted the development, which was primarily based on demolishing neighborhoods and relocating their residents—mostly by force—to housing estates in remote locations, as we see in chapter 7. Where the 1993 project had slated twenty areas for demolition, the majority of the four hundred 'unsafe areas' were due to be cleared under a mechanism called 'land value capture,' with the high-value land the shacks were built on being sold to cover the costs of giving the residents supposedly better homes.

On one hand, less than one million households in informal homes would receive electricity and benefit from the amnesties from the mid-1990s through 2011. On the other, over 41,000 would suffer the demolition of their homes and forced displacement, under the government's 'upgrading' and 'development' projects.[116]

Limbo: 2011–2019

Both informal self-building, as well as speculative building, capitalized on the January 2011 uprising and the subsequent withdrawal of the police. Again, informal builders would represent a constituency that it would be foolish for a politician to ignore, especially in a race to become Egypt's first new president in three decades. In May 2012, former prime minister and presidential hopeful Ahmad Shafiq promised regularization for all informal housing if he won the elections, "but it would be the last time."[117]

And how big was this constituency? The Ministry of Electricity received one million requests for formal electricity in 2011 alone, of which an unprecedented 880,000 units were connected by 2012.[118] Most of these were of course not built in a year and included older buildings whose applications had been rejected previously. The ministry instituted a paradigm shift in semiformalization, devising a new coded electricity meter, so-called because it does not carry the name of the owner, but a numbered code instead. The significance of this change was that connection to the grid would no longer give any legitimacy to the building, as there would be no contracts between providers and clients,[119] and thus no paper trail connecting owners to their properties.

This constituency included many more developers than ever before, as well as those who bought from them. The developers were also greedier than before, with thirty-one hastily built informal towers collapsing and killing over sixty people in one year.[120] While several of these had still been empty or under construction, they were built in dense neighborhoods, which meant the structures that were between ten and twenty stories high toppled on smaller, occupied structures around them.[121]

Shafiq lost to Muhammad Mursi, who in his year in office did not make any changes to the housing status quo before being deposed by the military in July 2013. It would be almost another year before the government moved to demolish some of the newer informal buildings, with the dramatic use of explosives in a well-publicized show of force.[122] It should be noted that these were not on privately owned land, which the majority of informal homes are built on, but rather were mostly speculative towers on state-owned land in the heart of Cairo. Al-Sisi, who had served as Mursi's defense minister before leading the military ouster, then ran for president in mid-2014. In an interview with *al-Ahram*'s editor, one month before the elections, he said, "We will confront the *'ashwa'iyat* with determination," explaining that it would take several years to raise standards of services and infrastructure.[123] He did not, however, promise formalization of around three million units built since 2011.[124]

In March 2016, in the middle of al-Sisi's four-year term, the government fully legislated the connection of coded meters, despite resistance from local government to their use [125] (possibly because it signaled an end to a source of income through fines). The new legislation initially only covered buildings on private agricultural land, but was amended nine months later to include those on state-owned land.[126] While this move has certainly eased the troubles of many, it is far from a guaranteed proof of tenancy.

But in May 2017, al-Sisi ordered the removal of all transgressions on state-owned land because "no one is above the law. Whoever places his hands illegally on the nation's land is a thief and a land-grabber, no matter who he is."[127] He pointed to the newly formed Committee to Recover State Land (CRSL), which was already inventorying adversely possessed state land, as we see in chapter 7. A month later, during a ceremony parading the recovery of some of this land, al-Sisi mentioned buildings on a Nile island that he left unnamed, claiming that they were leaking sewage into the river. He declared, "Any buildings on the banks of water channels, drains, or the Nile should be removed. Yes, there are residents. We should find a solution for them, but they have to be removed."[128] Ten days later, Central Security Forces stormed Warraq Island in Cairo by ferry, armed with bulldozers in an attempt to demolish more than seven hundred buildings on the island, which is home to ninety thousand people.[129] The residents clashed with police, and one local was killed and fifty from both sides injured. While officials claimed they were demolishing illegal buildings on state-owned land, residents disputed this claim. They produced documents showing that most of Warraq Island is privately owned, and that many buildings have permits and legal connections to electricity, while the remainder has the government's coded electricity meters. In what can only be seen as an official recognition of the residents' formal ownership, the government later issued an exportation decree for all the land on the island's perimeter, as well as land within it, estimated to affect twenty thousand people.[130]

Big developers remained immune from the law. For example, while a demolition order was issued by the governor of Matruh in 2018 for a large resort under construction on the northwest coast for not having the required permits, the order was ultimately frozen. But unlike the al-Sallab–Wazir standoff in 'Izbit al-Haggana, here it was pleas from the developer and the minister of investment that prime minister and minister of housing

Mustafa Madbuli responded to. But he went a step further than Prime Minister Nazif and brought in the Administrative Control Authority to investigate the governor's actions.[131]

While the semiformal electricity was being extended and the demolitions were raging ahead, a draft law was leaked in 2015 outlining a process of *tasaluh* (reconciliation) of some forms of illegal buildings for a hefty fine, equal to the cost of construction.[132] This would echo the 'temporary' amnesty laws issued between 1956 and 1986, particularly given that it would suspend, for six months, the relevant building code article stipulating the demolition of informal buildings. The scope of formalization provided for under the law was heavily limited, as it did not include buildings on agricultural land—which made up the vast majority of infringements—nor those on state-owned land. This implied that the government would be demolishing literally millions of units.

Four years and many drafts later, the Construction Violations Reconciliation Law 17/2019 was passed, setting a range of fines of between LE50 and LE2,000 per square meter from remote rural areas to central urban neighborhoods in big cities, as well as including buildings on agricultural land. The ninth amnesty since 1956 followed its predecessors in excluding a number of infringements, such as those on *tanzim* lines, as well as building on state land, unless legalized through the CRSL. In July 2019, its executive bylaws were published, giving owners or residents of informal buildings six months to apply for reconciliation.[133] It remains to be seen how many millions will apply and become formalized, and how many billions will line the treasury's coffers.

(Anti)-Social Production of Habitat

Looking back at six decades of elaborate de facto tolerance of informal self-building, it appears to be less a series of cobbled-together knee-jerk reactions than a deliberate policy on the part of the government. In cases where there were official efforts to help support self-builds—such as the Helwan project in the 1980s and Ibni Baytak in the 2000s—the government still managed to find a way to scuttle them. If you are a small owner-builder who is ethical or simply does not want to take risks, the government's message has been 'good luck,' because sticking to the rules might not get you very far either.[134]

Instead of recognizing self-building as a legitimate form of housing provision—and so designing policy that accommodates and encourages it—successive regimes have sought to trap builders, and lately buyers of informally built homes, in a manufactured informality. Government creates a demand for infrastructure and recognition, which is met only through criminality. It is an informality that people have cut their teeth learning to negotiate, in order to provide themselves with decent homes. At times, residents have been able to literally win land, resisting repressive legislation and practicing their right to housing and the city, but at other times, when a regime is strong, it claws back lost land and establishes a skeletal authority, leaving many hanging in limbo waiting for the state's next move.

This waxing and waning of authority is reflected in the varying forms of recognition extended by different governments—from discretionary extension of infrastructure between the 1950s and 1980s, to the full, legalized electricity extended to the *'ashwa'iyat* between 1993 and 2011, through a diluted semiformal recognition by way of the coded electricity meters from 2011 onward. As the government has been actively commodifying the housing market over the last decade,[135] informal housing has also evolved from being almost exclusively owner-built by the marginalized to real estate that can be capitalized on by developers. Government has responded in an increasingly arbitrary way, legalizing particular infractions, while demolishing others using the very same laws. Even formal but poor communities are not immune.

The contradictory, almost paradoxical, rafts of legislation and their abuse by government has meant that the rule of law has been diminished, bringing to mind philosopher Michel Foucault's theory of how governments use laws as tactics, and "consequently law recedes."[136]

3

OLD TO NEW RENT

In conversation with city dwellers in their eighties, you would be forgiven for thinking that renting is the only tenure option available in Egypt, as almost every home they have lived in, including the present one, has been rented. They are 'generation Old Rent'—beneficiaries of rent control, which kept prices generally affordable. Talk to urban Egyptians twenty years younger, and you will get a mix of responses. Most of those who grew up in cities were probably renters when they got married, though they had to pay large fees called *khiliw rigl* (key money) to acquire an Old Rent apartment. This could sometimes be as much as the price of a more modest home. Many of them now live in homes that they own, bought through savings made after spending a few years working in the Gulf.

From the 1990s onward renting came into disdain. If a young man were to propose to his bride-to-be, offering to live in a *shaqqa igar* (rented apartment), he would probably be seen as unable to provide a stable future and would be refused on the spot. Indeed, as New Rent came into force in the 1990s, deregulating prices and contract terms, rents have become increasingly expensive, eating up chunks of income that could better go toward saving up for a home.

The experiences of these generations are but a mirror of official policy toward rent over the last eight decades, which the statistics throw into stark relief. Rent has been losing popularity on a massive scale over the past forty years, dropping from two-thirds of urban households in 1976, to barely a quarter in 2017. Over half a million households abandoned renting altogether in the past decade alone.

Regionally the changes have been striking. In Cairo, the city where rent is most popular, the share of renters has dropped by half. In 1976, an overwhelming majority of 80 percent of the population rented, and were mostly Old Rent tenants, while today the rate is 39 percent, two-thirds of which rent under Old Rent. The case is even more dramatic in Port Said, where renters dropped fivefold from a little over 80 percent of households to barely 16.2 percent, less than half of which are Old Rent tenants.

To understand why we are seeing such a strong retreat of rent, especially given the liberalization of rent control two decades ago with the specific goal of catalyzing the market, we need to explore almost one hundred years of rent legislation.

Seeds of Rent Control: 1920 and 1942

Government regulation of rent was rather lax during the first half of the twentieth century, except for a brief price freeze just after the First World War, lasting from 1921 until the market was deemed stable in 1926 (table 3.1). Come the Second World War, a shortage of building materials inflated real estate prices, leading to massive price hikes by landlords as well as high vacancy rates.[1] This was also exacerbated by an influx of American military personnel in 1942 that trebled prices in certain Cairene neighborhoods.[2] Thus, a barrage of prime ministerial orders were issued between 1942 and 1945, and citing martial law, they fixed rents at no more than 8 to 12 percent of their 1941 values (table 3.1). More importantly though, the legislation abolished fixed-length contracts (terms), allowing only for the eviction by court order of nonpaying tenants, or if the owners needed their property back for personal use, in which case a six-month notice period was required. The 1945 order also saw the further tightening of control over private property, stipulating that any vacancy was to be reported to the local council within a week, thereby forcing the rental of vacant homes. Overall, rent control was only enacted in the cities, leaving villages, where rent probably did not exist for the most part, out of the equation. Much of the legislation was copied from the British colonial rulers, especially the Rent and Mortgage Interest Restrictions Act 1939.

After the war, instead of reverting back to market rents, most of these temporary provisions were enshrined by the king through Law 121/1947. Again, this was following in the footsteps of Britain, which only decontrolled rent a decade later with the Rent Act 1957. Rents for contracts in buildings constructed before 1944 were increased slightly, but still fixed, while there were no rent limits imposed on buildings constructed after 1944, so that the private sector would still have an incentive to build new

Legislation	Rent Values	Terms/Eviction	Scope	Controls on Private Property	Advances/ Deposits/ Key Money
Law 11/1920 & others	Temporary rent freeze until June 1925				
PM Orders 151, 164, 199 & 315/1942	From May 1, 1941, rents fixed to April 1941 values plus 8-12% depending on value	Terms abolished, eviction only - By court order for non/late payment or misuse - By notice of six months in case of need for personal use.	In cities, specified by Ministry of Interior Order.	None	None
PM Order 598/1945	From May 1, 1941, in Alexandria only, rents fixed to August 1939 values plus 8–12% depending on value		Adds certain provisions for the cities of Cairo, Giza, Alexandria, and the Suez Canal.	Vacancy reported within one week.	None
Provisional Laws 97 /1945, 140/1946, & Law 121/1947	For buildings built before January 1, 1944, rents fixed to April 1941 values, plus 10–15% depending on value	Adds: -Court order in case of sublet without permission, imminent building collapse, and need to rebuild.	Provincial capitals and list of cities. Possibility of extension by Minister of Interior Order.	Property vacant for more than three months must be rented out at legal value if there is a request.	Any payment other than that stipulated in the contract must be reimbursed (though without penalty).

3.1: Highlights of rent legislation between 1920 and 1947.

homes. Reasons to evict tenants and end contracts were also expanded. These included the need for major structural repairs, if a building was condemned for demolition, and if a tenant misused the property or sublet it without the owner's permission.

'Socialist' Rent Control: 1952–71

The Free Officers took little time in announcing their socialist revolution when they swept to power in July 1952. Barely two months after deposing the monarchy, a 15 percent reduction in rents was passed on all buildings exempted from previous legislation (table 3.2). As before, buildings constructed after the law was passed were exempt, and were rented out at unregulated rates. This was not to remain the case, however, and three further reductions to rent were enacted over the next decade to "relieve the *azmit al-masakin*" (homes crisis).[3] President Gamal Abd al-Nasser saw these surprise reductions as "tangible socialist legislation that the people noticed right away, so they knew that there is socialism and that socialism benefits all."[4] Indeed, 1961 was also when Arab socialism was consolidated and codified as the ideology of the regime.

But these laws did not "relieve the homes crisis," and actually led to rents higher than market rates for the exempted buildings, as landlords were found to hedge against future price hikes.[5] To address this, the more elaborate Law 46/1962 was passed (table 3.2), assigning Rent Valuation Committees in each governorate to regulate all future rents at an annual value of 5 percent of the value of the land and building, in addition to 3 percent of the value of the building to cover maintenance and repairs (depreciation). This was prorated to each unit by surface area, and was seen by the government as sufficient to encourage private sector building, especially given that annual interest rates on bonds were only 4 percent.

However, because the law stipulated that the committees reviewed each rental contract, and only after it was signed, the committees were overwhelmed with work that took years to process.[6] Landlords again asked for higher rents to hedge against the committees' foreseeable reductions, which even members of the Arab Socialist Union (ASU), Nasser's political party, found to be excessively low—committee members had feared they would be seen as corrupt if they did not sufficiently lower the rents. To emphasize the problem, one senior party member quoted to Nasser a poem by late-nineteenth-century judge and philosopher Qasim Amin: "I know people that ruled unjustly so that it is said they ruled justly."[7] There were corrupt committees in which members were also landlords who raised rents.[8] To tackle this, Law 7/1965 brought a swift end to the backlog of unprocessed reviews by reducing all pending contracts by 35 percent (table 3.2)—which was seen as the amount landlords hedged against the reductions[9]—retroactively to 1962. A separate reduction of 20 percent was made for contracts signed between 1952 and 1961, so as not to leave earlier contracts more expensive than the newer ones.

Despite all these regulations, there continued to be a 'homes crisis,' but not because there were not any homes. Public landlords—namely the now state-owned companies that were nationalized in the early 1960s—controlled thousands of nationalized properties assigned to them. Civil servants became powerful brokers, renting out choice properties to high-level government employees upon a formal request made by their employer,[10] though bribes were also accepted from the wealthy.[11]

The ability of private landlords to control property remained through the practice of *khiliw rigl*. The demand for upfront key money was by no means new; the initial rent control law issued in 1947 had tried to address the practice, though without criminalizing it.[12] The practice seems to have surged in the late 1950s and early 1960s, leading to the passing of Law 12/1962, imposing fines on landlords or their middlemen who were proven to have accepted key money.

Complaints about prohibitively expensive key money were still made personally to Nasser in 1966.[13] The president was averse to imposing any further restrictions on homeowners, arguing that "we also want to encourage the private sector to build housing, and, in all honesty, we imposed very large rent reductions on them."[14] But after the 1967 Six Day War—which saw the Israeli invasion of Sinai and the decimation of Egypt's army—government resources dedicated to housing were all but depleted and building materials were siphoned to rebuilding military bases. As such, there was a large drop in the production of government housing, while private housing was much more expensive to build, and landlords demanded higher *khiliw*, further exacerbating the housing shortage.

This prompted the government to set up Key Money and Resolution Committees in 1968, which received tenants' complaints about landlords, and managed to reimburse LE3.3 million worth of key money in Cairo alone.[15] When landlords complained that the committees were illegal, Cairo Governor Saad Zayid famously replied, "*Al-qanun fi agaza*" (the law is on holiday).[16] The government was able to enforce action against key

Legislation	Rent Values	Term/Eviction	Scope	Controls on Private Property	Advances/ Deposits/ Key Money
Law 199/1952 (Amends Law 121/1947)	From January 1, 1944, rents reduced by 15% (except new contracts or 10-year contracts)	As before (see *Table 3.1*)	As before	As before	As before
Law 605/1954 Unsafe Buildings		Temporary eviction with court order for major repair or without court order in case of imminent collapse			
Law 564/1955 (Amends Law 121/1947)			Exempts government housing for employees and workers		
Law 353/1956 (Amends Law 121/1947)		Rebuilding requires permission of special committee			
Law 55/1958 (Amends Law 121/1947)	From September 18, 1952, rents reduced by 20% (except new contracts or 10-year contracts)	As before	Extended to government-subsidized housing	As before	As before
Law 168/1961 (Amends Law 121/1947)	From June 12, 1958, rents reduced by 20% (except new contracts or 10-year contracts)	As before	As before	As before	As before
Law 169/1961 (Amends Real Estate Tax Law 56/1957)	Reduction of rents equal to exception of rented units from real estate tax	As before	As before	As before	As before

Law 12/1962 (Amends 121/1947)					Landlord/ middleman subject to fine (LE20–100)
Law 46/1962 (Amends Law 121/1947)	From November 2, 1961, annual rents fixed to 5% of land and construction value and 3% of construction value (for repair and maintenance) based on committee valuations	As before	As before	As before	As before
Law 7/1965 (Amends previous laws)	For places specified in Laws 199/1952, 55/1958, and 168/1961, reduction of 20% and reduction of 35% if final committee verdict not issued and if issued, the lower of the two, under Law 46/1962	As before	As before	As before	As before
Law 52/1969 (New Rent law, abolishes previous legislation)	From August 18, 1969, annual rents fixed to 5% of land and construction value, and 3% of construction value based on committee valuation during construction (not after, as before). Rents can be increased by 12% of value of major repair, up to maximum 50% of original rent	Bequeathal to first-degree family members, and to third-degree family members if cohabiting for minimum one year before death. Eviction by court order for non- or late payment (stopped if paid during ruling), sublet without permission, misuse. Temporary eviction for major repair or rebuilding (personal use omitted)	All provincial capitals and settlements designated as cities as per Municipal Law 134/1960. Extension to villages by Minister of Housing decree	As before	No payment other than two-month deposit and rent. Restrictions on tenants and middlemen. Six-month jail term and/or LE500 fine

3.2: Highlights of rent legislation between 1952 and 1969.

money for about a year, before the regime's mouthpiece, *al-Ahram* newspaper, ran a front-page report in February 1969 titled, "An Important Ruling on Key Money: Landlords' Admittance of Accepting Key Money under Pressure Inadmissible!" This enraged ASU member Abd al-Gabir 'Allam, who demanded an investigation into how the supposedly revolutionary newspaper could run such an "erroneous report," one which misleadingly cited an original verdict that had later been appealed in the government's favor. The newspaper "thus could only be interpreted as attacking the revolutionary governors who requisitioned the key money, or the ASU itself."[17] Nasser responded that he had spoken with his confidant and *al-Ahram* editor-in-chief Hassanein Heikal, and that an investigation had been launched by the ASU. When 'Allam brought the issue up a week later, Nasser assured him that in fact the plaintiff's building had been issued a sequestration order "so that we could rid him of lawyers, and save him their expense, because the case went back to court after the [last] ruling."[18]

The tumultuous road of rent legislation in the socialist era to relieve the homes crisis would reach its ultimate milestone in March 1969, when ASU member and former minister of local administration Abd al-Muhsin Abd al-Nur presented the draft of the second comprehensive law regulating rent at an ASU meeting. The new draft aimed to address a number of problems, chief of which was the need to streamline the work of the Rent Valuation Committees. The draft stipulated that landlords submit rent values during construction, rather than after; that committees combine tenant applications by building, rather than individually; that tenants rather than landlords pay for water use, as well as regulations of the proliferating market of non-rent-controlled 'furnished apartments.'[19] Nasser reminded the session of what socialism was, before stressing, "what we need is a housing law that does not prevent the building of homes . . . and we do not want exploitation, but we also want to encourage those with the means to build." In response, one member commented that in order for the law to be enforced it needed to be just, while another asked for an increase to the return on investment (for which rental values are calculated). Nasser agreed to the raise, while conceding that tenants may need to pay advances, as long as they are deducted from the rent. He told the meeting that he himself had not been able to find a place to rent in 1944 until he was "saved" by a landlord who accepted an advance to finish his incomplete apartment. He concluded:

> In all honesty many people cannot find apartments. One knows many people who cannot find homes . . . and want a home by any means. Can the government build housing for all of them today? . . . Honestly, we can't. Therefore we must encourage whoever constructs buildings, and I say these are the fundamentals of socialism, to build so that people can be housed . . . Those who will postpone their marriage two or three years have to be housed . . . We have to make the process easier, or they'll say we exhausted them. . . . They will say they said they'd build and then didn't, nor did they let the people build, and the result is that we can't find homes.[20]

Five months later, Law 52/1969 was passed with none of the pro-landlord changes agreed to in the ASU committee meetings (table 3.2). The rents remained fixed at the same rates stipulated in the 1962 law, though with some provision for raising them if major repairs were made to the building. On the other hand, furnished rents were heavily regulated, a jail term was introduced for landlords, middlemen, or tenants who accepted key money, and the fine was increased fivefold to LE500. The most significant addition to the law was the introduction for the first time of bequeathal of lifetime contracts, not just to immediate next of kin, but to up to third-degree family members, as long as they had been living with the original tenant for a year before his or her death. No limit on bequeathal was set, implying a perpetual tenure for tenants and their heirs.

By the end of the socialist era—marked by Nasser's death in 1971—and after more than three decades of rent control, almost two million families were tenants (figure 3.5), representing two-thirds of urban households (figure 3.4). This was the highest ratio of renters in Egypt on record, and would change dramatically over the next few decades, as Old Rent unraveled during the rule of Nasser's successor, Anwar Sadat.

Open (Back) Door Deregulation: 1971–81

The right of bequeathal of rental contracts almost indefinitely, introduced in 1969, must have contributed considerably to the rise in both value and incidence of *khiliw* in the 1970s. It also became standard informal practice that in the event of buying out an existing tenant, the *khiliw* would be divided equally between the tenant and the landlord. This led to rising discontent among new tenants, which prompted an exceptional decree in 1973 recriminalizing *khiliw* (table 3.3). This was merely a decorative piece of legislation, as it did not introduce anything not already enshrined in law four years prior. Governors also threatened noncomplying landlords with prosecution by the Socialist Public Prosecutor,[21] a much-feared political-judicial office that operated in parallel to the public prosecutor and the judiciary.[22] Despite this, by 1976, Prime Minister and Vice Military Commander Mamduh Salim conceded that some landlords were exploiting *azmit al-iskan* (the housing crisis), and that the practice of *khiliw* was "so widespread and breached all limits, urgently requiring that it be excised from its roots, so that the citizen can fulfill his housing needs without suffering, exclusion, or exploitation."[23]

The issue was not only about *khiliw*, as by then building owners were regularly circumventing rent control altogether, either by exclusively renting out furnished homes, or selling them outright to buyers. Cash was much easier to come by in the 1970s, with over one million Egyptians working in the Gulf sending back $3billion in earnings every year.[24] Using the powers of martial law to "urgently curb the housing problems that have accumulated,"[25] Salim issued his second military order in three years addressing rent (table 3.3), raising the fine on *khiliw* so that it became equal to double the amount paid, in addition to reimbursing the tenant. The decree also restricted furnished rent to one unit in any one city per owner, and for the first time restricted the sale of homes to 10 percent of units in multi-unit apartment buildings of ten units or more. This last provision was especially brow raising, as it was not conceived of during the socialist era, but amid newfound free market policies.

The rental housing crisis continued to worsen with an almost complete breakdown of the landlord–tenant relationship. The situation was so dire that the Chief Public Prosecutor Ibrahim al-Qalyubi submitted a draft rent law to parliament to "plug all the loopholes that have led to disputes and fights, and even transgressions between owners and tenants," and relieve his office of an inundation of reports by setting up special housing courts to resolve disputes quickly.[26]

Even though interwar austerity (1967–73) came to an end with the October War in 1973, the ensuing peace talks with Israel, and warming of relations with the West, inflation was at a record high due to post-war foreign investment in Egypt, rising interest rates, and the deregulation of Nasser's policies through the Infitah.[27] This of course had a tremendous effect on frozen rents, greatly diminishing any meaningful return for landlords. Inflation also meant more vacancies, as owners held onto their units for longer in order to reap potentially higher *khiliw* or sale prices in the future. Given that the rent law stipulated that units vacant for longer than four months must be rented out to a tenant willing to pay the legal rent, owner-builders started to deliberately slow or halt construction in the later stages, just enough to keep the units from being in a usable state. Units often remained without windows, doors, interior finishing, or elevators, so that their owners did not have to report them as vacant.

One year after the military order, the third of the elaborate rent laws was issued: according to Parliament, Housing Law 49/1977 was to "help the country exit the housing crisis . . . that burns the Egyptian citizen."[28] This time, its scribes invoked Islamic rather than socialist principles, as Sadat had by then gradually steered the country away from socialism toward the Infitah's market liberalism. Styling himself *al-ra'is al-mu'min* (the believer president), Sadat branded socialism as a secular and anti-Islamic ideology, and implied the Infitah was more Islamic. Politicians toed the party line, and parliamentary housing committee head 'Abbas Safi al-Din, who debated the new law, said, "In our country we must have a good example in Islamic law. Islamic jurisprudence balances between the rights of the owner and the tenant."[29]

The new law was not a departure from the previous socialist laws, however, just as Nasser's laws had not been much of a departure from the colonial-era rent control laws preceding his rule. It was rather one link in a continuum of politically driven knee-jerk evolutions. The new law simply modified, elaborated, and even complicated previous legislation (table 3.3). It was also intriguingly passed a few months after the deadly Bread Riots of January 1977, the pinnacle of a series of protests against Sadat's free market policies and the peace process he brokered with Israel. Since almost two-thirds of the urban population were tenants, rent was a powerful political tool (figure 3.4).

Ironically for a free market law, restriction on private property was expanded, supposedly to increase the availability of rental homes under the premise of "realizing [private property's] social function in the service of the national economy . . . where its use does not prevent the general good to the people."[30] The ceiling on selling units in new buildings was changed to 10 percent of the investment value,[31] rather than a set number of units as previous legislation had stipulated (table 3.3), in addition to both sellers and buyers made to buy government-issued economic housing bonds at 5 percent of their sale value. Vacancies still had to be reported, though within

Legislation	Normal Rent	Term/Eviction	Scope	Controls on Private Property	Advances/ Deposits/ Key Money
Law 65/1971 on investment of Arab funds			Exempts housing built under this law from rent control		
Vice Military Commander Order 6/1973				Jail term and/or LE500 fine for owners who refuse to rent out property vacant for more than two months, including deliberate delay of finishing units	Jail term and/ or LE500 fine for payments other than rent and two-month deposit, in addition to refunding tenant
Law 43/1974 on investment of Arab and foreign funds (Abolishes Law 65/1971)			Exempts housing built under this law from rent control		
Vice Military Commander Order 4/1976	Egyptians in furnished rent for more than five years prior to passing of law can rent it under rent control values but give up furnishings			Selling restricted to 10% of units, except housing co-ops. Prohibition of deliberate delay of finishing/preventing use	Jail term for excess payments in addition to fine equal to double the value, and refunding tenants

Housing Law 49/1977 & Executive Bylaws in MoH Decree 99/1978 (Abolishes previous laws)	From September 9, 1977, annual rents fixed to 7% of land and construction value and 3% of construction value. Real estate taxes paid by tenant. Allows change of use after permission from landlord with surplus of 50–200% of rent depending on building age	As before. Bequeathal to third-degree (ruled unconstitutional in 1995, and secondary bequeathal ruled unconstitutional in 2002) Eviction for repair or demolition. Superseded by Law 119/2008	All provincial capitals and settlements designated as cities as per Local Governance Law 52/1975. Extension to villages by Minister of Housing decree	Selling restricted to 10% of investment value for each level, except all public agencies and co-ops. Vacancy must be reported after four months. Expropriation of unfinished units to finish them. Prohibition of deliberate delay as before	Owners and middlemen prohibited from accepting payments other than rents and deposit stipulated in contract
Law 136/1981 (Amends Law 43/1977)	From July 31, 1981, annual rents fixed to 7% of land and construction value only upon tenant's appeal. Repair costs distributed between owners and tenants. Exemption from real estate taxes	Omits eviction due to misuse according to terms of contract	Exempts luxury units	Selling restricted to one-third of building area. Ruled unconstitutional in 2002	For new build at finishing stage can accept down payment of up to two years' rent, which would be deducted from the rent over the first four years

3.3: Highlights of rent legislation between 1971 and 1981.

four months instead of three. But if an owner was found to deliberately delay finishing works in order to keep the units off the market, governors were allowed to issue a warning along with a timeline to complete the work. If the timeline was not met, a form of temporary sequestration order would be issued, whereby a governorate-appointed contractor would be sought to complete the works at the owner's expense by renting out the finished units until the costs were covered.

To balance these restrictions and to maintain some incentive for the private sector to build-to-let, the rate at which rents were fixed was raised from 5 to 7 percent of land and construction value—in addition to the 3 percent of construction value to account for maintenance and depreciation, as interest rates for deposits were already at 5 percent in 1977. As further encouragement, the payment of real estate taxes was shifted from the owner to the tenant.

The changes brought on by the Housing Law belied its rushed and impulsive roots almost immediately, proving to be both unpopular with owners and burdensome on new tenants, although Sadat had claimed that its "stakeholders" were free to debate it "with the utmost freedom."[32] The effect of the hike in rents was quickly washed away as the Central Bank raised interest rates for deposits to 8 percent two years later, and to 12 percent by 1981.[33] The government was also in dire need of US dollars, so state banks were instructed to issue dollar deposits at 19 percent, further discouraging those with foreign currency from converting them into Egyptian pounds to invest in housing.[34] The exacerbated shortage of rental homes led to a surge in the incidence of key money despite the 1977 law upholding previous penalties[35]—from 9 percent of Cairo contracts in the early 1960s to 30 percent in the mid-1970s to a staggering 53 percent by 1980.[36] Tenants also had to pay higher rates of *khiliw*, which by 1980 represented a year-and-a-half's worth of savings for the average Cairene resident.[37] Tenants now also had to pay real estate taxes, another burden, which due to skyrocketing inflation, represented a 52 percent surcharge on their rents.[38]

The Housing Law also ignored the fact that older buildings, most of which were under rent control, were deteriorating at an alarming rate. In 1975, it was estimated that 700,000 homes[39]—or about 10 percent of the existing stock—were on the verge of collapse. Another contemporary estimate suggested that there were around 12,000 collapses a year nationwide.[40] The main cause was a lack of maintenance, as building

3.1: One of the neater examples of the addition of two floors to this 1950s rent-controlled building in Zamalek to boost revenue through their sale or rent at much higher values. (Photograph by Yahia Shawkat.)

materials were increasingly expensive, while owners who were legally obliged to conduct major repair and maintenance opted not to do so as the income from rent would barely cover the costs. They usually hoped that the building would ultimately collapse, as this was one of the cheaper legal ways the rent-controlled contract would end (figure 3.2). Rent control also allowed for additions to buildings, which was fully exploited by owners seeking to sell or rent out new units at much higher current market rates (figure 3.1). Some of these additions worked to hasten building decay and ultimate collapse, in addition to intentional efforts to affect the structural integrity of buildings.[41] There were also collapses of newer buildings, as owners or unscrupulous contractors sought to maximize their profits by ignoring building codes and using cheaper building materials.

In an attempt to address these mounting problems, Sadat's vice president, Hosni Mubarak, passed the last of the major rent control legislation, Law 136/1981, in July of that year, amending Law 49/1977. The 'housing crisis' had now been demoted to the 'housing problem' and parliament eschewed political ideology or holy teachings as the moral underpinnings of the legislation, instead invoking a participatory air of the "spirit of consultation and democracy,"[42] playing to Sadat's newfound political pluralism. Muhib Stino, head of the parliamentary housing committee preparing the law, lauded the legislation:

> It is assured that the people's participation in preparing this law on such a wide level, affords the power of enforcement to the law, drawing on the citizens' trust in it, and their understanding of it, a fact that has made possible the insertion of important amendments to the draft that reflected the orientations of the grassroots bases, as well as the meetings held over the draft in various fields of thought and opinion, in addition to citizens' opinions and recommendations and the political orientations of public opinion.[43]

Rents were still fixed at 7 percent of land and construction value, though this was soon to be offset by a host of new pro-landlord provisions (table 3.3). The law relaxed the restriction on private sale from 10 percent of investments to a third of the built-up area. So-called luxury housing was to be completely exempt from rent control—though after such construction was approved by a local housing committee, because they did not receive any subsidized building materials, unlike with the other categories of buildings.

The main pro-tenant provision was an exemption of all nonluxury units from real estate taxes, which the tenants had been obliged to pay under the previous law. Otherwise, this ultimate shred of rent control legislation invoked the "spirit of democracy" to (legally) relax active government regulation of rent control, in a bid to "reduce the burden on the Rent Valuation Committees and the courts." The fixed rent values became recommended rather than imposed, as owners were only required to make the tenants aware of the legal rents, now preset by the valuation committees, and it was up to the tenants to appeal to the committees within ninety days if they so wished. In a sellers' market, this provision actually meant a formal deregulation of rent, as tenants accepted rents higher than the legal levels, at times in lieu of paying key money, which had grown to counteract the fixed rents in the first place. In some cases, rents paid reached ten times the legal level.[44]

Key money was also implicitly legalized. Owners completing new buildings could now accept 'down payments' of up to 14 percent of the

3.2: A mostly vacant and decaying building in Downtown Cairo, with occupied rent-controlled shops on the ground floor preventing demolition. (Photograph by Yahia Shawkat.)

unit's legal cost, which would be deducted from the rent, as a way to finance construction. If tenants wished to change the use of their units from residential to commercial, surcharges of between 50 to 200 percent of the legal rent, according to the buildings' age, were permitted. This provision allowed for some flexibility in the use of units that had otherwise stood empty.

Law 136/1981 also added provisions to pragmatically address widespread building decay, caused in part by low rents. The amendments omitted the 3 percent surcharge on rent for maintenance and major repairs, as it was found that it was not used to this end.[45] Instead the costs were divided between landlords and tenants on a sliding scale based on the age of the buildings, with the tenant paying a higher share of the cost to repair older buildings (table 3.4). The law also provided for government cooperative repair loans at low interest rates to landlords and tenants, in the hope that they would be used for that purpose.

Building Age (Rent Laws)	Owner Share	Tenant Share
Up to March 22, 1965	One-third	Two-thirds
March 22, 1965 to September 9, 1977	Half	Half
From September 9, 1977 onwards	Two-thirds	One-third

3.4: Share of major repairs and regular maintenance after the first ten years of construction, according to the Landlord–Tenant Law 136/1981, Article 9, and Civil Law 131/1948, Article 651. (superseded by Unified Building Law 119/2008.)

Running Out of Steam: 1981–96

Amid economic turmoil and a retreating government it was too little, too late. The new law proved unpopular with owners, even with the raised limit on sales, and they claimed the rented units would not cover the costs of construction. The government argued that the rate of house price appreciation already meant additional value, but the owners wanted income rather than equity,[46] especially given that rent control with bequeathal effectively meant they were selling the unit. Some owners went as far as challenging the legislation in the Supreme Constitutional Court, striking down a considerable portion of both the 'Islamic' law of 1977, and the 'democratic' law of 1981, though over a span of two decades.[47] They eventually won several cases between 1995 and 2002 on restriction of sale, bequeathal to relatives, and perpetual bequeathal (limited to once only).

Urban economist Stephen K. Mayo foresaw the limited impact of the new amendments on improving rent for poorer households only one year after they were enacted,[48] a prediction later borne out by statistics. Between 1976 and 1986, urban renting households increased by 500,000, comprising less than 40 percent of the 1.4 million households formed in that period (figure 3.3). If we also take into account the 2.4 million new homes produced, rent control was being circumvented altogether, where instead of an average of about 80 percent of private production earmarked for rent control, as stated in the 1977 and 1981 laws, only one-quarter of that target was met. In the succeeding decade, a meager 10 percent of new households, and 5 percent of new homes, were rent controlled (figure 3.3). New rent-controlled housing, even with key money, effectively disappeared.

How was this possible with the barrage of legislation controlling rent? Underneath their straightjacket exterior, existing laws simply allowed for more new housing not to be rented out in the first place. Individual and small-scale investors were able to exploit a loophole around the sales caps

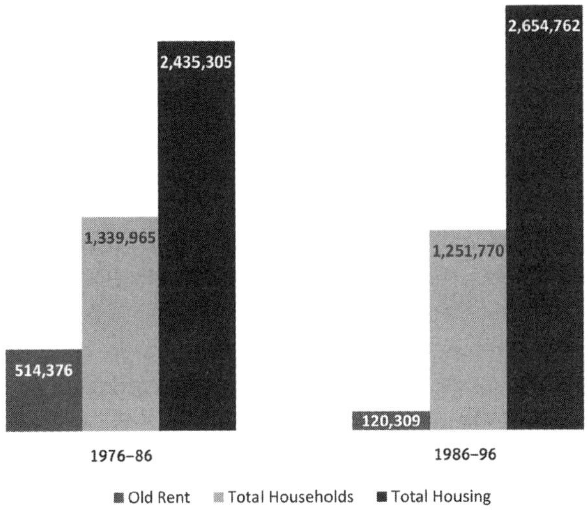

3.3: Comparison between new urban households living in Old Rent to total households formed, and total new housing built in the intercensal periods 1976–86 and 1986–96. (Sources: CAPMAS Censuses for Housing Conditions and for Buildings 1976, 1986, and 1996.)

by shifting from straightforward direct sales to buyers, including them as shareholders from the beginning of a project. The rent control laws allowed for building through *ittihad mullak* (owner unions), whereby multiple owners of a plot of land could apply for a building permit, as each owner was allowed one unit to be exempted from rent control, and immediate family members, including underage children, were registered as individuals. Of course, the number of owners was made equal to the number of units being built, which was not difficult given how large immediate and extended families are in Egypt. In larger undertakings, further 'shares' were given or sold to friends and acquaintances, thus rendering the sales caps almost useless.

Significantly, the caps had never been enforceable on large investors, whether public or private. The 1977 and 1981 caps did not apply to any government investment in housing, which took the form of state-owned developers, cooperatives, or housing funds. Furthermore, as we see in chapter 5, from 1978 onward, tenants of existing government housing were allowed to buy their units, while the tens of thousands of new low-income housing units were sold to applicants instead of rented out. (That was quite the example that policy makers set there.) Big private investors were also exempt from rent control, including private insurance funds, and all Arab and foreign investment projects, which had been exempted from as far back as 1971,[49] Sadat's first year of rule.

Geographically, the law mainly applied to urban areas—cities and towns—exempting villages unless annexed by the housing minister or governor. This may have fueled informal housing construction on cultivated land adjacent to cities, as small-scale investment shifted to these areas. This dynamic might be described as a cat-and-mouse game between builders and the government, as a string of decrees annexing villages in Giza in the late 1970s and early 1980s[50] sought to bring Greater Cairo's periurban fringe under control. But it was largely fruitless, as homes were already rented out or sold by the time the decrees were effected. On the other hand, how would the government enforce rent control on buildings it was already powerless to prevent from being built in the first place? Tenants in informal areas rarely had contracts and did not find resorting to the police helpful, as homeowners often had more local power.[51] Overall, Old Rent tenants were low in areas designated as rural, while they would experience the most rudimentary form of gentrification, as utilities and home improvements were introduced, pushing up rents to levels they could not afford.

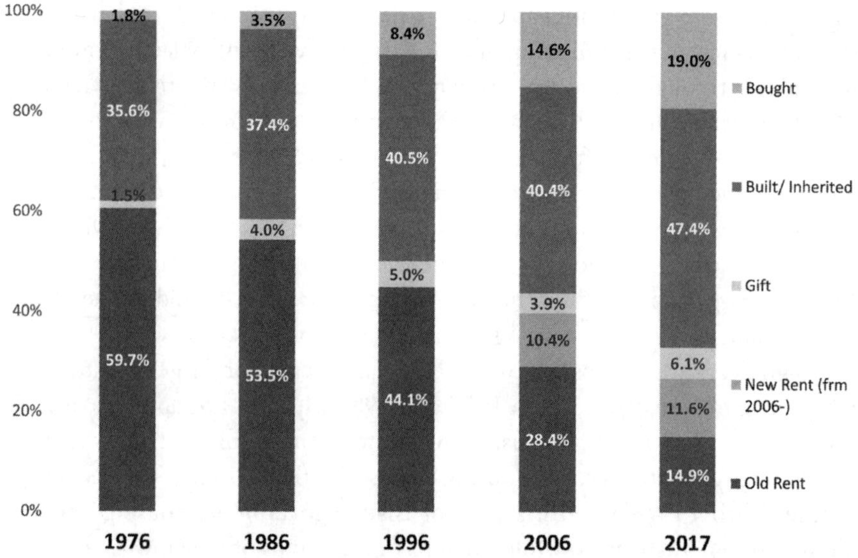

3.4: Change of household tenure for urban Egypt 1976–2017. (Sources: CAPMAS Census for Population and Housing Conditions 1976, 1986, 1996, 2006, and 2017. Also see section on methodology in Chapter 1.)

With an ever-shrinking number of rent-controlled homes, key money skyrocketed to unprecedented levels, making it impossible for most to rent. In the 1980s, *khiliw* could reach LE10,000—more than the price of a public housing apartment in the suburbs.[52] In 1993, an apartment in an old building in Downtown Cairo fetched LE19,000 in *khiliw*.[53] It was not just newly formed families that were not able to get into Old Rent, with many families being evicted in ever increasing numbers, as thousands of buildings collapsed or were made precarious during the final decade of rent control. The early 1980s saw a series of fatal collapses of both old and new buildings, which took the lives of 185 people and rendered hundreds homeless.[54] In 1992, a medium-strength earthquake near Cairo killed 560 people, destroying over five thousand homes, and badly damaging around eleven thousand others,[55] the majority of which were rent controlled. Many of those made homeless were ultimately rehoused in remote government housing, while those in damaged buildings continued to live in them, in some cases for up to two decades, despite eviction and demolition orders, because they could not afford to live anywhere else.

Formal Deregulation by New Rent: 1996–Present

A little over three years after the earthquake, on a Tuesday in the middle of Ramadan, President Hosni Mubarak passed his first and only law on rent during his rule, as "a step on the path to solving the housing problem."[56] Law 4/1996 abolished rent control on all new buildings (table 3.5), as well as vacated Old Rent units to encourage private owners to "rent out vacant units," and investors to "build-to-let" by way of restoring "the natural relationship between individuals and enforcing the law of supply and demand."[57] Mubarak's NDP party members echoed these goals, pointing to how they would add two million vacant housing units to the market, but they were also quick to emphasize that tenants of Old Rent would not be affected.[58] Even the token opposition MPs supported the law, with the liberal Wafd's Yasin Sirag al-Din breathing a sigh of relief that the law was finally passed after nine years of foot-dragging because "the government always trembled before presenting it."[59]

In reality, it was more like twenty years of foot-dragging, as official calls for the abolition of rent control can be traced back to the mid-1970s. A joint research team of experts from the Ministry of Housing and United States Agency for International Development (USAID) recommended abolition as well as revising the low rates of rents as far back as 1976.[60]

Legislation	Normal Rent	Term/Eviction	Scope	Controls on Private Property	Advances/ Deposits/ Key Money
Law 4/1996 New Rent (Reverts new and vacant units to Civil Law 133/1948 Articles 558–627)	Values and annual raises freely set by landlord (informal default of 10% per year). Tenant bears all regular maintenance and utilities costs	Terms set freely with maximum 59 years. Notice to end minimum of two months for contracts longer than four months, and half the term if shorter. Subletting allowed unless expressly prohibited in contract Contract automatically renewed for open-ended term (59 years) if landlord does not request tenant to vacate at end of term. Term does not end with death of tenant	All of Egypt	None	Tenant must place belongings/ furnishings equal to two years' rent, or both parties may agree to waive this. (Informally deposit is one to two month's rent)
Law 137/2006 (Amends Law 4/1996)		Administrative eviction (rather than with court verdict) in case of late rent or end of contract if contract is registered			
Building Law 119/2008 (Supersedes repair and demolition in other laws)		Temporary eviction in case of major repairs. Costs for repair and temporary housing covered by owner, or can be paid by tenant and then deducted from rent and deposit. Permanent eviction in case of demolition			

3.5: Highlights of rent legislation from 1996.

In 1980, in another USAID-funded report, a team of Massachusetts Institute of Technology and Cairo University professors laid out the shortcomings of rent control and presented a number of scenarios and recommendations, from full decontrol to a partial compromise.[61]

It was this compromise that was passed a decade and a half later. In addition to the compulsory blessings of public opinion in the form of approvals from political parties and local councils, the law had a new backer—the Egyptian Businessmen's Association.[62] This was the first time that an organized group, independent of the ruling regime, had any influence on rent legislation. Rather than a grassroots or public interest group of tenants or individual landlords, the EBA was a self-described "lobbying power on behalf of the Egyptian business community to protect its interests and enhance the private sector existence."[63] The 1990s was, after all, the second coming of neoliberalism in Egypt, and the New Rent law—as it was dubbed—was not a stand-alone law. It was part and parcel of an International Monetary Fund and World Bank–led market liberalization structural adjustment package that saw public sector companies privatized, farmers' rents liberalized, and trade tariffs eliminated. The law of supply and demand was hawked by free market lobbyists as the holy grail to all market ills, and the new law unshackled every existing control on rent.

This elimination of regulations was intended by the law's proponents as a return to *pacta sunt servanda*—Latin for "agreements must be kept"—a Roman legal principle of civil law, delegating relationships to the terms agreed to in a contract, as long as they are not illegal. It is a much-touted phrase in the Arab world in the form of "*al-'aqd shari'at al-muta'aqidin*" (the contract is the law of the contract signatories), where Egypt's civil law enshrined it as such in 1948.[64] Most people interpret it as whatever is written in a contract holds, regardless of whether it is illegal or not. For owners, this was music to their ears, as the civil law's articles on rent were very liberal indeed (table 3.5).

New Rent saw an initial heyday in its debut decade, when the total number of renters increased by one million to an all-time high of 3.3 million urban households. Over 120,000 Old Rent households disappeared during that same decade (figure 3.5). More importantly, this record growth in rent was far outstripped by growth in owned homes, with the overall share of urban renters actually dropping by 5 percent compared to the preceding decade (figure 3.4).

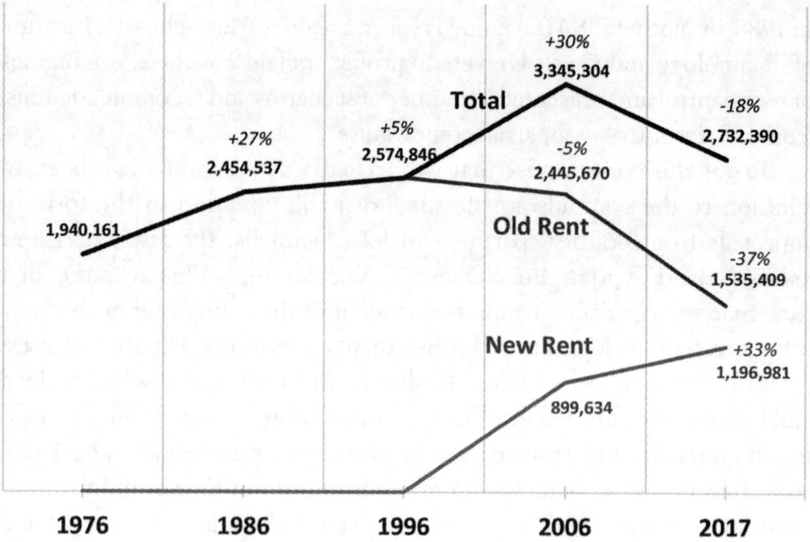

3.5: Comparison between the number of renting households in urban Egypt by type 1976–2017. (Sources: CAPMAS Census for Housing Conditions 1976, 1986, 1996, 2006, and 2017.)

Exercising their right to *pacta sunt servanda*, landlords wrote whatever rents they pleased, which were of course much higher than any Old Rent tenants were paying. A large urban study in 2008 that included both formal and informal homes found that rents were averaging 20 percent of income, which was still affordable, though poorer households were already near the affordability threshold of 25 percent.[65] High rents were not the only issue for tenants—even with the new law in their favor, landlords were overly cautious, demanding between 25 and 50 percent of the entire rent upfront in one-third of cases.[66] As opposed to the almost perpetual terms of Old Rent, most New Rent contracts were extremely short, at between one and three years.[67] The contract length became much less significant in any case, as the law also allowed for a break clause, whereby either party could end the contract with a minimum two-month notice period. However, there was also the practice of landlords with partly finished units making out long-term *'aqd maftuh* (open contracts) of fifty-nine years at lower than market rents, in order to fund the finishing of them.[68] These are sometimes confusingly also called Old Rent contracts because of their length, although they are legally regulated by New Rent.

While a majority of tenants had written contracts, barely 15 percent registered them.[69] It would be mistaken to understand the remainder as informal, as the law does cover standard contracts, though it does not cover so-called *istidafa* (hosting) contracts, which do not stipulate any exchange of money between the parties. *Istifada* contracts are used widely in thousands of public housing apartments as a loophole, since owners are not allowed to rent them out due to legislation restricting the rent or sale of subsidized government housing by beneficiaries, as we see in chapters 5, 6, and 7. Paying tenants can be evicted at any time, and may end up losing significant amounts of money, as in practice the value of the entire duration is paid upfront.

Landlords also came up against the practical limitations of *pacta sunt servanda* when they found eviction of noncomplying tenants to be slow and arduous.[70] Indeed, some only rent out to relatives or friends, or prefer to keep their units vacant for this reason.[71] In an effort to address the problem, an amendment was passed in 2006 allowing landlords to go directly to the police to evict noncomplying tenants (table 3–5), instead of waiting for a court order, though this was only an option if the contract was registered. On the other hand, illegal evictions are also known to occur. In February 2011, during the police vacuum in the wake of the January 2011 revolution, hundreds—possibly thousands—of tenants in the Nahda housing estate, northeast of Cairo, were evicted by their private landlords who feared

3.6: "Thank God… we're not bothered by these issues." A caricature in the leading state-owned daily parodying the public debates around rent control as being unimportant to the poor and homeless. (*al-Ahram*, February 2, 1996.)

local government would notice that they were illegally renting out their apartments.[72] The evicted families went on to squat in hundreds of nearby vacant government housing units.

In terms of accessibility, if you are single, especially young or female, good luck finding a landlord willing to rent out an apartment to you, as it will be assumed that you will be performing *a'mal munafiya li-l-adab* (immoral acts), such as having parties, doing drugs, and engaging in extramarital sex. There are no regulations against discrimination by landlords based on religion, social status, or ethnicity. In fact, some landlords with properties in expensive neighborhoods prefer to rent to non-Egyptians because they feel expats are easier to deal with—or take for a ride—and more importantly because some pay in dollars and euros.[73]

Contrary to the government's claims, New Rent did not so much as make a dent in vacancy rates, which more than doubled from 3.2 million units in 1996 to almost 7 million units in 2006. By 2017, there were 11.7 million empty homes in Egypt.[74] Indeed, Ragab al-Banna, a prominent *al-Ahram* columnist writing a few days after the new law was passed, could not have been more prescient when he suggested, "Those who say that the forces of supply and demand will bring rental values to a balance, do not understand the nature of the housing problem in Egypt."[75] He explained how the market was monopolistic, and that commodities and services were in short supply. While there was no quantitative shortage of housing, he was accurate in predicting that the law alone would not be a sufficient catalyst to entice owners of vacant units to put them on the market.

The shortage of rented homes is particularly apparent in how values have ballooned over the last decade. Median rent in Egyptian cities was around LE1,200 in 2017, a full six times higher than it was in 2008.[76] Incomes on the other hand have grown much more modestly, resulting in an almost threefold decrease in affordability where the national rent to income ratio climbed from a manageable 20 percent in 2008, to a phenomenal 39 percent in 2017.[77] Port Said, Damietta, and Fayoum were among six cities where people had to spend close to or more than half their income on rent, while Cairo was close to the national average.

Rising unaffordability, along with waning confidence in the rule of law, has contributed to the decreasing popularity of New Rent, which in its second decade added a paltry 300,000 households (figure 3.5). In fact, the 2006–2017 decade was the first time rent experienced negative growth, as the number of those leaving Old Rent outstripped New Rent tenants three to one, leading to a net loss of over 600,000 tenants. In 2017, renting households were less than half those of 1976. If this trend continues, renting will all but disappear by the next census, due in 2027.

Pacta sunt servanda?

Looking back at eight decades of rent policy, Nasser's trial-and-error attempts at providing affordable housing through the private sector seem to have had the biggest impact, though only during his governance. Rents were affordable for tenants, and at the same time still close to market values, as inflation was largely in check, while the many actions against key money meant that overall incidence was low.[78] If it were not for the strong influence of politics on rent control, whereby almost every reduction in rent accompanied a political event,[79] as well as a few miscalculated moments of grandstanding—chief of which was the bequeathal of contracts—a balanced rent regime may have flourished.

The record of the rules of Sadat and later Mubarak show how rent control without regulation in a heated property market simply does not work. Again, politics was a key deciding factor. The fear of destabilizing support for their regimes prevented any meaningful legislative change, while tightening controls on paper that were routinely circumvented on the ground only served to squeeze the rental market further, almost obliterating it in the late 1980s and early 1990s.

Pacta sunt servanda has not helped either. After two decades of New Rent, we can see how complete deregulation has meant that it is increasingly unaffordable and insecure for tenants. Owners also rely on the appreciation of the value of their property in the deregulated housing market, rather than on rent as a return on investment, making it easy to ask for high rents, or simply keep the units vacant. On the other hand, the growing erosion of the rule of law in Egypt[80] has contributed significantly to keeping properties empty, as owners rightly fear government inaction when it comes to evicting nonpaying tenants. For some, *pacta sunt servanda* has meant taking the law into their own hands. In one week in March 2018, a husband and wife in an Old Rent apartment were severely injured after their landlord stabbed them during an argument in Khusus just outside of Cairo, while a landlord in a nearby village fired shots in the air to evict a nonpaying tenant.[81] A week earlier, during an argument between a landlord and his Old Rent tenants over utility bills, a bystander was killed by a stray bullet when the landlord fired his gun in anger.[82] The list of injuries and deaths in arguments over both Old and New Rent goes on.

The retreat of government in managing landlord–tenant relationships has led to other deaths and injuries. As recently as 2013, almost one-third of 390 building collapses in Egypt, which killed almost two hundred people and made over eight hundred homeless, were found to be of old, dilapidated buildings that could have been repaired.[83] This was largely the result of continued lax implementation of the laws that regulate building repair and maintenance. More ominous though was the collapse of structurally sound buildings due to an internal or external action that violated their structural integrity, leading to 15 percent of building collapses. Many of these cases are blamed on landlords looking to evict tenants of rent-controlled buildings.[84]

Since 2015 parliament and the government have yet again been touting deregulation of Old Rent law. The main changes mention rent increases of 25 percent over four years before they are decontrolled altogether.[85] The delay debating the law for at least three years seems to have been largely political, as the current government cannot handle hundreds of thousands of families being made homeless overnight, while 2018 was also an election year for President al-Sisi. This has only led to insecurity for tenants and frustration for owners, and by early 2019 it was nowhere near ready.[86]

With incomes low, the general absence of mortgages and the fact that millions of residential units stand empty should make renting the most popular form of accommodation in Egypt. The main advantage of renting—as opposed to buying—is that it is dependent on income rather than on wealth. A renter pays a set monthly value, rather than saving up for a lifetime or depending on already existing savings, inheritance, or another property that can be exchanged for a home. But renting, and indeed ownership, cannot operate without a minimum of government regulation, be it balanced or in either party's favor. Absent from the debates on rent is any talk about the vacuum of official authority in governing property values and relations—while energy is wasted on building empty units and lives are wasted defending occupied homes.

4

'MODEL' VILLAGES FOR 'MODEL' CITIZENS

Looking at the countryside today, most people get the impression that the home of the fellah has remained unchanged for thousands of years, as some guidebooks proclaim. Egyptian universities teach this to architects and planners, instructing them to see villages as an act of spontaneous organicity, either romantically, but mostly abhorrently as unplanned and unsanitary slums that are the sole creation of 'ignorant peasants.'

While rural settlements have been mostly self-built, drawing on centuries of traditional knowledge passed down through generations, the various governments and regimes that ruled Egypt over the last two centuries have nevertheless shaped much of rural housing through policy. As such, large portions of the houses some see today as rural and backward are the direct result of policies designed by politicians, planners, architects, and social scientists.

The royal family and the feudalist landowners, and later banks and corporations, would build *'izbas*, private hamlets located on large estates, which gradually housed a significant proportion of the rural population between the 1840s and 1952.

Epidemics and social unrest gave rise to the model village movement of the 1930s and 1940s, whereby the government, leading architects, and private enterprise aimed to reconstruct rural housing throughout Egypt. While the movement only managed to build a handful of villages, it would survive the end of the monarchy and come to set the stage for rural mass housing over the next half century.

Gamal Abd al-Nasser's 1952 land reform would bring a temporary end to the *'izba* system. The new regime would also launch mega land reclamation schemes in the New Lands—the expansive desert that the thin Nile

Valley plows through—and tens of thousands of people would be resettled to officially planned model villages.

By the end of the twentieth century, neoliberal government would still build model villages, though ones that would never be used. The reclamation in the New Lands had moved to take the form of super estates, much larger than those in the feudalist nineteenth century. With them came the reincarnation of the *'izba*, though this time around as primitive barracks for workers built by large landowning corporations.

The *'Izba*, a Private Village: 1840s–1952

The systematized exploitation of Egypt in the 1800s, alongside state control over the population for military conscription, tax collection, and crop mix spawned the first modern large-scale, state-controlled mass housing typology that would define how a significant number of Egyptians lived.

Forced conscription by the military in the 1820s, as well as the enforcement of growing cash crops two decades later, led tens of thousands of fellahin to abandon their villages and move to rural areas outside government control.[1] Initial efforts failed to prevent desertion by policing—whether through village sheikhs, officials, local notables, or Bedouins. Between 1847 and 1862, a series of laws were passed allowing the state to expropriate abandoned land. During the same period, the ruling elite were starting to establish large estates, seizing abandoned land, as well as pastoral land on the fringes of the floodplain from the *'Arab* (settled Bedouin).[2]

This led to even more desertion, and an elaborate response was needed to force labor back onto the fields and curb resistance. This came in 1863 when the newly crowned Khedive Isma'il would start reorganizing Egypt into a system of agricultural estates. He created government departments to manage the ruling family's landholdings, while giving tracts of expropriated land to anyone close to him, from high officials to servants and even Bedouin tribes.[3] These Bedouin settled around Lake Qarun in Fayoum, and though they would reclaim thousands of feddans over the coming years, they did not forget their nomadic origin—so much so that during his rule, Libyan dictator Muammar al-Gaddafi would make sure to visit his tribal kin there whenever he was on a state visit to Egypt.[4]

Feudal estates were seen as an efficient, decentralized way to establish proxy control over the fellahin who tilled the land. The landowners would accumulate (further) wealth in return for ensuring profitable crops were grown, the military was furnished with fit conscripts, and taxes were deducted from the already miniscule wages the fellahin were paid and sent to the Treasury. Within three decades, a little more than 1 percent of the population would come to own two-fifths of cultivable land,[5] and arguably control how a significant proportion of the population lived.

This control took the physical form of the *'izba*. While some existing villages were incorporated wholesale into the *shafalik* (private estates), the once uncultivable swamps and marshes on the fringes of the Nile floodplain were now beginning to be reclaimed as *ib'adiyat* (wastelands 'excluded' from the cadaster). These new estates of course needed housing arrangements, and here the *'izba* was born, as a rural workers' camp built to house the laborers and their families, who were mostly brought in from neighboring villages or provinces.

In the 1840s, Joseph Hekekyan Bey, a civil engineer, planner, and surveyor, would instigate the paradigm of patronizing top-down housing for the masses. He built a number of model villages on royal estates arranged in a street grid, with homes segregated by order of importance, starting with the owner's manor house and *diwan* (guest house) overlooking the road, and then rows of homes for the well-to-do sheikhs and merchants, followed by rows of homes for what he called 'middling' fellahin, probably those with agricultural knowledge, and then huts for a lower class of fellahin that would bear the menial labor (figure 4.1).[6] In between the manor house and the other houses, was a row of commercial buildings—shops, a mosque, an inn, and a house of prostitution.

Hekekyan was not a pioneer in model villages, for the concept had been applied in Britain from the eighteenth century, initially for aesthetic reasons, where on some estates, villages were demolished and rebuilt elsewhere simply to improve the owner's view.[7] British educated under Mohamed Ali's patronage,[8] Hekekyan imported the concept to Egypt, and it became widely established by the late nineteenth century. The hamlet on the estate belonging to Princess Fatma, Khedive Ismail's daughter, had over two hundred houses. It has since been swallowed by the neighborhood of Dokki, her palace surviving as the Agricultural Museum, and the remains of the hamlet, since renamed 'Izbit Awlad 'Allam, can still be found off Mussadak Street to the southeast.[9] Private feudalist *'izba*s were shrunken versions of model villages. Mona Abaza provides a rare account of an early twentieth century *'izba* in her book, *The Cotton Plantation Remembered.* The *'izba* of Mustafa Bey Fuda, built in the Delta in 1927, had a mansion, a house for the *nazir* (the main overseer of the *'izba)*, a *duwar* (livestock barn), and

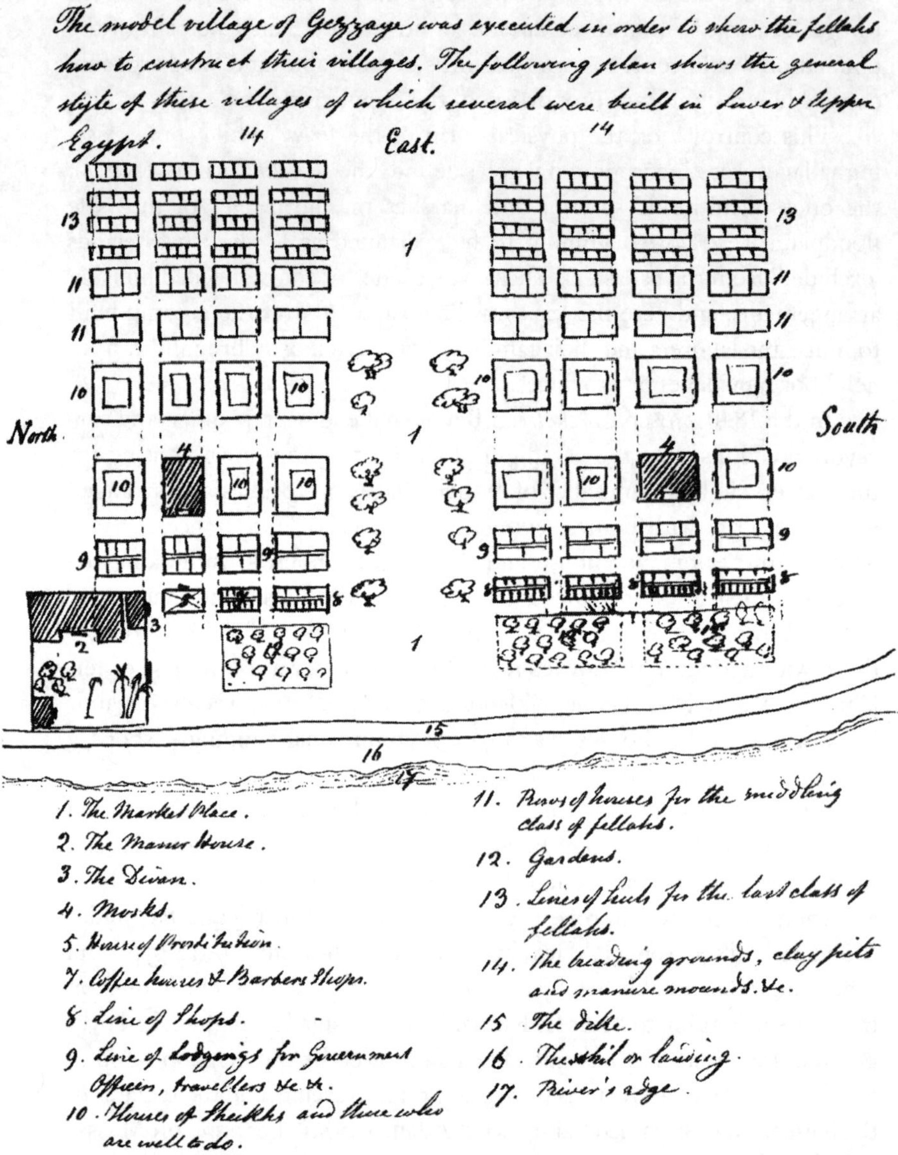

4.1: The model village of Gezzaye, designed by Joseph Hekekyan in 1852. (Hekekyan, Journals
1851–1854, Folio 355, British Library Add Ms. 37452, Vol. 4. Used with permission of the British Library.)

4.2: Aerial view of the *'izba* of Mustafa Bey Fuda in Daqahliya, built in 1927. In 2005, the mansion could be seen with its own walled garden in the middle. The rectangle directly to its east is the *duwar* (livestock barn), and the one northwest is the original hamlet of ninety houses, now an expanding village. (Image dated March 28, 2005, ©2018 Digital Globe/ GOOGLE.)

4.3: One of the original sandstone houses in 'Izbit Tunis in Fayoum. December 2018. (Photograph by Yahia Shawkat.)

a separate hamlet of ninety houses for the fellahin (figure 4.2).[10] Identical houses were a feature of most *'izba*s, their quality reflecting the wealth of the owner of the estate. In 'Izbit Tunis in Fayoum, now famous for its annual pottery festival, the original houses were much more austere than those of 'Izbt Fuda, their local sandstone and mud façades bare from any brickwork or ornamentation (figure 4.3).

The planning of the *'izba*s was not an act of benevolence. Abaza describes them as "total institutions"—a term coined by sociologist Erving Goffman for prisons—where "bonded labor" that was neither slave nor free produced a "military agriculture."[11] Living in an *'izba* meant living under the overwhelming control of the landowners. Inhabitants could only leave with permission and were not allowed to work anywhere else.[12] Walls and gates existed on some *'izba*s, though they were not really needed as *ghafar* (private security guards) would terrorize the inhabitants,[13] and escaping from the *'izba* meant being both landless and homeless.[14] *'Izba* residents had no rights or title to their homes[15] and could be evicted with any disagreement.[16] If the landowner no longer saw the need to house the fellahin on

	Feddans	Families	Individuals	% of Rural
Total rural population and cultivable land in 1952*	**5,982,000**	**2,791,262**	**13,956,308**	**100%**
Estimated maximum population living on estates over 50 feddans in 1952**	2,043,000	854,602	4,273,008	31%
Area of land and number of families living on *'izba*s that benefited from land reform between 1952 and 1970***	817,538	341,982	1,709,910	12%

* Projection from 1947 and 1960 censuses based on CAPMAS, "al-Kitab al-ihsa'i al-sanawi li-jumhuriyat Misr al-'arabiya 1952–1973," 7.

** Land area as in CAPMAS, 60. Estimate of families based on average 2.4 feddans/family ratio of redistributed land. Individuals based on five individuals/family ratio of rural population in 1952.

*** CAPMAS, "al-Zimam wa-l-masahat al-munzari'a fi jumhuriyat Misr al-'arabiya 'am 1970," 78.

4.1: Rural land ownership and *'izba* population estimates in 1952.

his land, he would demolish the *'izba*. As one *'izba* resident would remember years later, "*'izba*s disappeared, and then would revive again."[17]

On the other hand, the fellahin were bound to the *'izba* itself when it changed owners or banks moved in to repossess it after owners defaulted on their debts. They would also seize the fellahin's holdings, even though they were only laborers.[18] Far from being the sole creation of the landowners, the planning of the *'izba*s was regulated as they grew in number. Several laws were passed between 1885 and 1950 to regularize existing *'izba*s and define standards for how new ones should be established, including provisions for housing and sanitary conditions.[19]

The influence of the *'izba* over the population would grow throughout the second half of the nineteenth century, and last about a century. In 1882, 701,000 people were living on five thousand estates.[20] By the eve of land reform in 1952, this population had swelled to anywhere between 1.7 and 4.3 million 'totally instituted' people—making up almost a third of the rural population (table 4.1).[21]

The Model Village Movement: 1930s–1952

The model village concept would be revisited in the 1930s and 40s in the context of increasing rural resistance against the regime, deadly epidemics, and a wave of nationalism. The fellahin clashed with landowners or local officials over rents, evictions, and taxes in almost sixty collective actions from the 1920s through to 1952.[22] Malaria and cholera epidemics would infect over 1.1 million people between 1940 and 1947, killing over a quarter of a million.[23] The suffering was blamed on squalid rural living conditions, rather than the social inequities of life in the *'izbas*[24] or temporary labor outside of them.

This response mostly followed how the model village in Western Europe evolved from aesthetic landscape redesigns to playing a paternalistic role. In the mid-nineteenth century, conscientious landowners in Britain who saw that "property has its duties as well as its rights" would build model villages on their estates that were picturesque, as well as providing more sanitary living conditions.[25] In Egypt, model villages would become a national political pursuit after 1936, when Nahas Pasha, prime minister and the head of the ruling Wafd Party, announced their construction in parliament as part of a larger manifesto for reform that also included the supply of drinking water to rural areas.[26] Leading architects and social scientists of the time responded to this call—as well as government bodies, large landowners, and private enterprise. Much theorizing ensued around 'village reform,' which the architect Omar Azzam split into schools of thought that ranged from the evolutionary—those that sought to improve life in the villages through a range of gradual interventions—to the radical—those that focused on the complete rebuilding of the countryside into model villages.[27]

The early 1930s would witness the birth of the Radical School, when two institutions started experimenting with model villages. In 1933, The Royal Agricultural Society built a block of single-story brick and concrete houses on its estate in Bahtim, hoping to protype a model for replication across the country.[28] Besides using modern building materials, the models featured indoor toilets and taps for drinking water but omitted the baking oven for fear it was a fire hazard. But the fellahin that used it added an oven, while landowners found the houses too expensive, so in 1936 the society built another set of prototypes with wooden roofs as well as mudbrick domes instead of concrete, and ovens inside for cooking and heating.[29] Even though the newer homes were cheaper to build, they were still considered expensive.

After a fire destroyed almost half the houses in the village of Mahallat Ziyad in the Samanud district of Gharbiya in 1934, the newly founded Department of Village Affairs at the Ministry of Health planned a village extension to rehouse the homeless fellahin. [30] Other families would be relocated there after two main streets and a plaza were built through the original village to improve its fire safety. It was designed for 250 'modern' houses in semidetached clusters of two and four on wide streets on a gridiron plan. Public buildings included a mosque, a rural school, a clinic, and a market.[31] These modern fellah houses would not be built by the government as initially intended, as it was ultimately considered too expensive an endeavor.[32] Instead, the government gave the displaced fellahin priority in buying the new plots, as well as zero-interest loans from the municipality to build the houses, but only according to official designs.[33] It seems that while everybody agreed that the quality of village life needed to be improved, neither landowners nor the government were willing to pick up the tab.

Another of the Department of Village Affairs' model villages would be built in 1941 near what was then the village of al-Marg in the northern peridesert fringes of Cairo.[34] This village was based on Sayyid Karim's extensive research and lobbying for what he called the 'transitional village,' citing the problems he had with the "superficial model villages" built at the time, describing them as the "model of what should not be done."[35] He stated that

> reforming the village does not mean rebuilding houses in expensive redbrick and concrete, building houses on decorative geometric layouts, building schools that have resulted in the fellahin abandoning the village for the city, building hospitals that have not improved healthcare, and in fact have increased the burden on the fellah's expenses.[36]

Despite his critique of top-down superficial design, Karim took an even more ominous position by stating that the model village was the wrong concept, not because he opposed the idea itself, but "because first we must prepare the model fellah and the model citizen," to be able to "appreciate" the "model house" and not "turn it into a model of his living conditions."[37] Many of his fellow architects shared this view, as we see in the *Majallat al-'imara* articles of the time, no doubt influenced by the then prevalent social engineering theories. For example, there was the Viennese social housing that in the 1920s worked to "indoctrinate their residents in socialist values" by way of socializing previously private residential practices such as cooking, washing, and bathing.[38] The Dutch Woonschools, literally housing schools, were even more extreme, where building new housing districts to forcibly resocialize families it saw as antisocial was normal practice from the 1920s through the 1960s.[39] To that end, Karim proposed plans for a transitional village based primarily on 'healthy zoning,' dividing the village into a "clean side," comprising the main plaza, mosque, lodge, the house of the *'umda*, *kuttab* (religious school), clinic, and toilets, and a "dirty side," comprising the animal pens, mill, store houses, and animal market. Laid out in V-shaped grids, the houses would follow suit, with one side opening onto the clean street and the other onto the dirty street (figure 4.4).

The village built by the Department of Village Affairs in 1941 to Karim's design was not intended to house any fellahin though. At first it was an emergency shelter for *al-muhaggarin* (displaced)—would-be Cairo evacuees during the Second World War—but having received no migrants by the end of the war, it was turned by the Ministry of Health into a tuberculosis colony for the sick and their families.[40] More than seventy years later, al-Marg is now a teeming Cairo neighborhood, and the Tawfiqiya Canal that fronted the village has long been filled in and turned into the Mu'assasit al-Zakat highway. While most of the model village has been demolished to make way for the neighborhood's public buildings including a hospital, municipal headquarters, and some schools,

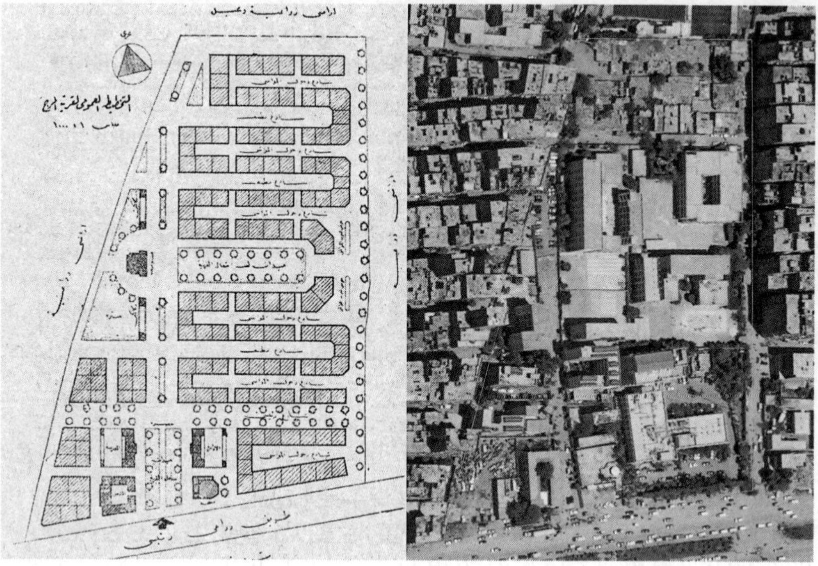

4.4: Left: Plan of the al-Marg *muhagirin* (migrants) model village showing U-shaped clusters of houses opening on a 'clean street' for people, and a 'dirty street' for livestock. Right: Six decades later, only traces of the model village remain. Most of the houses have been replaced with public schools and buildings, while the surviving two rows (top) are now 'Ishash al-Muhaggarin (Shacks of the Migrants) (Left: 'Abd al-Gawwad, "al-Maskan al-sihhi li-l-fallah." Special Collections, Fine Arts Library, Harvard University. Right: Image dated April 2017, *©2017 GOOGLE.)*

a cluster of the original houses still exists as *'ishash al-muhagirin* (shacks of the migrants) (figure 4.4). In an ironic twist of fate, Karim's healthy model village has become a "highly dangerous slum" that is a "social danger and a humanitarian disaster" in need of urgent upgrading.[41] So much for Karim's critique of the "model of what should not be done."

In the same year that the model village of al-Marg was built, Hassan Fathy—best known for his reinvention of Egyptian vernacular mudbrick techniques as a 'national style'—would build the third model village at the Royal Agricultural Society, launching a career in building model villages.[42] Most famous of these was New Gurna Village, built in Luxor in 1945 as a flagship for the National Program for Rural Reconstruction, and the centerpiece of his book *Architecture for the Poor*.

The book would be a blockbuster success, mostly because it is a rare and candid insight into how an Egyptian architect with deep-seated social leanings viewed his work. His model village would ultimately fail. This is partly because it was sabotaged by the would-be inhabitants who opposed being forcibly relocated to it and never invited Fathy to design their new village. It was a commission by the Department of Antiquities, which wanted the people resettled from their village. But the failure was also due to Fathy's attempt to artificially and single-mindedly recreate an organic village devoid of any input from the would-be residents, and without any interest in what made their own homes appropriate for them in what Timothy Mitchell has called an "oxymoron of planned individuality."[43] It was yet another "model of what should not be done."

New Gurna was ultimately settled in by other people, and today, most of its mudbrick houses have been demolished and rebuilt in concrete and brick by their occupants, while a fraction of the original houses, as well as most of the public buildings, remain. These are to become part of the Ancient Thebes UNESCO World Heritage Site, a conservation plan that aims to "valorize the pioneering ideas and philosophy of Fathy's work."[44] However, the plan is creating a new oxymoron. Completely overlooking the violence that the community of Gurna were put through over decades on their way to being forcefully relocated to another site, the plan recommends the resettlement of 120 households living in New Gurna in order to "rehabilitate" Fathy's village and "reduce the present housing densities."[45] They will of course be moved to a new housing development that is "consistent with the Conservation Area planning principles,"[46] with no mention of any participation or consultation with the families that will in all probability also be relocated by force, as we see in the case studies of chapter 7.

Finalizing the Model

One of the more revolutionary proposals that emerged from the evolutionary school of village reform came from 'Ali al-Miligi Mas'ud, a town planner who wrote extensively on housing and sanitary conditions. In an article published in 1941 titled "al-Muwatin al-namuzaji" (The Model Citizen),[47] Mas'ud described his vision of the model village, which was based on the fellahin becoming model citizens—not through top-down social engineering, but through the dismantling of the feudalist *'izba* system. The fellahin, he argued, should have the agency to build their own homes, and grow their food on land they owned—albeit small parcels of 1,000 square meters, or a little less than one feddan.[48] Mas'ud would go on to become one of the pioneers of urban public housing in Egypt. Ironically, though, his article on the model citizen was published in the very same issue of *Majallat al-'imara* that featured Sayyid Karim's village reform article.

Mas'ud however, was not treading unchartered waters all on his own in calling for agrarian reform. The malaria epidemic had energized parliamentarians to argue for the redistribution of wealth as the primary solution to social inequity, proposing a number of laws between 1944 and 1951 to limit landholdings to fifty feddans.[49] These never gained the majority to pass, as most parties still very much represented the landowning elite, but they did put enough pressure on King Faruq to force him to take notice.

In 1947, the Taftish Kafr Sa'd project to reclaim around 7,000 feddans of saline swamp land that belonged to the Department of State Property (Maslahat al-Amlak al-Amiriya), on the northern most fringes of the Nile Delta, was ready, and the government had decided to distribute this land to two types of beneficiaries to cultivate. The first were from the lower middle class, the *kharigin*, or graduates of the agricultural schools, who were selected by a special committee based on their record of "good behaviour and manners,"[50] and who would receive loans from the Treasury to help finance their endeavors.[51] The second were the landless and "destitute" fellahin, who were the target of King Faruq's "desire . . . to help raise the level of the poorer classes and realize calls for social justice."[52] Around 1,412 houses were distributed in Taftish Kafr Sa'd between 1948 and 1951, along with a monetary contribution and five feddans of land.[53] The main distinguishing feature of this project was that a relatively large number of rectilinear model villages, at least nine, were built by a government authority in a remote area unrelated to any existing villages. Another feature was the clear sign of royal patronage, whereby the villages were all named after Faruq and his dynastic predecessors (figure 4.5).[54]

In twenty years of playing model village, the architects and social scientists would build less than twenty villages, housing around seven thousand people. While landowners expected the government to build the villages, it claimed a lack of funds. None of the model villages were reconstructions of older ones. The new Mahallat Ziyad village was built in response to a fire. The three *'izba*s of Bahtim were showcases for technology, probably in an attempt to lure construction contracts. Al-Marg village was not even built for fellahin to live in, while the only village built for the fellahin, New Gurna, was sabotaged by its would-be inhabitants as it was part of a government effort to forcefully relocate them.

What the government did build, which were settled in by fellahin, were the nine super *'izba*s of the Taftish Kafr Sa'd reclamation scheme. It seems that government interest in model villages lay in building new housing in remote sites for agricultural labor, in order to expand the area, and with it the production of cash crops. Rebuilding existing villages, or even upgrading their services, would not rake in revenue for the royal coffers, as there would be no increase in agricultural production, while land reform was strictly off the table.

But it was too little, too late. Rebellion by the fellahin living in *'izbas* on the large estates rose significantly between 1950 and 1952, helping to usher in the Arab socialist revolution.[55] Ironically, it would be the government model of new remote villages, land reclamation, and patronage that would survive regime change, evolving into mega models of total social control.

From Private 'Izba to State Model Village: 1952–1977

The government created the *'izba*, and also dissolved it. Agrarian land reform began in September 1952, barely two months after the revolution deposed the king and established an Arab socialist regime. Between 1952 and 1963, five laws would see the redistribution of about 800,000 feddans to 342,000 families (table 4.1).[56] This was primarily done by expropriating the land of large estates that were initially over 200 feddans, then 100 feddans, then 50, and redistributing plots of 2 to 5 feddans to the fellahin that worked them.[57] The government's Agrarian Reform Agency (ARA) either rented out the expropriated land or sold it through lease-to-own contracts over thirty years to fellahin willing to buy.

This reform would only affect two-fifths of the area controlled by the large estates (Table 4.1). Landowners, including other government agencies, still controlled the rest, and so rents were fixed at seven times the land tax, and leases became almost perpetual. Overall, around one million tenants would benefit from these rents.[58]

But the reform of the 'old lands,' the traditional Nile Valley and Delta, would not be enough for the Nasser regime, which envisaged the resettlement of millions of people away from the apparently overcrowded valley to thousands of new villages on reclaimed desert in what would be called the 'new lands,' the successor to the *ib'adiyat* of the previous era. There was after all food sovereignty to consider, and the fact that hundreds of thousands of fellahin were still landless (table 4.1). Consequently, not one, but three large-scale projects were launched during the Nasser era, prompting

4.5: Recent aerial view of the former royal estate in Kafr Sa'd, showing the names of the model villages built there from 1947. (Image dated May 2, 2016, ©*2017 GOOGLE. Place* names based on IDSC, "Dalil al-taqsim al-idari li-l-muhafazat hatta mustawa al-shiyakha wa-l-qarya.")

the building of dozens of new model villages in the desert and the resettling of thousands of fellahin. The first was the United States funded Egypt American Rural Improvement Service (EARIS) project. It was planned a year before Nasser came to power and implemented in 1953, to reclaim 80,000 feddans south of Alexandria and in Fayoum, and resettle 16,000 landless families from neighboring regions on smallholder farms.[59] The Free Officers would go one up on the American project in 1954 with the Mudiriyat al-Tahrir (Province of Liberation) scheme, which had the much more ambitious targets of reclaiming 600,000 feddans of desert in the West Delta to sustain 120,000 families on state farms.[60] In an exponential evolution of targets, the New Valley project sought to literally create a new valley running parallel to the old Nile Valley, of between half a million and three million feddans,[61] where four million people were imagined to live.[62]

The new model villages in all three reclamation projects were designed by architects inspired by the radical school following the template of the model villages of their forebears—model redbrick and concrete houses grouped in rectilinear clusters on relatively wide street grids, around public buildings—usually including a school, a clinic or hospital, social center, and mosque, with a separate area for livestock (figure 4.6). An EARIS brochure proudly proclaimed, "EARIS built 262 redbrick houses for settlers in the first village (all supplied with potable water), a mosque, a school, a public laundry, a social center, and more."[63]

In Tahrir, the new inhabitants received two-bedroom houses built out of hollow concrete blocks and roofs to insulate them from the heat and the cold.[64] In addition to the requisite running water, a government report stated that "for the first time the peasant could use electricity in his day-to-day life, as well as in the first time in the history of the Egyptian village, sewage is drained away in a modern manner where it is used to make organic fertilizer for cultivation."[65] The regime was so proud of these homes, that in a major speech in 1964, Nasser himself would laud them as "buildings that are contemporary and good for the fellahin" *(mabani 'asriya wa mabani kwayisa bi-l-nisba li-l-fallahin)*.[66] And unlike in previous projects that just stopped at building the homes, in Tahrir the new residents were "supposed to resign themselves to a better life already planned, organized and continually supervised for them."[67] Forty of the three hundred houses in one model village would be set aside for the government employees who would be responsible for this supervised life.[68]

But while anthropologist Helmi Tadros saw that the fellah could not have dreamed of a better house than those at Abis, an EARIS model village, he observed that "gradually he starts to feel the inadequacy and inefficiency of the house in relation to his living facilities and other needs."[69] So stark was the dislocation from traditional rural life that visiting American reporter Bill Downs would write, "[The village of] Om Saber and the Liberation province now has about it the atmosphere of a pioneer American town of the West—except for the first completed buildings: the mosque and the filling station."[70]

Patronage and control through housing were thus reinvented for the Arab socialist era. The *'izba* on the private estate, thought to have disappeared with the land reform of the 1950s, would be revived within the same

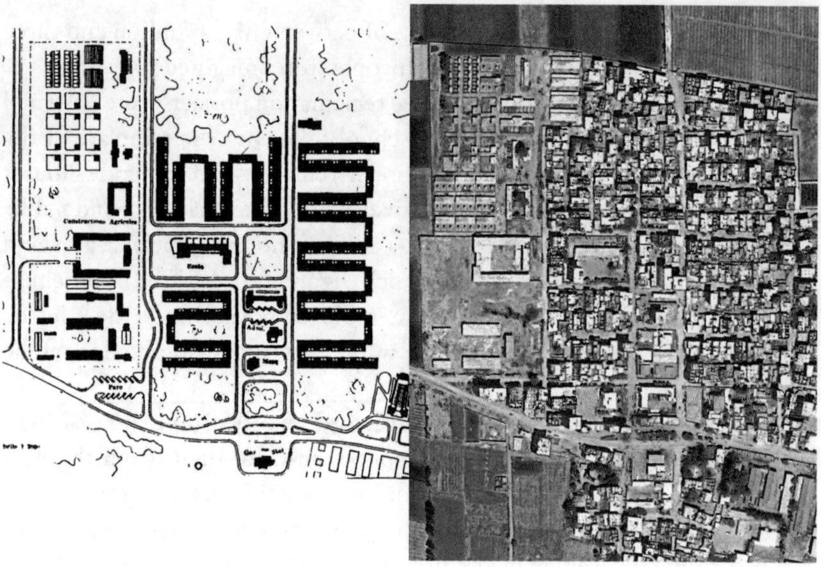

4.6: Left: Original plan of Umm Saber model village in Mudiriyat al-Tahrir. Right: Aerial view of the model village sixty-one years after it was built, where homes appear modified, and organic additions fill the once empty spaces. (Left: Ministry of Agriculture and Land Reclamation. Right: Image dated September 2, 2016, ©2017 GOOGLE.)

decade—and especially in Tahrir, as a national socialist model village on a state-owned estate, a village ten times the size of a landowner's *'izba*.

Patrimonialism and Social Control

Beneath the pragmatic goals of food sovereignty and employment, there were ideological goals as well as loyalty to secure. In what has been termed a bid for total social control, the Nasser regime created a Department of Social Planning to 'recondition society.' The minister of social affairs perceived the situation as follows: "It is impossible to build a society whose people have not been trained to be good citizens."[71] These 'good citizens' would have to eschew their 'chaotic' traditional dress for 'model clothes,'[72] such as shirts and trousers for men, and skirts and blouses for women, as part of life in a 'model society.'[73]

And what better place than in the new lands to breed the 'good citizens,' where another social affairs official saw that "both people and land" were under reclamation.[74] Here, the paternalistic notions of model citizens living in model villages were transplanted wholesale from the model village movement of the preceding two decades, and in fact evolved into a model of nation building and control. In an address to the employees of the Mudiriyat al-Tahrir's Social Guidance Unit, the project's chief architect and Nasser ally, Major Magdi Hassanein, would plainly state:

> Your job is to teach the fellahin that will settle Mudiriyat al-Tahrir how to love their country, to inform them of their nation's patronage toward them . . . that will give them the land, the house, and the ample living—they are to appreciate this patronage. And with that, we create the good citizen who is ready to work and sacrifice for his nation, . . . for the goal of establishing Mudiriyat al-Tahrir is to create an Islamic national socialist union on a scientific basis.[75]

As with any social engineering experiment seeking to forge entirely new communities, those to be resettled in the model villages were chosen according to set criteria for "the most promising farmers and settlers."[76] This differed slightly from project to project, but the new settlers were generally expected to be literate, able farmers, twenty-one to fifty years old, with a family no larger than five, no police record, and ready to join the agricultural cooperative.[77] They would then take part in rehabilitation programs aimed at the "economic, social, and political advancement of communities."[78] In Tahrir, would be residents were put through both physical as well as mental health tests, which only a small number passed.[79] An official there went as far as saying that mothers-in-law would not be permitted residence as, "We want to make it a utopia."[80] The Viennese and Dutch social engineers of the 1920s would have been proud.

The selection of candidates for settlement somewhat favored people naturally inclined toward the military regime. Early on in Tahrir "a concerted effort was made to recruit former soldiers,"[81] mostly veterans of the 1948 Arab–Israeli War who were relocated in army trucks. Veterans would also be part of the first batch of beneficiaries of the EARIS project.[82]

Village names were ideologically chosen—or deliberately kept neutral. In the EARIS project that was funded by the United States at a time when the relationship between Cairo and Washington was cooling, the villages in all three localities were chronologically numbered. The satellite hamlets of the main villages would follow suit, so one person would be from Abis the Third, while another would be from '4:3.' Indeed as Hilmi Tadros would wryly ask, "Can man develop loyalty to a number?"[83]

In military-managed Tahrir, names were chosen to reflect a host of different narratives.[84] Villages in the first phase were named to honor symbols of popular resistance in the lead-up to the 1952 revolution. Umm Saber was a peasant woman who was the "first Egyptian female martyr in the [Suez] Canal," killed by the British because she refused to be searched at a checkpoint in 1951.[85] Popular poet Salah Jahin would immortalize her in 1956 with the song "Ya hamam al-barr" (O Righteous Dove). Umar Shahin was another Suez Canal martyr, who was a student activist, killed in clashes with British troops in January 1952.[86] Some settlements were named in relation to battle, paralleling military action with land reclamation. The main town acting as the administrative center for Tahrir was Badr, named after a key battle in early Muslim history and one of the few mentioned in the Qur'an. Other names chosen in a similar vein included al-Kifah (Struggle), al-Tahadi (Challenge), al-Ma'raka (Battle), and al-Nagah (Success).

The names of villages built in the 1960s, in both Tahrir and the New Valley, commemorated pan-Arabism. Driving down a desert road in the New Valley you would see sign posts in the middle of nowhere for villages with names of Arab capitals and major cities, including Baghdad, Jeddah, and Sana'a. Tahrir also had villages called Baghdad, al-Fallujah, Khartoum, and Palestine. Other villages in Tahrir were named after prominent figures in the history of pan-Arabism, such as Nabil al-Waqad, known as the first Egyptian officer killed in the North Yemen Civil War of 1962–70, and 'Abd al-Salam 'Arif, a president of Iraq who rose from the Free Officers of Iraq, and who many believed to have been assassinated in 1966. In the 1970s, reflecting President Anwar Sadat's Islamic leanings, new villages in Tahrir would be named after Muslim caliphs Abu Bakr al-Saddiq, Uthman ibn 'Affan, Umar ibn al-Khattab, and 'Ali ibn Abi Talib. When ideologies ran out, they simply resorted to Arabic letters—Seen (s), Ye (y), Hah (h), and Tah (t).

The hybridization of model villages, model citizens, and patronage would pay off early on, and the workers of Mudiriyat al-Tahrir would play a key role in cementing Nasser's rule. During a power struggle between Nasser and the installed president Muhammad Naguib in 1954, Hassanein's "good citizens" of Tahrir were called on to show "their appreciation" of the "land, the house, and the ample living" given to them.[87] He trucked the men to Cairo from the state *'izba*s to join the National Guard and the Military Police in civil disobedience against institutions that supported Naguib.[88] In his memoirs, Naguib would recall how the Tahrir workers were directed, along with the Military Police, to storm the State Council

(Administrative Court) to disrupt an emergency session upholding the pro-democratic reforms that he had called for.[89] The members of the meeting were beaten, the council's decree torn up, and the judges forced to sign a declaration upholding the rule of the Revolutionary Council.

The success of the orchestrated rebellion against Naguib would mean that Hassanein now had a private civilian army that saw him as "the father and leader of all of us."[90] It was an army that could be utilized not just for the advancement of the regime, but for personal gain. In a bid for parliament in 1957, Hassanein registered all the Tahrir workers in his Cairo constituency of Qasr al-Nil[91] and instructed them to carry placards that read, "Elect Magdi Hassanein, the Creator of Mudiriyat al-Tahrir!"[92] Hassanein would win the seat, but was forced to resign before long when his corrupt tactics and overspending in the running of Mudiriyat al-Tahrir would be too much for the rest of the Free Officers.

This was by no means the end to the co-optation of the Tahrir workers, who in 1964 would find themselves at the center of a global power play. Mudiriyat al-Tahrir had impressed Soviet premier Nikita Krushchev, who during a visit there saw in the large model state *'izba*s an opportunity to scale up the existing model of patronage.[93] As relations between the two countries warmed, the Soviet Union would fund the reclamation of a further 10,000 feddans in North Tahrir according to the Russian model of large collective state farms, as part of a package of assistance in exchange for "re-creating the country in the Soviet image."[94]

Illusion of Control

Model villages would not house anywhere near the numbers predicted. The plans to redistribute the population—as if Egypt was populated by pawns, ready to be nudged, carried, or pushed at the players' will—would stall due to a number of problems plaguing the overambitious reclamation and resettlement targets.

In the first twenty years, barely 170,000 people would be resettled to 438 new towns, villages, and hamlets in the new lands[95]—less than 2 percent of the more than 11 million people added to Egypt's population during that time. More significantly, less than 1 percent of the rural population of 1976 would be living in new villages.

The fellahin obviously did not quite like the model life designed for them, and mass resettlement failed spectacularly. Living off the land in these villages was not quite the utopian dream, and within the first three decades of resettlement, many families had to take on other jobs, since income from cultivation alone was insufficient.[96] They also saw returns on their land shrink, since the smallholdings were not enough to sustain second and third generation members. As one beneficiary put it, "history repeats itself."[97] Besides the logistical challenges and the limitations of a purely agricultural economy, soil and irrigation problems became a heavy burden. Frequent power outages meant water shortages, as irrigation of most new lands depended on electrical pumping stations rather than gravity.[98] Water shortage issues meant that the livelihoods of between 90 and 100 percent of the 1,650 families in the Quta and Kom Oshim lands of the EARIS project were dependent on family members working as migrant labor, sometimes in Cairo.[99] Some fellahin abandoned the villages altogether.[100]

Even the model houses broke down. Water supply was a major problem in the villages of Tahrir and EARIS. All EARIS villages experienced inadequate water supply, with severe water shortages in Kom Oshim and Quta,[101] and in the Tahrir villages, sanitation infrastructure became so overloaded that sewage water overflowed into the streets.[102] Houses were also too crowded since entire extended households migrated to the new lands, where

4.7: Houses in Sayyidna al-Khidr, a *kharigin* model village in Wadi al-Rayyan, Fayoum, completed in 1999, follow similar designs to those developed in the 1930s and 1940s. Many houses stand empty, sixteen years after the village was built. November 2015. (Photograph by Yahia Shawkat.)

thirteen to seventeen people lived in dwellings built for five.[103] It was not only people who crowded the small houses. Fear of theft, poison, and the evil eye, as well as the burden of walking in the cold and rain to the designated stables, meant that the fellahin moved their livestock into their courtyards.[104] Cultural attachment was also a factor, and animals had to be cared for if they were sick or pregnant.[105] As one horse-cart driver put it to me previously, "*fa'l al-husan fi al-bayt hilw*" (the omen of a horse at home is good).

Ultimately, it is difficult to imagine a more complex, challenging, or risky human endeavor than designing communities from scratch.[106] Planners sitting in offices must have pretty big egos to believe they could successfully re-create lives that had taken decades, even centuries, to evolve. The settlements that were successful worked because of the sheer grit of the settlers. Hanne Kirstine Adriansen's study on a later project, the *qura al-kharigin* (graduates' villages), shows how some were motivated out of true religious or nationalist beliefs, seeing opportunity in the new lands, where women and the poor felt empowered,[107] though her research also showed that some left their original villages because "there was nothing there to make them stay."

Most settlers persevered because they had nothing left to lose. The 1950s schemes were directed at those still landless after the land reform and people who were evacuated from Sinai and the Suez Canal cities after the 1967 Israeli occupation of Sinai. One of the larger projects to cultivate 27,000 feddans was to relocate the homes of 50,000 Nubians displaced by the construction of the High Dam in Aswan.[108]

Neoliberal Ghost Villages: 1977–Today

Despite the failures of the grand reclamation schemes, President Sadat, Nasser's successor, would initiate new ones, though not before a short break to build his power base.[109] Foreign loans, aid, and investment started trickling back in the latter half of the 1970s, which Sadat would try and direct to his "new map of Egypt," one that envisioned populating the "strategic vacuums" of the desert with new cities and industry.[110] In 1977, in a barren expanse south of the Ismailia Canal, amid chants from would-be beneficiaries proclaiming him the "initiator of a civilizational renaissance in the desert," Sadat launched the Wadi al-Malak project, aiming to reclaim 21,000 feddans.[111] Most of the headlines were similar to the grand reclamation schemes that harked back to the 1940s: a remote location, rectilinear plots of smallholdings surrounding a new village, and so on. But one glaring difference stood out: instead of distributing the land for free, Sadat expected to fund it through the fellahin's "savings," in order "to involve the people in managing and funding the projects to achieve the best results."[112]

This was of course the era of the Infitah, the newly introduced free-market open door policies that would align Egypt with the West and airbrush out the "Soviet image" that the state farms of the previous decades had painted. The Ismailia-Misr Agricultural Development Company was set up, with the government only owning 20 percent of its shares, while the remainder was owned by "Egyptian, Arab and foreign investors."[113]

Also absent were any preparations for social engineering. Indeed, in the contemporaneous World Bank funded New Land Development Project in West Nubariya, started in 1980 near Mudiriyat al-Tahrir, 4,000 smallholders were expected to buy "minimal houses," which had two rooms within a walled courtyard, so that they could expand as needed and connect to communal water taps "at their own expense."[114] This expense would be underwritten by loans to be paid back over a twenty-five-year period, and were to cover buying the desert land and cultivating it.[115]

The one model village Sadat was interested in was his own village, Mit Abul Kom, in the Delta govornorate of Minufiya. On his sixtieth birthday on December 25, 1978, he laid the cornerstone for the rebuilding of the village he grew up in, describing it as his "most joyful celebration" and where his "dream of building a house turned into a dream of building [his] village."[116] The fellahin would also receive homes for free, as Sadat personally donated $1 million from his Nobel Peace Prize to build the new houses "for every citizen of Mit Abul Kom," along with taps with running water and proper sanitation.[117] Over the next two years, Sadat would visit the village a number of times, including on his sixty-first and sixty-second birthdays to hand the deeds of 125 new houses to their residents.[118]

Sadat would not give out any deeds in December 1981, as he was assassinated two months prior to this. President Hosni Mubarak, who succeeded him, would pour cold water over the investor-based large landholdings and rehash the old monarchial reclamation schemes that targeted graduates because of a growing cadre of 'educated unemployed' that the government did not have the resources, nor the need, to employ.[119] A key difference between the 1987 Mubarak Project for Youth Graduates, also known as *qura al-kharigin* (graduates' villages), and the earlier ones, was that applicants did not have to be graduates of agricultural schools, although those with a degree in agriculture from a rural background were preferred.[120] As with the contemporaneous New Lands project, "minimal houses" were allotted, along with a five-feddan land plot, which the applicants bought through subsidized loans.

Qura al-kharigin would not only accept graduates, though. When agrarian reform was undone in 1997 as part of the IMF and World Bank structural adjustment program, around 6 million fellahin, many of whom lived on the old *'izba*s, faced the threat of being made both landless and homeless within months.[121] While the land rent liberalization law 97/1992 stipulated rehousing evicted fellahin, less than 2 percent of families facing eviction were given alternative housing, all in the remote new villages of *qura al-kharigin.*[122] Not only that, the government had decided that five feddans was too much for them, and so allocated each family half a standard plot, which also meant half an already "minimal house," though they "soon realized that sharing houses was a bad idea" and built some extra ones.[123]

In the latter half of the 1990s, Mubarak would shift policies, launching a torrent of publicly-funded mega-land reclamation projects. The infamous Toshka and the lesser-known Darb al-Arba'in and East 'Uwaynat reclamation projects, initiated in 1997, promised to reclaim 2 million feddans[124] and resettle unspecified millions as part of the formally titled South Valley Development Project (SVDP). A year later the development project of Salam Canal in North Sinai was to reclaim 400,000 feddans and resettle about 21,000 families. In 2005, a project to build 400 *qura al-Zahir al-Sahrawi* (desert fringe villages) and reclaim one million feddans was launched as part of Mubarak's electoral campaign.[125] The January 2011 uprising and regime change did not stop the onslaught of large-scale reclamation schemes, where President Abd al-Fattah al-Sisi launched a project to reclaim 1.5 million feddans. Launched in 2015, the official government tag line states that it "will be a model for a series of villages . . . to establish an integrated residential community that attracts residents."[126]

The Procurement Regime

Using Google Earth, one can see a desert littered with government-built *qura ashbah* (ghost villages) that have mostly never been settled (figure 4.8).[127] In the span of sixteen years, the Mubarak Project for Youth Graduates would see at most 350,000 people abandon the Nile Valley for the slowly greening desert.[128] As with the older projects, this signified only a paltry 'redirection' of the population to what Sadat called the 'vacuums

4.8: Ghost village—one of the larger *al-zahir al-sahrawi* villages, Wadi al-Rayyan in Fayoum, standing empty six years after being built. (Image dated July 23, 2016, ©2017 GOOGLE.)

of the desert'—a mere 1.3 percent of the rural population at the time, and 2.2 percent of rural population growth from 1960.[129] Toshka, which should have had over 1 million people living on its greened land within two decades of its 1997 start date, had barely more than 2,000 people in 2006, and zero in 2017.[130] Out of 400 *qura al-Zahir al-Sahrawi* that should have been built by 2011, only 40 have been built, and almost none have ever been inhabited.

Sadat's and Mubarak's projects would also break down, some almost instantaneously, and others that never worked at all. The World Bank's New Lands project did not receive enough water to keep its fields cultivated barely two years after it was completed.[131] The parastatal Salhiya reclamation project that started reclaiming tens of thousands of feddans in the desert east of the Delta in 1979 was abandoned in 1990, after incurring massive losses on its government and private financiers.[132]

Mubarak's *qura al-kharigin* villages were no different. While one study of ten villages in the Western Delta found "the positive image was by far the most prevalent," where the majority of residents were found to be "satisfied with their new life,"[133] they still faced numerous challenges, including a lack of public services and insecure tenure. Many were also bound to land as they were already deeply in debt from loans taken out to cultivate them because of the high costs of reclamation, low yields, and the fact they could initially not sell their land to repay their loans.[134]

Other *qura kharigin* experienced the same problems of water shortages, soil trouble, infrastructure breakdown, and lack of services found in the older projects. Five villages in the Husayniya area in Sharqiya were found mostly abandoned, fourteen years after they were built and the land distributed.[135] In the new village of al-Siddiq al-Minshawi in Suhag, only a fifth of the 1,100 houses built in 1985 were inhabited twenty-nine years later. In addition to the standard set of troubles, armed thugs had forced the smallholders off their land.[136] Various news reports over the last ten years have described the twin villages of Sayyidna al-Khidr and Sayyidna Mousa in Fayoum as *mansiya* (forgotten), *kharig nitaq al-khidma* (out of service), and *guhannam* (hell) (figure 4.8).[137]

The majority of the dozens of *zahir sahrawi* villages built in the late 2000s and the early 2010s were an absolute disaster, and have never been lived in. A 2016 report found six villages in Minya to be lacking in both drinking water and irrigation, as ground water was found to be unsuitable, while most had become inundated by sand dunes, with sand blocking the doorways of the brand new houses as well as the streets.[138] Cultivable land had evidently not been part of the original plan, as beneficiaries in other villages were told only the homes were ready, which they refused to accept, as without land, there was no point in moving in.[139] In Aswan, the Central Auditing Authority produced a scathing report showing that half a billion Egyptian pounds had been squandered on 58 villages that stood empty years after they were completed, two of which were built in flash flood zones that required extra millions to be spent on dams to save them.[140]

Squandering money that just had to be spent seems to have been the main objective of all of these projects from the start. A procurement regime, where public finance is meant to underwrite the construction of massive infrastructure, but not economic or social success. The much-critiqued reclamation projects of the 1950s to 1980s were stellar achievements in land reclamation and resettlement in comparison. The urgent need to redirect population growth out of the old lands, meanwhile, turned out to be mythical, as the core problem lay in the management of population densities and land use, not the actual area of land.[141]

Present in almost all of Sadat's rural projects was Osman Ahmed Osman, former housing minister, then parliamentarian, and, more importantly, contracting tycoon of the Arab Contractors and Osman Group fame. Osman cofounded the company that ran the Wadi al-Malak project using the pension fund of the Arab Contractors company.[142] He was head of the committee to rebuild Mit Abul Kom, which the Arab Contractors was also entrusted with. The Arab Contractors was also majority shareholder of the Middle East Company for Land Reclamation, which ended up owning some 150,000 acres of the Salhiya project in 1979.[143] The late leftist housing critic Milad Hanna called this period the "sovereignty of the contractors,"[144] with special reference to Osman, whom David Sims described as a "crony capitalist par exellance."[145]

Easy money—part credit, part grants from international donors—was a major factor. The *qura al-kharigin* project was funded by American and Danish agencies to support cooperation between Egypt and Israel according to the 1979 Camp David peace accords.[146] The Japanese and the Kuwaitis paid for the North Sinai project,[147] and Japan and other Arab states funded Toshka.[148] The World Bank, the African Development Bank, and the World Food Programme paid for the New Lands Development Project in the Western Delta,[149] and the United Arab Emirates funded the Hammam Canal in the northwestern coast.[150]

Propaganda was another factor. Sadat laid the cornerstone of the Wadi al-Malak and Mit Abul Kom projects himself, visting the latter many times to give new owners their deeds. A prominent feature in some *zahir sahrawi* villages was the helipads attached to them—concrete red carpets for Mubarak's entourage of four to six helicopters to touch down as he was whisked from one photo op to another. Toshka also came with the requisite helipads: a major installation at the mouth of the Toshka Canal, at least three others at pumping stations, and one near the experimental farm where the first pivot irrigation was installed. Not much changed after the January 2011 revolution. The site in Farafra associated with the one-and-a-half-million-feddan project also came replete with a helipad for three, as well as a purpose-built grandstand. In her master's thesis titled "Designed to Deceive," Emma Deputy posited that these large-scale projects were "designed to fail because the regime received the largest benefit by starting them—not by completing them."[151] The spectacle of massive public funding would be strong enough to convince lower- and middle-class Egyptians that food, jobs, and homes would be provided, while in effect the money went to buy the patronage of the business elite through consultancies and construction contracts.

The mythical premise that the Nile Valley was too crowded ticked the boxes of donor reports, made handsome profits for consultants and the construction industry, and bought some years of legitimacy for the authoritarian regime.

Today: Reincarnation of Private *'Izba*s

A regular feature of the grand reclamation projects was quietly omitted from the larger post-1997 projects: the model village. While the smallholding projects were spluttering out of steam, the government reapplied the blueprints of desert reclamation through large landholdings of thousands of feddans distributed to private corporations that it had attempted before in the late 1970s. In Toshka, 100,000 feddans were given to Saudi Prince Walid bin Talal's KADCO.[152] Another Saudi firm, Al Rajhi, was given 100,000 feddans also in Toshka, as was the Emirati firm Al Dahra,[153] which also owns 16,000 feddans in East 'Uwaynat. I use the word "given" because the land was priced at LE50 per feddan, whereas it had cost the government around LE11,000 to extend the massive irrigation infrastructure to it.[154] James Last's serenade of the "Lonely Shepherd" playing on the website of the South Valley Company for Development will help you ease into the fact that the Egyptian state owns the remaining land in Toshka—120,000 feddans that are considered a "nature reserve with no disease or pests."[155] In East 'Uwaynat, the Ministry of Defense owns 110,000 feddans, and the Awqaf (Religious Endowments Authority) owns 48,000.[156] The remaining 50,000 feddans are owned or rented by fifteen companies, most of which are Gulf based.[157] The so-called smallholdings of the 1.5 milion feddan project, launched after the January 2011 uprising, come at a minimum of 238 feddans, and young investors have to set up companies of at least ten shareholders to buy them. The large landholdings start from 2,000 feddans.[158]

If all these private and state-owned companies own the land, why would the government build any villages, let alone schools, hospitals, and all the other services associated with communities? (This is not to imply that the government did this well when it built model villages). In Toshka, even though model villages were promised as well as a new Toshka City, none of the villages have been built. The 'city' is but a number of social housing blocks, built eighteen years after the project started.[159] It is in the middle of nowhere, where none of the homes have been sold. Indeed, the 2006 census

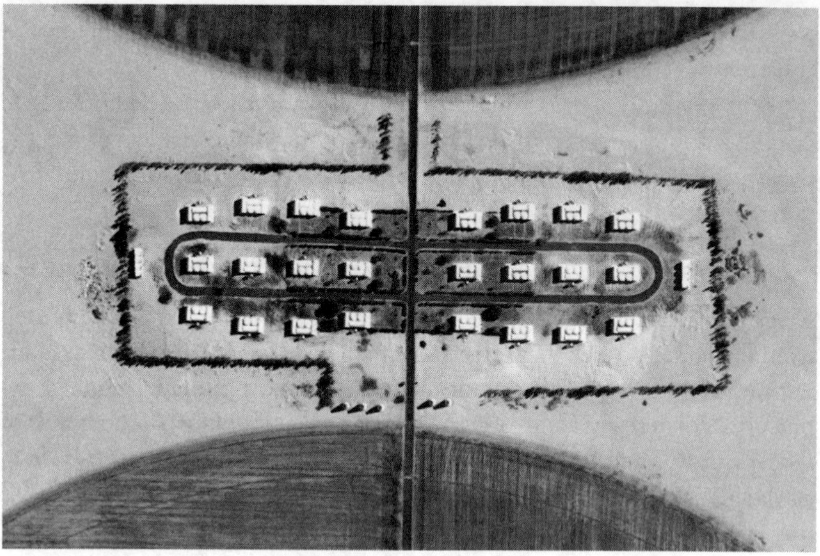

4.9: The *'izba* reincarnated—a large workers' compound, one of many, on a super farm in East 'Uwaynat. (Image dated December 2014, ©2018 Digital Globe/GOOGLE.)

counted 2,655 people in the New Toshka city *shiyakha* (the smallest census block) and found them all living in barracks of different sorts.[160] Of these residents—which did not constitute even 1 percent of the millions that were supposed to have resettled there—only three were women. Interestingly, the 2017 census showed the same *shiyakha* to have zero residents, the only plausible expalantion being that the workers were moved deep into the large estates that were inaccessible to census staff.

With massive private or quasi-private landholdings, the private *'izba* has been reincarnated, albeit in its more primitive form of housing for male rural workers. The housing ranges from tents and shacks to scattered rooms and rectilinear designed compounds, depending on the size of the corporation and the image it wants to project. The super-sized farms in East 'Uwaynat have neat rows of domed housing interspersed between the cultivated pivot irrigation circles (figure 4.9).

In over a century and a half of officially sanctioned rural housing of one form or another, the stability associated with having a permanent home has remained elusive for the country's fellahin. During the nineteenth century, many were displaced from their villages either protesting forced labor or accepting it on the private *'izbas* on the new, remote lands. Mass rural housing thus started out as a way for government—though funded by the private sector—to physically control the lives of large swaths of the population by fixing them to a defined location.[161]

In the second half of the twentieth century, destitution forced many to move to the government-built model villages of the new lands. For a significant portion of them it was a risky move, and many would return to the old lands if they could, or were compelled to continue to work as bonded labor to repay the mounting debts they took out to reclaim the land in what was a quiet step toward intangible methods of control.

The last two decades have seen much of the fellahin reduced yet again to *tarahil* (migrant agricultural labor). Instead of walking to the nearby fields as they did in the nineteenth century, or riding a truck for an hour or so as they did in the twentieth century, the *tarahil* of today waste entire days traveling hundreds of kilometers to work on super farms located in the middle of nowhere. The move from physical to intangible control has thus been completed in the form of a fixed destabilization. Today, much of the youthful rural workforce spend most of their lives in remote desert 'institutions,' far removed from communal activity. The remoteness of these *'izba*s allows for abuse, as indicated by the trickle of news that comes out of these desert outposts. Local news site *Akhbar al-Wadi al-Jadid* covered incidents in which ninety-two people were either killed or injured in East 'Uwaynat over a four-year period.[162] Most were involved in accidents on the dilapidated East 'Uwaynat–Dakhla highway, but the rest were work-related incidents. In one of these, a twelve-year-old boy was killed while harvesting potatoes.[163] Child labor on these super farms appears to be rife, with another article reporting that children are regularly seen on microbuses going to East 'Uwaynat or working on farms, especially during harvest.[164] The *'izba*s that had disappeared for over half a century have been revived in all their terror and control.

5

GOVERNMENT HOUSING, A BRIEF HISTORY

Urban government housing has been a staple of the Egyptian cityscape since the 1950s. Identical apartment blocks dot every city and town, as well as some villages, where they run along railway tracks and canals. Beneath the uniformity of this housing lies a harlequin patchwork of policies, laws, and circumstance that drove their construction.

Urban government housing is the most appropriate term—rather than public or social housing—because not all of it has served a social purpose. Many of the housing blocks were not built for the poor but for designated target groups—usually those closest to the ruling regime or poor residents who happened to be in the way of urban gentrification. In the three decades preceding the 1952 revolution, most mass housing was not even built by the government but by privately owned companies to house their employees. While the socialist 1960s saw the flourishing of so-called cooperative housing, it was built by profession-based cooperatives close to the state and even by a state-owned agency. Upper-middle and luxury[1] housing has also been a feature of government housing, as the state set up its own urban developers, in addition to nationalizing the largest ones in the 1960s. Over the last century, the state's quest for properly built houses that the poor could afford could not have been more fleeting.

Modern Origins: 1860s–1926

From the nineteenth century, the monarchy built a smattering of rural model villages to house farmers, as we see in chapter 4. As early as the 1860s, some housing for civil servants working in the government's vast infrastructure in remote areas started to appear on government *fawriqat* (industrial estates).[2] Besides housing employees, the government also sought to rehouse the poor and destitute in an effort to establish some semblance of public health. Two slum clearance and rehousing projects in Alexandria were planned in 1867 and 1897 but failed to materialize, while one housing project in Helwan to the south of Cairo was only partially built in 1870.[3] Urban government housing schemes would splutter into life during the latter half of the nineteenth century before going full steam in the 1950s.

The first half of the twentieth century saw a little more government housing activity, though still centered around its employees and slum clearance. In a fascinating work, architecture historian Mercedes Volait tracked down a considerable portion of these.[4] No less than seventy expropriation decrees would be issued between 1904 and 1952 to acquire land to build housing for the employees of the railroad and irrigation departments (figure 5.1).[5] Most decrees were for a handful of dwellings at most, though one rare project comprised fifty homes for employees of the government's al-Amiriya Press. In the 1920s and 1930s, six different housing projects comprising a little over one thousand units were planned by government agencies, but only half were realized. One project was again for government workers, though this time it comprised a two-hundred-unit compound for railway employees in Abu Za'bal, just north of Cairo. What was different was that the Ministry of Public Works organized a design contest in 1932 overseen by a committee that chose the winning design according to criteria of "economic and healthy housing."[6]

The other projects were all preoccupied with slum clearance in Cairo and Alexandria. In 1921, a one-hundred-unit 'model municipal colony' was planned on Alexandria's outskirts, as was a much larger one seven years later, but neither were realized because they were too costly—something that would dog housing projects over the coming century. When Prime Minister Muhammad Mahmud laid the first stone of a three-hundred-unit scheme of *masakin sihhiya* (healthy homes) in the popular Cairo neighborhood of Sayyida Zaynab in 1930, he was also laying the first stone in the foundation of government patronage of low-cost homes. However, he only managed to build sixty units, which remained mostly vacant because they were too expensive for the working class, even after a 40 percent subsidy. Eight years later, the cabinet initiated a five-year plan to build a 244-unit workers' town in Imbaba. While it was indeed built, it was subsequently requisitioned for Second World War migrants from Alexandria before it could house any workers, and later became part of a hospital.

5.1: A row of old single-story railway housing near Aswan. January 2018. (Photograph by Yahia Shawkat.)

A lack of interest in housing as a social good has prevented government-sponsored schemes from becoming policy, and indeed from being implemented. Mahmud Riad, an architect who would later become Egypt's first ever housing official, summed it up in his notes on the Alexandria colony, observing, "One considerable difficulty is that the people living in the slums cannot, in most cases, afford to pay an economic rent for properly built houses."[7] The monarchy, as well as the colonial British, had no intention of subsidizing homes that brought no economic return, while working-class wages were meager at best. Even the liberal governments that came in the late 1920s after nominal independence were unable to build housing such that they could be rented at rates that would both cover their costs and be affordable to the working class.

Mass urban housing thus remained the preserve of top government employees. Interestingly, the largest housing scheme for government employees at the time was built by the private sector—albeit accidentally. In 1907, the Cairo Electric Railways and Heliopolis Oases Company (Heliopolis Company), famous for building what was then the suburban desert district of Heliopolis to the northeast of Cairo, had agreed to supply the government with four hundred villas and apartments that would be rented out at subsidized rates to government employees.[8] The developer's interest lay in making its vacant buildings appear occupied after a market crash in 1907 shrunk housing demand, leaving much stock without owners or tenants.[9] A similar agreement was made in 1921 to supply six hundred units at predefined rents for thirty years.[10] This time it was high inflation after the First World War leading to spiraling rents and an uprising in 1919 that pushed the government to move to secure housing for some of its employees by financing a loan to the Heliopolis Company.[11]

Rise of Workers' Housing: 1926–1945

It was the private sector, rather than the government, that built most of the low-cost urban housing in the few decades preceding the 1952 revolution. The government was not a significant employer and did not have much incentive to supply low-cost housing to the poor, as labor unrest in the 1930s targeted the industrialists and not the government. There were some rare instances of private industrial housing before the 1930s that set the template for later schemes.

In 1874, the Suez Canal Company built a small compound in Port Tawfiq in Suez, though the reason for this was that the port was too far from the town.[12] The Heliopolis Company built around two hundred units for its own workers in 1911, again due to the remote location of the project, in what it labeled the 'native quarter,' which residents renamed 'Izbit al-Bustan,[13] invoking the hamlets built for workers on rural estates (see chapter 4). In 1926, Port Fouad on the eastern bank of Port Said raised the bar by becoming the first company town in Egypt, and one that was designed along the lines of the garden city movement that was in vogue in the early twentieth century.[14] Financed by the Suez Canal Company to address a severe housing shortage in Port Said after the First World War, it was inaugurated by King Fouad among other dignitaries.[15] The king even issued two limited edition commemorative stamps to mark the creation of his namesake town (figure 5.2). The stamps were only on sale for a few days, however, and only through the post office to ensure they remained rare, causing a five-thousand-strong riot and speculative buying by government employees.[16] Port Fouad's plush villas were designated for high-level management (figure 5.3), while it had small houses for European workers, and a caravanserai-like compound for the locals in a zone that ensured they did not "spread through the European Quarters."[17] In the eighty years between its inception and its nationalization, the company would build 1,500 housing units for managers, staff, and workers along the canal.[18]

5.2: Two commemorative stamps issued by King Fouad to mark the inauguration of Port Fouad in 1926.

5.3: One of the villas in Port Fouad's 'European Quarter' housing Suez Canal Company employees, built along the lines of the garden city movement in 1926. October 2010. (Photograph by Yahia Shawkat.)

With the company town, the Suez Canal Company also introduced the model of a compartmentalized colonial world, as the philosopher Frantz Fanon saw it, one where "the 'native' sector . . . confront[s]" the European one following the "dictates of mutual exclusion," for "the colonized man is an envious man" that dreams of taking the place of the colonist.[19] It would be transplanted—initially along racial lines and later according to class—to the oil towns that started springing up in the late 1930s, such as the Anglo-Egyptian Oilfields company town in Ras Gharib.[20] Segregation would also make its way to industrial housing, where over twenty workers' housing estates would be built from 1939 to 1950, mostly comprising health, social, and educational services.[21] One of the earliest of these was at the Beida Dyers factory complex built in 1939 in Kafr al-Dawwar, designed by the Anglo-Swiss, Egypt-based Serjeant and Zollikofer Architects.[22] It was followed three years later by the neighboring Misr Silk Weaving Company's housing for employees, designed by Egyptian architect 'Ali Labib Gabr.[23] Most famous of these, however, was the Misr Spinning and Weaving Company's workers' housing in al-Mahalla al-Kubra, which was another 'public–private partnership.' This time the company approached the government to co-finance an emergency *muhagirin* (migrants) village in 1941, on the condition that it would be used as workers' housing when the Second World War would finally end.[24] It would indeed house workers from 1945, and that same year the company would build better housing for its staff at a separate location.[25] The *musta'marat* (colonies), as they came to be known, would witness quite a few changes with the rise of socialism in the 1960s, before almost completely unraveling in the neoliberal twenty-first century.

But why the sudden interest in workers' housing? Industry had been around in Egypt for over a century, while the concept of model villages was of equal vintage. In Britain, model villages had started to morph into industrial model housing much earlier, at the turn of the nineteenth century, following their same paternalistic and aesthetic drivers.[26] But while the government in Egypt was neither provider nor regulator of housing, the British had a raft of workers' housing laws that started with the Artisans and Labourers Dwellings Act of 1868, which created a system to report dwellings "unfit for human habitation."

Living conditions had badly deteriorated in the Egyptian factory towns in the 1920s and 1930s when nationalist industry boomed and the towns could not absorb the large influx of workers. This led to severe overcrowding where up to twelve families would gather to afford the rent of one

5.4: Originally built as a village for *muhagirin* displaced by the Second World War in 1941, these houses in al-Mahalla formed one of the earliest modern workers' colonies in Egypt. (Photograph by Yahia Shawkat.)

home, sleeping three to four at a time in shifts.[27] Others lived in cheap hotels or built informal shacks. When they could not afford any of these options, people slept on the street, a criminal offense that subjected offenders to arrest.[28] Complaints about housing were made, and a committee was formed by the residents of al-Mahalla, which sent a petition to King Fouad in 1930 highlighting the housing shortage and high rents.[29] But it would take a burgeoning labor movement some time before it could force the postindependence governments to make better housing conditions a priority.[30] The Wafd Party proposed legislation in 1927 to regulate working conditions and have employers provide housing, food, and social welfare for workers—a proposal resisted by the heads of industry who claimed that Egypt was not ready for European standards.[31] Two years later, the rival Liberal Constitutional Party proposed another remedy—direct government intervention through a five-year plan to build workers' housing itself. Its experiment became one of the expensive and partially completed schemes described earlier. This blip in labor rights would be washed away that year when antilabor Prime Minister Isma'il Sidqi came to power and would not see a resurgence until 1937, when trade unionists established the

Commission to Organize the Workers' Movement, and waves of strikes forced part of their rights agenda through.

The housing eventually provided by business owners helped alleviate some health and social concerns. Families lived in small houses that they did not have to share with others, while unmarried male and female workers slept in adequate dorms, resulting in decreased rates of overcrowding and much improved health conditions, evidenced by lower infant mortality rates. The accommodation hardly made a dent in demand; in al-Mahalla it housed barely 10 percent of the workforce.[32]

It also came with its own strings attached. Workers in al-Mahalla complained that the company "housing units were designed to be prisons," as inspectors could enter unannounced under the pretext of checking on cleanliness.[33] Arguably this was a reinvention of the controlled life of rural workers on the pasha's *'izba*.

Birth of a Housing Policy: 1945–51

Responding to labor unrest and a new wave of literature on the inequities of working-class life,[34] and perhaps smelling an opportunity to expand their work, architects and planners of the 1940s started transferring their concepts from the model villages they had spent the last decade or so perfecting (see chapter 4) to designing "the ideal way that each poor and middle-class family could acquire a healthy home . . . known all over the world as workers' homes."[35]

One of the earliest policy notes centered on *mushkilat al-masakin* (the homes problem) and was written by an architect. Mahmud Riad's 1945 article, "Tahdid al-manatiq al-sina'iya wa insha' masakin al-'ummal" (Identifying Industrial Zones and Building Workers' Homes) in the influential *Majallat al-'imara*, described how the Egyptian government had developed industries but "left the question of workers' and poor people's homes without any serious attempt to solve it." It was a question that he saw as a "major national problem that should urgently garner the lion's share of attention to ensure the peoples' development."[36] His response was studied, drawing upon analysis of policies in the West, singling out Austria as a leading country on the question of workers' housing.[37] It had passed a raft of legislation including rent control, thirty-year tax breaks on low-cost homes, and a progressive real estate tax, where most of the revenue came from more expensive properties. There was also monetary support to build workers' homes in the form of long-term low-interest loans for municipalities, the use of local building materials, and the expropriation of land needed for such projects. Riad used the Abu Za'bal railway town competition, which he had entered over a decade earlier, as an example of how expensive the homes were relative to workers' wages, and demonstrated how applying subsidization policies like those in Austria could slash costs by half, thereby enabling the provision of homes that were affordable to the poor.[38]

Two years later, the Third Arab Engineers' Conference was held in Damascus, with almost half of its presentations devoted to the subject of "economic and healthy homes."[39] It addressed what it described as *mushkilat dayqat al-sakan* (the problem of the shortage of homes) with recommendations echoing those of Riad, in addition to more radical concepts including regulating the profits of real estate companies and the prices of building materials.[40] 'Ali al-Miligi Mas'ud—who only a few years earlier had the radical concept of redistributing land to the fellahin as a way to create the 'model citizen' and would then go on to create the 'model village'[41]—took Riad's views a few steps further. As head of the Town Planning Department, Mas'ud advocated the complete rebuilding of "unhealthy areas" (slums) as well as the building of new suburbs as a preventative measure "that delays the need for treatment and is a sure tonic for a host of bodily and social diseases."[42] He saw that this should take utmost priority, even over the building of hospitals. Echoing Riad, Mas'ud recommended a host of government measures to support municipalities, co-ops, and factories, including free land, cash subsidies, and low-interest loans to build rent-controlled homes for "working-class people in public services and companies, small shop owners, and all who are of limited income." He also recommended making it mandatory for companies to build homes for their employees.

Glaringly absent from his recommendations were any of the soft measures that did not involve construction, as described by Riad. There also seemed to be some government interest in piloting these hard measures, and so Mas'ud—who was not shy in blowing his own trumpet—was chosen to present the Imbaba Workers' Town, which he designed, as the "first and grandest of these projects in the Middle East."[43] Imbaba broke ground in 1947, with the aim of building six thousand units over five years. The homes were to be rented out to government workers who met certain employment, familial, and geographical criteria. These residents would be required to adhere to a set of rules, any violation of which would result in immediate eviction.[44] Imbaba's main departure from previous schemes was not its government finance but that it was the first to apply Riad's subsidization model in an elaborate plan that took into consideration workers' wages and what proportion they could spend on rent that "would not burden them" (table 5–1).[45] It seemed like a heyday for government-funded homes, especially when in 1949, the king's name would grace plans for a second government-funded project. Farouk the First City was to be an industrial estate in the Upper Egyptian town of Kom Ombo, replete with a flour mill, pasta factory, homes for workers, and a garden city for employees.[46]

Type	Ground floor	Typical	All	
Bedrooms	1	1	2	3
Cost per room	0.45	0.55	0.5	0.5
Total monthly rent	0.9	1.1	1.5	2.0
Average income	13.3	13.3	13.3	13.3
Rent-to-income ratio	7%	8%	11%	15%
Deposit	Case-by-case			
Compulsory co-op subscription	2.0	2.0	3.0	4.0

Source: Ministry of Social Affairs Decree 7/1950.

5.1: Imbaba housing rents in 1950.

Riad's contribution to affordable housing would not go unnoticed. In 1949, the government commissioned Riad and Ahmad Hussein, a senior official at the Ministry of Social Affairs, to prepare a comprehensive plan to provide homes to families of "limited income."[47] Riad was then appointed head of Egypt's first official office for housing, the Department of Popular Homes within the Ministry of Social Affairs, in 1950.[48] The following year, the Popular Homes Law 206/1951 would be passed, relying on a hybrid of the recommendations from Riad and Mas'ud, though it was centered solely on the construction of homes, ignoring any measures to regulate existing accommodation or the real estate industry.

The Popular Homes Law regulated construction by municipalities, housing cooperatives, and private business when it came to the provision of workers' homes, as well as the construction of new villages. Government would provide state land, or expropriate private land, which would be leased for free to the agencies or businesses for forty years, after which it would revert to the government. Provisions were made for government-subsidized long-term loans for construction at rates of 2 percent, though this was to be regulated by a separate law. Other government support included a five-year real estate tax break, tax exemption for investments made to build the homes, as well as a provision for the government to pay the owners of the popular homes the difference between the set rents and those affordable to the tenants on a case-by-case basis. The tenants would benefit from a pre-set rent contract, though they would be evicted immediately if they failed to pay the rent.

We will never know whether this relatively progressive law would have helped stem the 'homes problem.' Its executive bylaws, which were to detail much of its provisions, were never passed, while nine months later social unrest and a military coup unseated the monarchy and ended colonial rule. The pioneering Imbaba project would barely see a fifth of its target of six thousand units realized,[49] strongly indicating that government finance and support for affordable homes never fully materialized.

Popular Housing Explosion: 1954–67

The Law of Popular Homes found favor with the socialist regime of the Free Officers that supplanted the monarchy in July 1952. Mahmud Riad was replaced a year later by the capable and construction-centric 'Ali Mas'ud as head of the Popular Housing Department,[50] while Riad went on to become an influential state architect as well as director general of the Cairo municipality. Application for government-built homes was opened in August of that year,[51] although construction of the new homes was delayed because a design could not be agreed on. In early 1954, two pilot projects of one hundred units each were put to tender in Telal Zeinhom in Cairo to test the economics of different housing models. Four-story and five-story apartment blocks were chosen,[52] and would then be built at five sites in Greater Cairo and Alexandria.[53]

A year and a half later, in a public speech marking the revolution's third anniversary, Nasser announced that 4,310 homes had been built in Hilmiyyat al-Zaytun, Imbaba, and Helwan in Cairo, and were to be delivered to their owners within days.[54] He explained how the "popular homes were being built to relieve *azmit al-masakin* (the homes crisis), outlining plans to build over 12,000 homes for both blue- and white-collar government employees in different parts of Egypt that would be sold or rented at affordable rates.[55]

Within a socialist regime, workers were a key constituency, and by the early 1960s, much industry had been nationalized. New compounds were built in the Shubra and Helwan industrial estates around Cairo, the sugar factories in Dishna and Hawamdiya, the new Kima Fertilizer plant in Aswan (figure 5.5), as well as the expansion of the older workers' compounds in al-Mahalla, Imbaba, and Abu Za'bal of the 1930s and 1940s.[56] The 1960s also saw the construction of the High Dam in Aswan, which meant that it became a boom town, with workers, traders, engineers, and public servants and their families pouring in by the thousands. This created a severe housing shortage, one that was met by the construction of six thousand cramped rooms for workers by the now nationalized Arab Contractors, as well as one thousand modern apartments and villas in the Sahari colony for Egyptian and Soviet engineers working on the dam (figure 5.6).[57]

Finally, housing was recognized as a social good and was affordable to most of the population. A considerable proportion of the popular homes were built to rehouse masses of people in response to crises or major projects rather than as part of a general social program to rehouse poor families. Around 4,000 homes built in Cairo in the 1950s rehoused families whose neighborhoods had been demolished as part of a grand slum clearance and beautification project for the capital.[58] In the early 1960s, another 10,000 units were planned solely for Cairo's slum clearance projects,[59] as were most of the homes in Alexandria. After the Tripartite Aggression in 1956 destroyed swaths of Port Said, killing 1,400 civilians and leaving 25,000 homeless,[60] 4,460 homes were built as part of the reconstruction efforts.[61] In Aswan's Kom Ombo, 17,000 homes were hastily built between 1963 and 1965 to relocate the Nubians displaced by the building of the High Dam.[62] In 1967, mass forced migration of almost one million residents of the Suez Canal cities and Sinai in the aftermath of the Israeli invasion of Sinai created a severe housing shortage in many Delta towns as well as Cairo. Many of the displaced were housed in thousands of tiny one-, two-, and three-room huts with shared bathrooms, called shelter housing *(masakin al-iwa')*.

This social good would also extend to a new middle class, as prerevolution segregation of housing between workers and employees continued under socialism, varying mainly in quality, design, tenure options, and prices. At first the Development and Popular Homes Company (Sharikat al-Ta'mir wa-l-Masakin al-Sha'biya) was responsible for all government-built housing. Founded in May 1954 upon "government concern" to "solve the homes crisis," it had a paid-in capital of LE250,000.[63] The company

5.5: Kima Fertilizer Company's workers' colony built in the 1960s in Aswan. January 2018. (Photograph by Yahia Shawkat.)

5.6: One of the villas in the Sahari colony built for Soviet and Egyptian engineers working on the High Dam in the 1960s in Aswan. January 2018. (Photograph by Yahia Shawkat.)

was allowed to issue bonds, as well as borrow up to LE2 million from the government. Riad reappeared as one of three government representatives on its board, with powers to oversee design and standards, and to define beneficiaries of the new homes. It built the first new batch of working-class housing in Cairo on both state-owned and expropriated land.[64] The Development and Popular Homes Company was not solely focused on working-class accommodation, and also built widely for government employees and military personnel, as well as dorms for al-Azhar University students.[65] However, it would build a mere 8,000 of the 150,000 homes constructed during Nasser's rule.[66]

As with previous attempts, the economics of 'properly built' homes that were affordable to the poor proved elusive. The 32,000 homes built by 1960 had cost the public purse LE22 million,[67] with little return, as most dwellings were rented at very low rates. The Development and Popular Homes Company fell into severe debt and stopped building affordable homes, focusing instead on the middle-income category of homes to balance its budget.[68] But the socialist government tapped into previously unimaginable resources, and by 1960, state-affiliated institutions that were revenue generating—such as the municipalities and the Awqaf—were instructed to earmark portions of their revenues and use their land banks to build popular homes (table 5.3). A year later, both private and public industry would be required to build homes for their workers and employees under a profit share scheme funded through the companies' revenues.

For the middle class, it was private developers, newly founded state-owned developers, and housing cooperatives that were corralled to build housing through government support in the form of subsidized land and low-interest loans. In 1955, the Cairo Electric Railways and Heliopolis Oases Company was instructed to prepare 1,500 plots of land in five new neighborhoods on its desert concession northwest of Cairo.[69] The 400-square-meter-plots would be sold at LE1.45 per square meter primarily to government employees or members of housing cooperatives approved by the Cairo municipality, half of which would be paid off over twenty years at 3.5 percent interest.

Another middle-class neighborhood in Cairo broke ground also in 1955. Madinat al-Awqaf (Awqaf City), which was originally intended as a 1,000-feddan upper-class development in the 1940s,[70] was re-appropriated to twenty housing cooperatives with over two thousand members, including those set up for the military, navy, police, judges, medical doctors, and engineers.[71] Large land plots of 500 to 1,000 square meters were sold after a 30 percent discount, which the Awqaf bore, at LE2–3 per square meter, paid off over fifteen years without interest, while members of the cooperatives were able to access soft loans to build at 3 percent interest.[72] Today we know the district simply as Mohandiseen—meaning engineers—based on the Engineers' City cooperative housing subdistrict planned and built by leading architects of the time.

The Madinat Nasr Organization was established in 1959 to build the new namesake district,[73] as well as the initial housing estates there, and would later assume responsibility for two housing estates for military personnel annexed to its concession.[74] By 1960, 1,300 homes had been built by cooperatives, receiving LE2.5 million in low-interest loans,[75] in addition to the embedded subsidies in state-funded infrastructure and public land.

During Nasser's rule, almost 150,000 government-built homes were constructed (figure 5.7), averaging 8,200 units annually—possibly forty times greater than the highest prerevolution rate. More importantly, that figure represented over two-fifths of formal housing production in urban areas, the remainder built by the private sector. In just under a decade, the state had gone from a bit player in housing provision to the main provider of formal homes for a significant proportion of the urban population, from the poor to upper middle class. It is not clear though how many homes were built for the working class, as higher-earning professionals and civil servants had access to finished government-built apartments and were also able to receive support to build through unions or housing cooperatives. From the available numbers it could be that around half of the government-built housing, perhaps a little more, was available to the working class. While one plan reveals that the government had a target of almost three-quarters of all new housing built to be of the economic type, this does not appear to have been implemented.[76] In the late 1960s, Nasser conceded that more housing was built than needed for the middle class, while the government was not doing enough for the poor.[77]

Rents for the different types of housing varied, particularly in relation to location. A small two-bedroom economic housing apartment was being rented out for LE5.6 per month in Sayyida Zaynab in 1969, while the same size apartment as a middle housing unit in al-Alf Maskan project was one-and-a-half times more expensive (table 5.2). There were also three- and four-bedroom apartments built for the middle class.

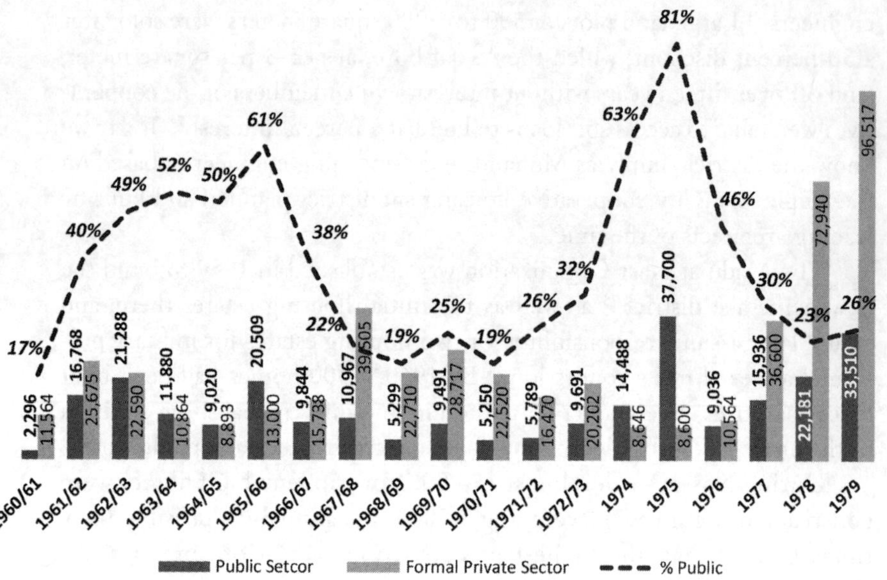

5.7: Government versus private production of formal urban housing 1960/61–1970/71. (Source: "Ministry of Housing and Reconstruction" in Joint Housing Team, "Immediate Action Proposals for Housing in Egypt—Statistical Appendix," 51.)

While government-built housing exploded in the socialist era, it was vulnerable to a number of factors. In the early 1960s, building materials and labor were heavily focused on building the High Dam, one of the largest construction projects of the era. This created a housing shortage in the major cities, including of government housing (figure 5.7), leading to a public outcry that "the government has taken our cement!"[78] In an effort to remedy this, production would be boosted in 1965 with lower-quality construction—which was cheaper and faster—through the Nasser Rapid Housing Scheme *(iskan Nasser lil-iwa' al-'agil)*. It would be initially earmarked for LE5 million, which would rise to LE7 million as 14,000 homes started to be built in thirty-one sites in Greater Cairo aiming to have them ready within eight months,[79] an unprecedented timeframe. Two years later, the 1967 Israeli occupation of Sinai robbed the state of revenue from the Suez Canal. Diminished public resources were redirected to the ensuing War of Attrition and rebuilding the military. Government housing dropped to around half its 1960–67 annual average (figure 5.7) and remained at this level for a decade.

Level	District	2 bedroom	3 bedroom	4 bedroom
Economic	Old (Rent controlled)	3.0	4.0	
	Sayyida Zaynab	5.6	-	-
Middle	Old (Rent controlled)	4.5	6.0	
	al-Qal'a	7.5	-	-
	al-Alf Maskan/ Misr al-Gadida	8.2	11	
	Madinat Nasr	-	-	11.25–14.6

Sources: ASU, February 5, 1969. 96–97 and Prime Ministerial Decree 110/1978.

5.2: Monthly rents for a range of government-built homes in Cairo in 1969 (LE).

Housing Becomes Political

On July 24, 1955, Nasser gave two separate addresses in Hilmiyyat al-Zaytun and Imbaba in Cairo to hundreds of government housing beneficiaries, marking the third anniversary of the 1952 revolution. He reminded his audience of the early days of the revolution: "We were fighting [battles] on two fronts—one against the allies of colonization and one for *al-bina' wa-l-ta'mir* [construction and development] . . . This revolution represents . . . the nation's dreams in the city and in the village, in both urban and rural areas . . . This is your revolution!"[80] While Nasser was not the first ruler to co-opt government housing development for political or promotional purposes, he went beyond Fouad and Farouk, who attended the occasional inauguration and had towns and villages named after themselves. For Nasser, it was also personal, as he shared the same social background and had lived through similar challenges to the crowd he was addressing:

> This project was a big dream, rather it was an unattainable dream. I remember in 1950 how there was a land subdivision project in al-Zaytun to distribute these plots to [government] employees. The project was considered one of those that do not get advertised—they did not say that they were going to distribute, so that they could distribute the plots [to those close to the regime]. I found out about the project, handed in my application in 1950, and to this day I have not received a response! This was a hope, and I felt it. I hoped that I would be able to own a plot of land that I

> could pay off in installments every month and build a home. And so today I really feel your happiness, and it is also mine.[81]

When Syria joined Egypt to form the United Arab Republic, Nasser, as president of the union, did not miss the opportunity to inaugurate a project to build popular homes in Aleppo, proclaiming that "the basis of a socialist democratic and communal community . . . is to work and build until we realize the life we hope for."[82]

Nasser's personal involvement also extended to the minutiae of housing policy, as with much of national policy during his rule. He regularly discussed details of housing projects in cabinet and party meetings, while his personal diaries included many entries, one of which laid out a complete and thorough plan to restructure government housing provision. In a six-page entry in 1961, Nasser noted how state-sponsored housing was expanding in post-war Germany, Russia, and the United Kingdom, and proceeded to divide beneficiaries in Egypt into four groups depending on their sector of employment.[83] Housing for the first group—industrial workers and employees in both the private and public sector—would be the responsibility of their institutions. Each large factory or group of small factories would have a housing department, with housing financed through low-interest loans along with profit contributions, and then rented out. To Nasser it was evident "that the capitalists in these industries enjoy comfortable and healthy homes, while at the same time the workers that bear the burden of work are deprived of them."[84]

Government employees, because they were based in different parts of the country, were to receive "healthy, comfortable, and cheap homes" from decentralized providers—the local municipalities. Central government would regulate the standards and rents, as well as extend loans to the governorates based on a housing plan that used municipal land. Agricultural workers and peasants, the third group, would be provided for through the agricultural cooperatives of which they were members. Each cooperative would set up a housing organization that would receive contributions from its members or borrow from the state-affiliated General Union of Cooperatives, and issue bonds to members.

Finally, Nasser did not forget those who were neither employed by institutions nor members of cooperatives—the self-employed traders, artisans, and craftspeople whom he called *al-qita' al-ahli* (roughly translated as the popular sector), which were probably the majority of citizens then and now. The state would also be responsible for them, though they were required to contribute through bonds to governorate-level housing organizations, receiving returns of 3 to 3.5 percent, while the organization could borrow from banks at 3 percent to fund construction. All housing organizations were to include representatives of the beneficiaries on their boards—heads of unions or cooperatives—and "thus the housing operation [would] flow automatically." Nasser also wanted the homes "to be elegant from the outside and the inside, whether a one-room apartment or more, as they would last a long time."

Nasser's plan was discussed in parliament in January 1961, and before the end of the year, his handwritten notes had transformed how housing worked in Egypt as a torrent of laws and decrees were issued—dissolving, establishing, and restructuring a plethora of institutions (table 5.3). In March, the Higher Council for Housing was established to oversee all housing policy, planning, and coordination. The following month, the General Organization for Cooperative Housing (GOCH) was founded, affiliated directly to the president's office. By August, it would have control over the three major developers and eleven main contractors, as well as building material companies operating in Egypt, when most big business was nationalized by the July Decrees as Nasser moved to firmly establish the Arab socialist state.[85] The decrees also put Nasser's grand plans for workers' housing into motion when the Investment Companies' Law was amended, enforcing a workers' profit share scheme (table 5.3). Workers would receive 25 percent of profits, of which 5 percent would be earmarked for social services and housing.

August saw the birth of Egypt's first ever Ministry of Housing (and Utilities), elevating the housing portfolio from a subsidiary ministerial department to its own executive agency. By October, the General Authority for Desert Development (GADD) became responsible for housing on reclaimed land in the new villages. The popular sector that Nasser had included in his notes was left out of the formal structure, though it would receive a series of amnesties for informal self-builds.

This template of forming a ministry and providing executive subsidiaries, along with oversight of governorate departments, cemented the official approach from a wider policy of providing homes to housing—synonymous with both the act of construction and the act of putting people in shelter. The use of *masakin* (homes) would disappear from official discourse, replaced by *iskan* (housing), and the die would be cast, with politics shaping the act of shelter provision in Egypt to this day.

Legislation	Details
Marsum of August 17, 1950	First official office for housing: Department of Popular Homes established in Ministry of Social Affairs
Law 206/1951	Regulates production of popular homes by government, co-ops, and private sector
Law 188/1955	Department of Housing renamed and moved to Ministry of Municipalities and Village Affairs (MoMVA)
Law 30/1960 amending Law 206/1951	Adds Awqaf (Ministry of Religious Endowments) as provider of popular housing
PD 1513/1960	Adds local councils as provider of popular housing according to general housing plan
Law 285/1960	Heliopolis Company is nationalized and becomes the Organization for Misr al-Gadida Suburb (Mo'assasit Dahiat Misr al-Gadida)
PD 107/1961	Establishes the Higher Council for Housing headed by MoMVA. To plan and implement housing policy, annual production plans
PD 319/1961	Establishes the General Organization for Cooperative Housing (GOCH) (al-Mu'assasat al-'Amma al-Ta'awunia li-l-Iskan) Affiliated directly to the presidency
Law 111/1961 amending Investment Company Law 26/1954	25% profit share scheme for workers and employees, of which 5% is earmarked for social services and housing upon agreement between company board and workers' union
PD 1202/1961 and 1331/1961	GOCH assigned nationalized companies: 11 contractors and building material companies, as well as Madinat Nasr Organization, Egyptian Delta Land & Investment Company (Maadi), and Misr al-Gadida Suburb Organization
PD 1325/1961	Vice President for Local Administration appointed (Kamal al-Din Hussein). Oversees implementation of public services' policy including housing and utilities
PD 1356/1961 and 69/1962	Establishes and regulates first ever Ministry of Housing and Utilities (MoHU). Transfers housing portfolio from MoMVA
PD 1515/1961	Establishes General Authority for Desert Development (GADD). Responsible for housing on reclaimed land (new villages)

Legislation	Details
PD 2905/1964 and 258/1965	Establishes Egyptian General Organization for Housing and Development (EGOHD) (al-Mu'assasat al-Misriya al-'Amma li-l-Iskan wa-l-Ta'mir). Oversees Madinat Nasr and Popular Homes organizations and subsidiaries
PD 4415/1965	Amends responsibilities of MoHU EGOHD and GOCH come under its supervision
PD 4419/1965	Amends responsibilities of EGOHD, transfers to it MoHU responsibilities concerning executing urban and rural development and housing policy
PD 4420/1965	Replaces GOCH with Egyptian Organization for Cooperative Construction and Housing (EOCCH) (al-Mu'assasat al-Misriya al-Ta'awuniya li-l-Bina' wa-l-Iskan)

5.3: Key legislation assigning responsibilities for government housing 1950–1970 (PD: Presidential Decree).

Battle of Reconstruction: 1973–77

The momentum of Nasser's restructuring continued under his successor, Anwar Sadat, until the October War in 1973 that saw the Egyptian–Israeli stalemate upended when Egyptian troops crossed the canal and retook land in the Sinai. Within two days of the ceasefire, Sadat created the Ministry of Reconstruction,[86] rehashing Nasser's anticolonial battle cry of *al-bina' wa-l-ta'mir*, alternating between *ma'rakat al-bina'* (battle of construction) and *ma'rakat al-ta'mir* (battle of reconstruction).

There was indeed much to be rebuilt in the Suez Canal area, where entire neighborhoods and small towns were leveled during the 1967 invasion, the ensuing War of Attrition, and the October War.[87] A government-sponsored repopulation effort had also started, enabling the *muhaggarin* (forced migrants) to go back to their hometowns. It was none other than Osman Ahmed Osman—self-proclaimed 'Builder of the High Dam,' construction tycoon, and Sadat's in-law—who would head the new ministry, immediately giving himself exceptional powers outside of "binding bureaucratic law" to "implement the many projects . . . without hurdles."[88] He was thus able to do what he pleased in planning new neighborhoods, expropriating land, and most importantly, assigning contracts, fully utilizing the millions of dollars in grants and loans that flowed in from the World Bank and Gulf states. Long gone were the days when planners or architects ran the show.

A plethora of state-owned housing and construction agencies would be corralled to the canal cities, including Uthman's nationalized Arab Contractors, where he remained chairperson.[89] Port Said, Suez, and Ismailiya rumbled with heavy machinery demolishing crumbling buildings, digging the earth, and raising concrete skeletons. Over 25,000 new homes were built and 55,000 repaired.[90] These three cities captured a third of Egypt's entire housing plan in the mid-1970s, contributing to a 25 percent hike in government housing production compared to the previous decade, averaging 14,500 units a year (table 5.4). Municipal governorate housing was the primary casualty, with its share dropping from almost 80 percent in the 1960s to around 50 percent.

	Governorates	Other*	Reconstruction	TOTAL	Annual Avg.
1960/61–69/70	101,786	15,576	0	**117,362**	**11,736**
	87%	13%	0%	**100%**	
1970/71–1975	36,415	11,639	24,864	**72,918**	**14,584**
	50%	16%	34%	**100%**	**+24%**

*Includes central housing agencies/companies, and cooperatives
Source: "Ministry of Housing and Reconstruction" in Joint Housing Team, "Immediate Action Proposals for Housing in Egypt—Statistical Appendix," 51.

5.4: Comparison of housing production by government agency between the 1960s and the first half of the 1970s.

Housing and politics also continued their love affair. Sadat supposedly responded to a "tearful" letter from a father of five who lived in a tin shack and had to walk three kilometers every day to get water by "immediately" assigning him a popular housing unit.[91] Sadat wanted everyone to have

> the happy Egyptian home, a big living room, that the family sits in, and that has space for expansive views for our children, as they grow up healthy and better. What brought me the greatest happiness was that I grew up in a village and that as far as the eye could see, there was greenery and endless fields.[92]

His "happy Egyptian homes" in the canal cities were to be found in King Faisal and Sabah in Suez and Sheikh Zayed in Ismailiya, districts named after their Arab Gulf benefactors. A Saudi prince visited one of the districts, while Sadat made a regular habit of visiting the canal cities at key national and religious celebrations over the second half of the 1970s, giving speeches and meeting the public as he sought to rally support for his increasingly unpopular policies.[93]

The politics of housing would not be just the preserve of the canal cities. Sadat's unpopular warming of relations with the West, the peace negotiations with Israel, along with his free market Infitah (open door) policies that saw socialist-era subsidies rolled back at a time of scorching inflation, ignited the January 1977 Bread Riots, which Sadat condescendingly called "the uprising of thieves." He was so irked and threatened by Cairo's protesters that he went as far as calling them *arzal* (rude or insolent) and proceeded to dish out his revenge on the narrow alleys of 'Ishash al-Turguman that sheltered many of them, giving orders to demolish the entire neighborhood.[94]

This was an opportune moment for the government to capture the new inflow of Arab and foreign capital and "remake" Cairo in a "modern image . . . a global metropolis that would meet the demands of tourists and foreign investors."[95] Out went any notion of social inclusion and in came the first capitalization of the rent gap—the difference between the current, low real estate values of the poor neighborhoods that Sadat saw

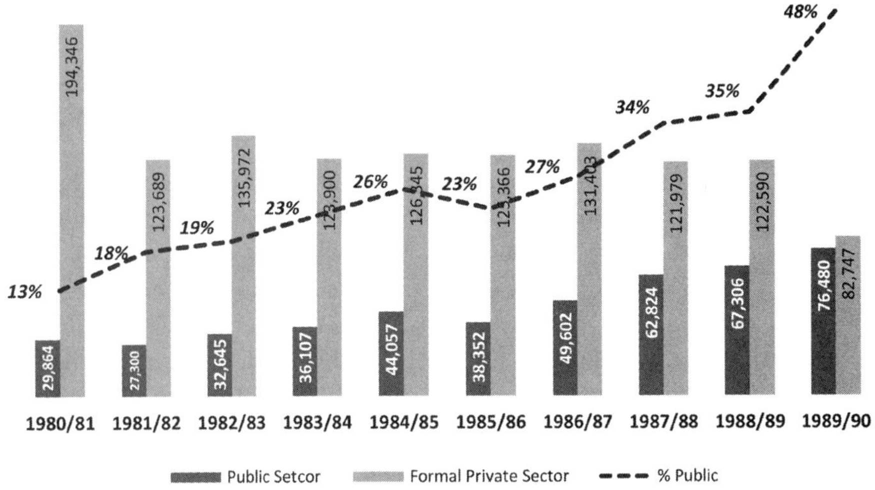

5.8: Government versus private formal urban housing production 1971/72–1981/82. (Source: "Ministry of Housing and Reconstruction" in Joint Housing Team, 51; Hanna, *Le logement en Égypte*, 227–49.)

as "cheap and dispensable" and the higher rates the government could sell the land at to private developers, minus the residents, which we see more recent cases of in chapter 7. In Bulaq's case, the rent gap was envisaged to be threefold.[96] Within eight months of the riots, 2,560 families had their homes razed and were squeezed into 2,020 hastily built housing units in al-Zawya al-Hamra on the northern outskirts of Cairo.[97] When asked how the residents found these overcrowded conditions, Cairo Governor Major General Sa'ad Ma'mun, who was proud of the swift forced resettlement, simply replied, "It's better for them than staying on the streets."[98] So much for the "happy Egyptian home."

Housing Sell-Off: 1977

While Sadat's slum clearance plans were resisted by both residents and leading intellectuals,[99] he was smart enough not to completely obliterate his public support. A few months after the Bread Riots, he gave a speech at the Transportation Workers' general assembly, in which he promised "access for every citizen in this country to own his home."[100] This promise seems to have been made as part of a political demobilization strategy, as in that very speech, Sadat also praised the head of the Workers Union for siding with the state during the January 1977 riots. By February 1978, legislation would be passed to transfer ownership of local government-built housing to tenants and designate all new government housing from that point onward to be sold to beneficiaries rather than rented.[101] It would be the first time that Egyptian government housing policy was ahead of its British counterpart, preceding Margaret Thatcher's neoliberal Right to Buy scheme by almost three years.[102]

Existing tenants of economic or middle housing units would be able to gain ownership of their units outright if they had been renting for fifteen years or more. Meanwhile, those who had been renting for less than that time would be required to pay the balance of fifteen years' rent, either up front with a 10 percent discount or in rent-to-own installments at values and a time frame to be regulated by each governor (table 5.5). Applicants to new economic housing would be required to meet income and eligibility criteria and pay the cost of the unit over thirty years without interest, while applicants for middle housing would be required to present a 10 percent down payment, paying the balance over thirty years—at 3.5 percent interest—though they would be exempt from eligibility criteria. Beneficiaries of both types of housing were allowed neither to own

Year	Rented for LE1 per room pre-September 9, 1977				Rented or built post-September 9, 1977			
Type	Economic		Middle		Economic		Middle	
Bedrooms	1	2	2	3	1	2	2	3
Cost (LE)[1]	360	540	810	1,080	3,500	4,500	5,250	6,750
Down payment (LE)[2]	Previously paid rent				None		525	675
Installments (LE)[3]	2	3	4.5	6	9.7	12.5	13.1	16.9
Maximum monthly income (LE)	(Already lived-in)				35	50	None	

[1] Pre-1977: Rent of minimum fifteen years, or the payment of the balance if rented for less than fifteen years, which can be divided into installments or discounted by 10 percent if fully paid in cash. Post-1977: Varies—Economic from newspaper announcement in 1978, Middle estimated at 50 percent higher, which was the norm. Discounted for both by 10 percent if paid in cash up front.
[2] Pre-1977: Rent paid. Post-1977: 10 percent of Middle unit's value
[3] Pre-1977: Current rent. Post-1977: Interest-free installments over thirty years for Economic, and at 5 percent for Middle (though later advertisements stated 3.5 percent interest for both).
Sources: Law 49/1977 (Article 72), Prime Ministerial Decree 110/1978, and al-Ahram, "35 million jinih li-da'm al-iskan al-'ummali."

5.5: General details and conditions of the government housing ownership scheme (LE).

another home within the same city nor to rent their units out furnished (a rent control circumvention covered in chapter 3). The revenues would be collected in a central Economic Housing Fund (EHF) that would use the money to build new housing in a "self-sufficient manner" because, as housing minister Osman observed, "Solving the housing problem requires a large amount of investment."[103]

In less than a decade, new government housing became a phenomenal 156 percent more expensive than old government housing, as average monthly installments rose fourfold over the original government rents, while income had only risen by two-thirds (figure 5.10).[104] This made new economic housing all but unaffordable to the poor, who were obviously not Sadat's target group for the "happy Egyptian home," as the maximum income for applicants was one-third higher than the median household income of the time.[105] Eligible applicants also had the option of buying the

5.9: Plaque commemorating the inauguration of 130 new housing units in the workers' colony in al-Mahalla on the occasion of the Mahalla Spinning and Weaving Company's golden jubilee on May 17, 1978, during the "era of the Believer President Muhammad Anwar Sadat." February 2014. (Photograph by Yahia Shawkat.)

units outright in cash, giving them a leg-up over less wealthy counterparts. Middle housing was even more inaccessible to the majority, as no maximum income was stipulated, while a 10 percent down payment had to be furnished.

But even for middle- and upper-middle-income applicants who could afford these units, there was a hornet's nest of caveats. Maintenance of the units for both current tenants and new applicants would now rest on their shoulders, offloading a considerable burden from the government onto them. Significantly, the ownership that Sadat had promised was just for the bricks and mortar, as the land the housing blocks were built on was not part of the deeds, effectively making this ownership a long-term lease of undefined length. This length would of course be more limited for the older housing blocks that tenants 'bought,' as they were already decaying. 'Owners' could not sell their units except with the governor's express permission, thereby opening the door for bribes and political favors.

And the caveats did not end there. Utterly confusing legal wording obscured exactly which old housing would be available for ownership by tenants, leading to lengthy legal battles between tenants and governors that would last a decade. The problems that arose from this manufactured

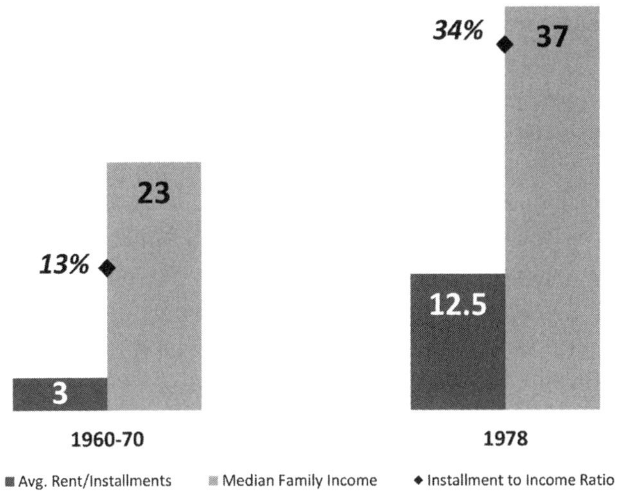

5.10: Comparison between rent and installment values for a two-bedroom economic housing unit and median incomes in the late 1960s and 1978 (LE). Notes: Incomes are from 1966 and 1976, rent and installment values are from 1969 and 1978. (Sources: Table 5.5 and CAPMAS Family Budget in Barrada, Wheaton, and Annez, "Public Policy and the Economics of Housing. Appendix A: Public Policy and the 'Shortage' of Housing in Egypt.")

informality, whereby government-written legislation deliberately obscured tenure, kept many transfers in limbo, and prevented full uncontested ownership, as we see in chapter 7.

From this point on, any notion of 'social' or 'public' to prefix government housing would disappear, reverting to the pre-Riad model where applicants had to be able to afford the housing units, rather than the unit prices being subsidized in order to not be a 'burden.' This was particularly well demonstrated by the ability of one investor to use these laws to acquire thirty economic housing units at once. The case ended up in court, where the buying spree was overruled after multiple appeals—a full twenty-three years later![106]

Housing 'Shortage' and Desert Estates: 1979–91

Building new districts and housing estates in the old cities would not satisfy the newly minted construction army, and new fronts for their battle had to be found. They prepared to invade no less than the vast, open desert—which officials, planners, and the media incessantly remind us covers most of the country. While the socialist mantra was invasion of the desert through agriculture (see chapter 4), here it was through urbanization. In May 1977, Sadat laid the cornerstone of the Tenth of Ramadan town exactly halfway between Cairo and Ismailiya, declaring that the new cities would "eliminate the housing crisis and relieve it from the widest of doors."[107] Indeed it had been decided that Egypt suffered from a housing shortage that the new National Housing Plan would address by building an incredible 3.6 million units over the next twenty years using both public and private resources. Critics countered that the housing crisis was not about a quantitative lack of homes, citing official statistics that showed that Egypt did in fact have a surplus of homes. It was rather a qualitative issue centered on the unaffordability of new homes and dilapidated conditions of old ones.[108] Milad Hanna even summarized the problem as a "housing trap," blaming "contractor" minister Osman Ahmed Osman for "baiting" the public for the benefit of the construction industry.[109]

Notwithstanding the critics, the reconstruction circus relocated to the desert to build not one, but six, towns out of the sand, all named to commemorate Sadat and his achievements.[110] Applications opened for the first batch of three thousand units in Tenth of Ramadan City in 1979, prioritizing those working in the city, business owners, or those who bought plots there but later changed their minds and wanted ready-built homes.[111] There were neither maximum income nor social need stipulations, and these units would also be slightly more expensive than their municipal cousins, costing between LE4,000 and LE7,000.

All this was of course managed by a host of new agencies. The Ministry of Reconstruction and New Communities (MoRNC) was established in July 1978, taking with it almost the entire construction portfolio from the Ministry of Housing, while a year later the New Urban Communities Authority (NUCA) would be responsible for all new city construction and management.[112] The responsibility of housing was devolved in 1979 from national government to a dual system in which governorates—local administration—provide housing in existing cities and towns, while the NUCA builds in new cities. The Economic Housing Fund was thus dissolved, barely three years after it was founded, transferring its assets and responsibilities to local Housing Accounts, the NUCA got its own housing fund,[113] leaving the Ministry of Housing to limp on as a redundant administrative appendage for some years. In the ensuing decade, the government would build almost 600,000 units, of which half were built by the governorates, and 13 percent the NUCA and its fund (figure 5.11).

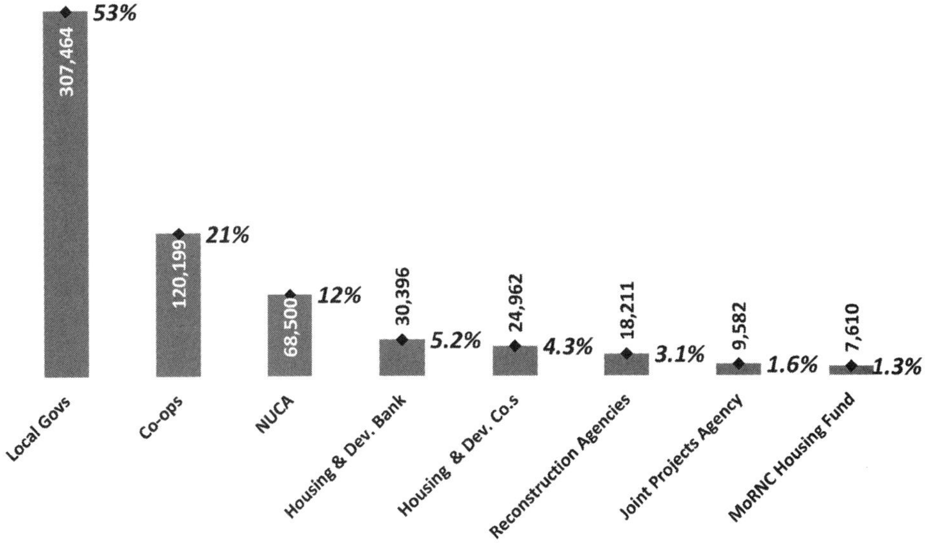

5.11: Urban housing production by sector, 1954–86. (See section on methodology in chapter 1.)

Although government housing production in the 1980s was almost two and a half times that of the preceding decade (figures 1.1 and 1.2), the government's share of total urban housing production remained at 12 percent, as private (especially formal) production surged. (For a complete overview of housing production, see chapter 1.) And while it seems paradoxical that this boost in the amount of government housing came during a free market era, it can only be explained by the understanding of housing as a commodity that the government and its agencies could profit from in a heated real estate market, effectively drawing the curtain on housing as a social good.

6

GOVERNMENT HOUSING TODAY

President Anwar Sadat's template for decentralized housing that was largely built by local government and sold to beneficiaries continued largely untouched for almost two decades after his death. Under his successor, Hosni Mubarak, government-built housing would surge by 250 percent in the 1986–1996 period compared to the previous decade, boosting its share exceptionally to a quarter of all urban housing (figure 6.1). It would remain largely unaffordable to a majority of Egyptians.

Mubarak directed academics and experts to "radically" solve the "housing problem."[1] Some of these experts saw him pushing a "quantitative" solution based on an "intensive provision" of units, ignoring the "qualitative" issue that centered around deregulation of the housing market and an acute "affordability crisis," whereby in 1983 it was estimated that 70 percent of Egyptians could not afford to rent or buy a home.[2] Singling out government-built units, the study found that only 0.1 percent of urban households could afford them if sold at cost at an installment-to-income ratio of 20 percent.

Architects Nasamat Abdel-Kader and Sayed Ettouney proposed an incremental self-build solution, whereby the government would provide land, utilities, and subsidized loans affordable to low-income families, while applicants would build their homes according to their needs.[3] While the proposal was piloted in the new city of al-'Ubur just outside of Cairo, much like similar sites and services or core housing projects in Ismailiya, Aswan, and Cairo, the government fought the concept, either by stifling the projects or neglecting them, as we saw in Chapter 2, since officials did not want to be seen to be "building slums." Cookie cutter medium rise housing blocks was all they were interested in. Taking that mentality into consideration, the architects acting as advisors for Minister of Housing Hasaballah al-Kafrawi were able to reach a compromise in the late 1980s that the minister termed "vertical core housing." These were five-story walk-ups with apartments of similar sizes to economic housing, though sold unfinished and without inner walls, save for a bathroom, reducing costs by 30 percent as a measure to make it more affordable for applicants to buy.[4] Residents would still have to finance finishing, but at their own pace.

The new 'low-cost' housing units initially benefited from subsidized loans paid over forty years, but the state-owned Housing and Development Bank stipulated formal jobs, thus blocking access to a majority of low-income families.[5] Even after it allowed the semiformally employed to take out loans, it reduced the repayment term to twenty-five years, thereby increasing the value of the installments which only lower-middle-income families could afford, and with that negating the entire advantage of the low-cost nature of the project. This would be the pattern of government-built housing for the coming three decades: politically driven promises of affordable homes, dashed because of bad planning, negelect of needs, and tailoring toward particular social groups.

Origins of Mubarak's Housing: 1995–2005

In the early 1990s, Mubarak would swap mounting debt and public spending for the IMF and World Bank's neoliberal structural adjustment program, which would see the share of government housing drop to an all-time low in half a century of 10 percent of urban housing.

The public funds for mainstream government housing were not saved, but diverted to bail out public and private sector banks, who had given out huge loans to a handful of businessmen who ironically had dabbled in real estate and could not pay back their debts.[6] Plans to privatize public sector companies under the structural adjustment program also meant that the government stopped them from earmarking employee profit shares for housing as they had done for the past thirty years, slashing overall profit shares from 25 to 10 percent.[7] Existing 'owners' of government housing were directly affected by structural adjustment as well, with the interest on their cooperative loans raised fivefold overnight, resulting in eviction for many because they could not afford the higher installments.[8] Needless to say, loans for those hoping to buy the now rarefied public housing became too expensive.

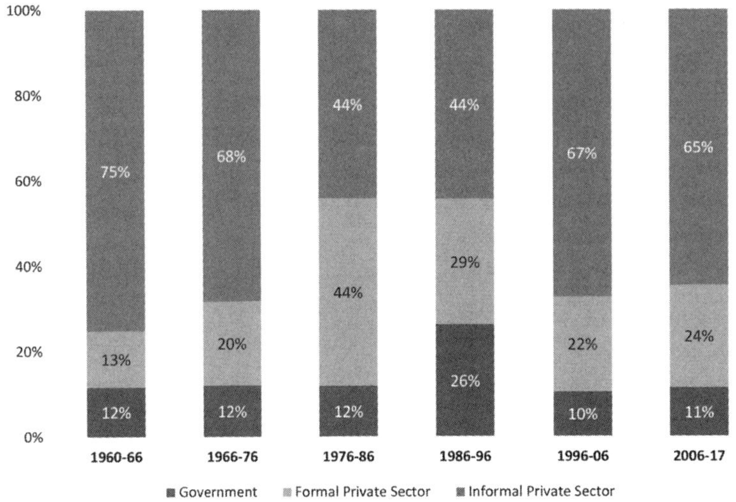

6.1: Urban housing production by sector, 1976–2017. (See section on methodology in chapter 1.)

It was a good decade and a half into his rule before Mubarak directly associated himself with a housing project. The first was the Mubarak National Youth Housing Project (Mashru‘ Mubarak al-Qawmi li-Iskan al-Shabab), or Iskan al-Shabab (Youth Housing) for short, that ran from 1995 to 2005. Around seventy thousand units were built in a decade, all in the new cities in the desert. In the first phase, these were one-hundred-square-meter apartments, and with each phase smaller units were built, dwindling to half that size in the fourth and final phase, mirroring a reduction in financing.[9] The one-hundred-square-meter-units, all of which were around Cairo, cost LE40,000, for which the government extended not one, but two, subsidized loans with different repayment conditions.[10] The remaining balance would be covered by a LE3,500 down payment, as well as regular payments until the unit was delivered, which would take between one and three years. At a later stage, two government agencies—the General Authority for Construction and Housing Cooperatives and the Ministry of Housing's Housing Fund—were assigned to build 'investment' units sold at profit to generate funds for the project.[11]

Iskan al-Shabab would mark the first in a series of measures that would see housing provision gradually recentralized since 1979, when housing production was largely devolved to the governorates' Housing Accounts. The local government economic and low-cost housing projects would continue in parallel to Mubarak's national project that was being built exclusively in the new cities. Although the target groups were those with incomes of up to LE300 a month, who were expected to pay an LE73 installment on the loans,[12] units did not necessarily go to the poor, since the bureaucratic "application regime," as housing expert David Sims describes it, handed out units through a random lottery that had very little to do with needs or income.[13]

Not to be outdone, Mubarak's wife and younger son started their own Future Housing Project (Mashru' Iskan al-Mustaqbal) in 1998, named after the foundation Gamal Mubarak chaired as the youth wing of their ruling National Democratic Party (NDP). With fifteen thousand units built in seven years,[14] it was much smaller than Iskan al-Shabab, which it ran parallel to, but it was never intended as a national project. Rather it showcased the face-to-be of the regime: Mubarak junior and his NDP business elite, who 'donated' half of the LE450 million cost.[15] The units were almost given away for free, with applicants paying a LE1,000 down payment, which was much less than Iskan al-Shabab, and then cooperative loan installments of LE67 per month, while the Future Foundation would subsidize the balance, covering half of the nominal LE30,000 that each unit cost.[16]

This politically funded cheap housing was not for everyone. In addition to the now standard 'application regime' conditions of not owning a home and being of a certain age range, applicants had to be covered by social security—formally employed, in other words—and have a clean police record.[17] The social engineering and control that pervaded housing in the first half of the twentieth century, as we saw in chapter 4, was rekindled by first lady Suzanne Mubarak, who oversaw the committees that set out the parameters for potential beneficiaries, and chose the design of the housing blocks herself in an effort to "break the monotony of traditional matchbox designs" (figure 6.2).[18] She would go on to spin off at least four housing projects of her own, funded by various charities and international aid organizations, all related to slum clearing and—often forced—resettlement in her bid to "build the Egyptian person."[19] This social engineering meant that in the Zeinhom project, for example, over half of the original residents did not receive new housing there under the ominous provision of having a police record, and were instead banished to al-Nahda housing estate on the outskirts of Cairo unless they could cough up a considerable bribe to be reassessed.[20]

6.2: Future Housing blocks, New Cairo, February 2013. (Photograph by Yahia Shawkat.)

Mubarak National Housing Project: 2005–2011

Mubarak senior would take back the mantle of housing provider from his wife and son in 2005, when he presented an electoral program for his coming six-year term that pledged to "confront the housing problem by building eighty thousand new homes a year . . . subsidized by the state to facilitate ownership through reasonable installments."[21] This was the first time that the four-term president would be elected by popular ballot—all the previous terms having been achieved by referenda—and the first time he had any semblance of an electoral program.

Initially, Mubarak's National Housing Program (NHP), colloquially known as Iskan Mubarak, was a half-baked extension of the Mubarak Youth Housing it replaced. But with no way of building the promised half a million units, and with low demand for the standard units already on offer, a seven-scheme program was fleshed out almost a year later to provide half a million 'housing solutions' rather than units,[22] with a host of both public and private agencies to deliver them (table 6.1). The housing minister would also bring in an award-winning architect, Hatem al-Said, to design the housing blocks, in a further effort to raise the profile of the presidential project.

The scheme would further centralize housing production, whereby unlike the previous Mubarak projects, the local Housing Accounts in all twenty-seven governorates would come under the national project's wing, along with the New Urban Communities Authority (NUCA). They were also made responsible for the largest of the NHP schemes, Tamlik (Ownership), with 199,000 units, making up 40 percent of the program (figure 6.3). NUCA was also to build 75,000 micro units under the Awla bi-l-Ri'aya scheme for those prioritized as 'in need,' mainly widows and retirees. The housing production of the Ministry of Religious Endowments (Awqaf) was also annexed, and it was to build 26,000 rental units, as well as a small gated compound of 3,000 Bayt al-'Ila (Family Home) units. The Housing Ministry's Central Agency for Construction (CAC) would build the Desert Hinterland Villages (*qura al-Zahir al-Sahrawi*) project on land reclamation sites. Except for this last scheme, all government agencies were to finance construction through their own funds and build on their own land. The Treasury, meanwhile, would foot the bill for the latter scheme with cash subsidies as well as low-interest loans or mortgages.

Overall, the public sector agencies were to finance just two-thirds of the original NHP plan. In an evolution of the Future Housing's model of public–private partnership, the remaining third of the scheme would be privately financed—ready-built units by companies and self-built units by individuals. The Mustathmirin (Investors) scheme was to comprise one-fifth of the NHP, whereby subsidized land would be sold at a variation of prices and conditions to large real estate developers, under the obligation that they would use at least 50 percent of the land for low-income housing units, as in the Tamlik scheme.[23] The second private sector scheme, Ibni Baytak (Build Your Home), was geared toward individuals, whereby 89,000 plots, making up 18 percent of the NHP, would be sold at subsidized prices, with a requirement to build a minimum of one floor of three allowed within the first year.

This was a time when international financial agencies were revisiting their neoliberal 'structural adjustments' in an attempt to boost stalled efforts to establish a mortgage market in Egypt, and with it to privatize low-income housing provision.[24] A Mortgage Finance Authority (MFA) and a mortgage Guarantee and Subsidy Fund (GSF) had been established, but were not really performing. It was in this context that the World Bank and the United States Agency for International Development (USAID)

Developer /tenure	Scheme Units		Planned*		Completed by Sept 2011**		
			% of Scheme	Units	% of Scheme	% change from planned	
Public sector ownership	1	Tamlik	199,000	40%	220,470	57%	11%
	2	Qura al-Zahir	8,000	1.6%	11,320	2.9%	42%
	3	Bayt al-'Ila	3,000	0.6%	3,020	0.8%	0.7%
	Total		**210,000**	**42%**	**234,810**	**61%**	**12%**
Public sector rental	4	Igar	26,000	5.2%	12,301	3.2%	-53%
	5	Awla bi-l-Ri'aya	75,000	15%	18,328	4.8%	-76%
	Total		**101,000**	**20%**	**30,629**	**8%**	-70%
Public Sector Total			**311,000**	**62%**	**265,439**	**69%**	**-15%**
Private sector ownership	6	Ibni Baytak	89,000	18%	93,405	24%	4.9%
	7	Mustathmirin	100,000	20%	25,511	6.6%	-74%
	Total		**189,000**	**38%**	**118,916**	**31%**	**-37%**
NHP TOTAL			**500,000**	**100%**	**384,355**	**100%**	**-23%**

Sources: * MoHUUD, "al-Mashru' al-qawmi." ** MoHUUD, "Al-Mashru'al-Mashru' al-qawmi li-l-iskan."

6.1: Distribution of planned and implemented NHP units by scheme.

funded the five-year Technical Assistance for Policy Reform (TAPR II),[25] with a housing sector reform component that aimed

> to put in place over the medium and long term the foundations of an efficient and well-functioning urban housing market, with the aim of making access to housing in urban areas more affordable to all, by making more effective use of Egypt's existing housing stock, maximizing the role of the private sector in housing production and financing, and targeting government assistance . . . to low, moderate and middle-income groups to access affordable housing solutions.[26]

The program also sought to improve the NHP, and consultants quickly put together a plan assigning the GSF the role of administering the entire project, overseeing private sector developers, and handing out subsidized mortgages to applicants.[27] They also had a champion of the initiative on

6.3: Typical NHP Tamlik blocks, Sixth of October City, December 2013. (Photograph by Yahia Shawkat.)

the inside: Ahmed al-Maghraby, minister of housing and real estate tycoon, who was part of the technocratic neoliberal cabinet.[28] He summed it up when he stated during a lecture before an audience of international business types at the American Chamber of Commerce in Egypt that he did not like monopolies, especially the "very serious . . . government monopoly on low-cost housing."[29]

Nevertheless, the scheme probably proved too alien for old-guard stalwarts, and a compromise was made, tacking on the private sector provision, and leaving the GSF and mortgages to play a minor role until late in the project when the World Bank financed cash subsidies through the fund.[30]

Social Housing Project: 2012–Present

In February 2011, barely a week into his tenancy as housing minister, Muhammad Fathi al-Baradei announced a new project to build one million housing units for low-income families,[31] double the target of its predecessor, Mubarak's NHP. But why, with the NHP still seven months away from its deadline, would the government undertake such a mega housing project devoid of Mubarak's name for the first time in sixteen years? This was during the eighteen days of continuous street protests that ultimately saw

Mubarak's end on February 11, and can only be explained as a distraction to demobilize the masses. Within days, thousands of applicants swamped the ministry's headquarters in Downtown Cairo, minutes from the iconic sit-in at Tahrir Square, leading employees to print out improvised applications for the crowds to fill in, promising that they would be formally accepted in due course.[32] On February 19, with a curfew still in place, and a government regime still in retreat, the Ministry of Housing, Utilities, and Urban Development ran a front-page advertisement in the local newspapers tagged "important," inviting applicants for the "new national housing project" (figure 6.4). Within a year, over 5 million people had applied.[33]

6.4: Original SHP advertisement, as it appeared ten days after Mubarak was deposed, and before it was officially named as the Social Housing Project. (*al-Ahram*, February 21, 2011, front page.)

In June 2011, the Housing Ministry ran an architecture competition to design 50- and 70-square-meter housing units according to a raft of social, economic, and environmental factors.[34] The trendy Medad practice won the competition by September with lush looking housing clusters.[35] Construction of the first Social Housing Project (SHP) units started in 2012, based on a much more austere design, and with promises of delivery within a year, running in parallel to the NHP, which had thousands of units still under construction or undelivered. But not a single SHP unit was delivered for four years as political turmoil continued. A military council ruled until Muhammad Mursi of the Muslim Brotherhood was elected in mid-2012, only to be removed a year later by Minster of Defense Abd al-Fattah al-Sisi. An interim government was installed and lasted a further year until another round of elections was held, during which time there were promises of delivering SHP units, but none materialized.

In March 2014, three months before the elections, al-Sisi—while still minister of defense, though in effect the country's de facto ruler following the ouster of the Brotherhood—launched an initiative to build one million units to "solve the housing problem."[36] This was not the SHP, but a completely different project to be built by the state-owned Emirati construction consortium Arabtec.[37] The new project had the blessings of the president of the United Arab Emirates, Sheikh Khalifa bin Zayed Al Nahyan, and banks would finance the required LE280 billion, though details about pricing and land provision were vague. Al-Sisi's initiative unraveled over the coming two years, shrinking to one hundred thousand units, then thirteen thousand, while filtering upward to middle- and upper-middle-income households, as disagreements between the partners escalated,[38] until the project ultimately disappeared before any units were built.

In the interim, someone must have remembered that there was another million-unit project already in the works, and in May 2014, just one month before al-Sisi was to be elected, the SHP was dusted off and relaunched with a fresh call for applicants, this time with more detail about prices, locations, and conditions (figure 6.5).

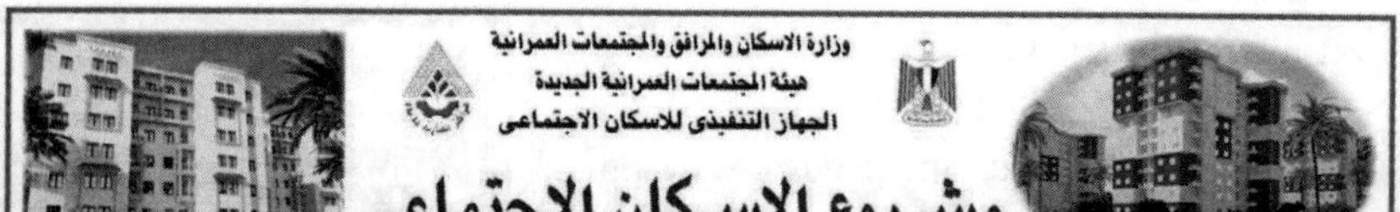

6.5: The first SHP advertisement after it was relaunched in 2014. Over ten more would follow until 2018. (*al-Ahram*, May 19, 2014, front-page.)

6.6: Brand new SHP blocks, New Cairo. January 2019. (Photograph by Yahia Shawkat.)

Between May 2014, when the SHP was relaunched, and October 2018, ten calls for application to the SHP would be made, 850,000 people would (re)apply, and over half a million units would be built (figure 6.6).[39] The project would become al-Sisi's solution for the "social housing problem in Egypt,"[40] a problem that his minister of housing, utilities, and urban communities pledged in 2017 to "radically solve within the coming three years."[41]

Affordability and Finance

Both access to and affordability of government-built housing, even if formally designated for low-income households, has been elusive since the inception of government housing provision almost a century ago, as we saw in this chapter and in chapter 5. It comes as no surprise that the NHP and SHP were no different in this regard. Using the index of a recent study on affordability in Egypt—which took into account international as well as local norms—it was found that, in order to be affordable to Egyptians, monthly installments should not exceed 25 percent of household income[42] and down payments should not be burdensome.

When the NHP was launched in 2005, most of its schemes were just about affordable to the poorest two-fifths of the population—low-income and poor families who should be the target of subsidized housing (table 6.2). Only the privately financed land plots and housing units were out of range. But this affordability was largely theoretical, as in reality access to the units was stacked in favor of particular income brackets and professional groups.

The NHP ownership schemes were the first to use legal definitions of income since the government began selling housing rather than renting it out in the late 1970s. These stipulations were to be used to set up subsidized bank loans and mortgages,[43] but the ranges were completely off the mark. The maximum a low-income household was allowed to earn was LE1,500 a month in 2005, which increased dramatically to LE2,500 a month in 2008, while the minimum monthly income was set at LE650 to qualify for the required bank loan.[44] This meant that the target range of the NHP effectively ruled out the poor, and focused on low-middle to high-income earners.

Compound interest was another risk for lower-income buyers, and the high rate of default in the first years of the program suggests that many were taken by surprise.[45] To make matters worse, costs increased in later phases, as the banks shifted to the mortgage scheme, which required a minimum income

			Costs				Cost-to-income ratio	
Developer /tenure	**Scheme** Size (m²)		Price	Up-front Payment	Monthly Pay-ments	Poor (LE600)	Low Income (LE800)	
Public sector ownership	1	Tamlik	63	50,000	5,000	160	27%	20%
	2	Qura al-Zahir	63	50,000	5,000	160	27%	20%
	3	Bayt al-'Ila	63				0%	0%
Public sector rental	4	Igar	63	Rent	180	180	30%	23%
	5	Awla bi-l-Ri'aya	42	Rent	0	93	15%	12%
Private sector ownership	6	Ibni Baytak	75	Land	1,050	5,733	956%	717%
	7	Mustathmirin	63	100,000	42,500	4,300	717%	538%

Adapted from Shawkat, "Mubarak's Promise. Social Justice and the National Housing
Programme: Affordable Homes or Political Gain?"

6.2: Quantitative affordability of the seven NHP schemes.

of LE1,080, and was thus only available for upper-middle-income earners and above.[46] Those who might have been able to afford these units but did not have a formal job to act as guarantor of the loans did not qualify unless they could pay the entire amount in cash, essentially rendering the units inaccessible to almost 60 percent of the working population with informal jobs.[47]

The rental schemes were equally inaccessible. The Awla bi-l-Ri'aya were small units of 42 square meters intended for retired couples or widows who would be expected to be living off a modest pension and not have children. The Igar scheme units—of an acceptable size of 63 square meters—were not available in all governorates and represented only 3 percent of the NHP as implemented. The Bayt al-'Ila scheme intended for families was downright discriminatory, as it was only made available to male applicants from professional syndicates or government agencies who had to prove that their wives had both a college degree and were employed, and that they did not have more than two children to "preserve the social status of the project."[48]

Both privately financed schemes were affordable only to the upper-middle and higher-earning households since the beginning of the project. The developer-financed units of the Mustathmirin scheme required three bulk payments—for reservation, signing of contract, and delivery—which would total between LE30,000 and LE55,000 within a one-year period, and that was only if the applicant had qualified for a LE10,000 subsidy.[49] In addition, there would be monthly or quarterly installments that averaged from LE7,500 down to LE1,100 per month on payment schemes lasting anywhere between one and ten years. It is not surprising that at one of the more mature developments, owners had the means to fence in the setbacks of the ground floor units in marble-clad fences and elaborate iron gates, as well as add small private gardens to their properties (figure 6.7).

The Ibni Baytak scheme was affordable only if you were buying the land plot, which required a LE1,050 down payment and seven annual payments of LE1,350 each. The rules were to build a semifinished unit within a one-year time frame from plot delivery (later increased to fifteen months), or else risk revocation of the land by NUCA.[50] Even with a LE15,000 cash subsidy, it cost an average of LE71,000 to prepare a habitable unit with a finished interior,[51] which amounts to an average of LE5,733 per month, driving many beneficiaries into debt to finance their units.

Unlike the NHP, which had three unit options under seven different schemes, the SHP promised its million units in just one option: ready-built and finished apartment units, that are overwhelmingly in one size and sold

6.7: A fenced-in 'villa' in Haram City, a low-income public–private development part of the NHP, Sixth of October City, Giza. December 2013. (Photograph by Yahia Shawkat.)

to applicants (table 6.3). There was a very limited run of rental units, as well as some rare two-bedroom units for ownership or rental, but otherwise there were just three-bedroom apartments in six-story blocks advertised as "up to ninety square meters" (figure 6.5).

Of the ownership schemes, the standard SHP subsidized scheme is the mainstay, covering almost all of the units offered until 2018. It has set income bands for "low-income" households to qualify for the Central Bank Low Income Mortgage Initiative, which has earmarked LE20 billion for interest rate subsidized mortgages.[52] A cash subsidy is still offered, though on a sliding scale in inverse proportion to income, reaching zero for higher-income applicants. Even so, almost a decade after the NHP, the SHP is characterized by similar affordability and accessibility issues.

The mortgage scheme favors formal private sector or government employees over the self-employed, the semiformally employed, and pensioners. At first neither the semiformally employed nor pensioners were accepted in the mortgage scheme at all, before a change stipulating that to access the scheme they had to pay almost three times the down payment that the formally employed pay, something that made total up-front costs prohibitive for most. President al-Sisi addressed the issue in 2016, instructing the minister of housing to accept all who applied to the SHP as long as they qualified because "every citizen should have a home."[53] The Central Bank modified the loan conditions accordingly, leading to an increase in the semiformally employed from 5 percent of beneficiaries over the first three years to 18 percent in 2017/2018.[54]

While this increase is significant, 18 percent remains small in comparison to the actual weight of the semiformally employed, who make up almost two-thirds of the workforce.[55] Another hurdle for lower-income applicants, whether formally employed or not, is that the up-front costs are the same for all income groups, equating to at least double the burden for lower-end earners compared to higher earners. This has forced many to borrow, mostly informally, from employers, family, or through rotating savings schemes in order to be able to afford the high down payments.[56] This borrowing increases the debt burden that will need to be repaid—apart from the mortgage—adding considerably to housing-related costs for the most vulnerable beneficiaries. In 2017, the project spread the down payments over a year until the delivery date of the units, but with no guarantee that the applicants would receive a unit, as the one-year mark was also when the applications were vetted against the criteria.

Unlike the subsidized scheme, the two other ownership schemes have no income restrictions and no cash subsidies, but applicants may qualify for the subsidized mortgages. The Unsubsidized SHP sells units at cost or with a small profit margin, and in one iteration offers exclusively to Egyptians abroad, stipulating payment in US dollars. The so-called Distinguished SHP (al-Iskan al-Igtima'i al-Mutamayyiz), also called Sakan Misr, is considerably more expensive, being sold for profit, but just falls within the subsidized mortgage parameters.

The Rental SHP scheme was introduced in 2016, with a plan that rentals would ultimately make up 12 percent of the program, in addition to a smaller scheme of rental cash assistance. The cash assistance scheme has yet to materialize, while 5,700 units were offered for rent, representing barely 1 percent of completed units, with the head of the Social Housing Fund (SHF) stating that they may not continue because of "low demand."[57] How affordable homes were in lower demand than more expensive homes defies logic. It has been the only generally affordable SHP option, with rental values ranging between an acceptable 21 percent of income to a burdensome high of 41 percent, depending on unit size and income level (table 6.3).

A—Ownership						
Scheme	Household Income Bands (LE/month)	Cost (LE)	Cash Subsidy (LE)	Payment Scheme	Units Offered in FY17/18	
A1 Subsidized SHP (90m^2)	wMin 1,500– max 4,750	184,000	0–25,000	16–40% down payment + 20 year subsidized mortgage at 5–7%	125,000	68%
A2 *Hurr* (unsubsidized) SHP (75-95m^2)	None	165,000–250,000	None	Cash or 25% down payment + 3 year yearly installments	18,061	10%
A3 *Mutamayyiz* (Distinguished) SHP/ Sakan Misr (115m^2)	None	425,000–575,000	None	Cash, 20% down payment + 5 year quarterly installments, or 20 year subsidized mortgage at 8–10.5%	40,000	22%
B—Rent						
Rental SHP 2-bedroom (75m^2)	Min 1,000 –Max 1,450	300/mth + 7%/yr	Embedded	LE1,000 deposit + LE3,000 utilities' hook-up		
Rental SHP 3-bedroom (90m^2)	Min 1,000– Max 1,450	410/mth + 7%/yr	Embedded	LE1,500 deposit + LE3,000 utilities' hook-up	0	0%
Total					183,061	100%

Sources: SHF, "Rental SHP advertisement"; SHF, "Ninth SHP advertisement"; SHF, "Egyptians Abroad SHP advertisement"; NUCA, "Kurrasat al-shurut al-khassa bi-hajz al-wihdat al-sakaniya bi-l-marhala al-ula bi-mashru' sakan Misr."

6.3: SHP schemes in 2016/2017.

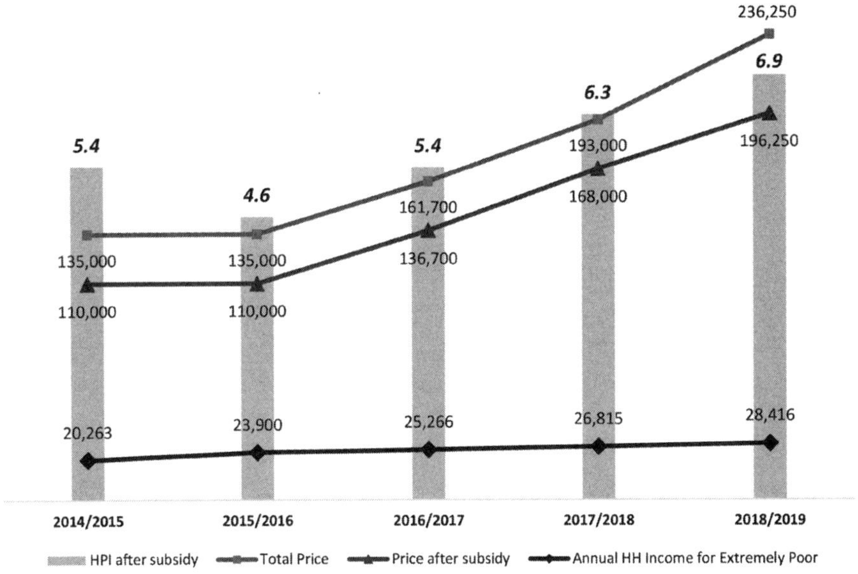

6.8: Inflation of SHP prices relative to income 2014/15–2018/19 in nominal LE. (Based on Shawkat, "A Million Units for Whom?")

Overall, the prices of SHP units have seen a shocking increase of 75 percent in the five-year period from 2014/15 to 2018/19 (figure 6.8). Even increasing the maximum allowable subsidy in 2018/19 only worked to keep the increase within the same average of 19 percent per year. Incomes remained relatively flat, increasing by 10 percent per year, if that. Thus, affordability has dwindled, with unit prices in 2018 representing a phenomenal 6.9 times the annual income of extremely poor households. The now renamed Social Housing and Mortgage Finance Fund (SHMFF) increased the maximum mortgage-to-income ratio from 25 percent of income at the start of the project to 40 percent, which can only mean an increased burden and higher risk of default for poor and vulnerable families.

Access and Corruption

Jumping through bureaucratic income hoops and hurdles is just one part of getting a government-built home, as there are always more obstacles lurking beneath the paperwork. The NHP had a host of minefields in its application regime. On the one hand, it was far from properly managed or monitored: not a single digital database was used so that it might have been possible to ascertain if an applicant had previously applied or had done so in another location, while income declarations were rarely investigated, and if they were, arbitrarily so.[58]

Two years into the project, the Housing and Development Bank, which up until that point had handled all the loans, transferred them to another state-owned bank, Banque Misr, which went on to add a new hurdle. Banque Misr stipulated a guarantor with a government job, no older than forty years, not an immediate relative, and who would have his or her salary paid directly into the bank on a monthly basis in order to have the value of the installment automatically deducted.[59]

The leading state-owned daily *al-Ahram* described the development as an "assassination of the dream of an apartment."[60] A black market of government employees started operating during application periods, offering their services outside of bank branches and charging LE15,000 per application or demanding co-ownership.[61] Those who could not find a guarantor had no choice but to cough up the LE30,000 in cash, otherwise the banks would put the units they had already reserved and qualified for to auction under repossession terms.[62]

The wheels were apparently coming off the financing mechanism, as costs spiraled out of control and there was not enough public cash to build the homes for which thousands had already paid down payments, leading local officials to play fast and loose with the rules. Some councils followed Banque Misr's lead in demanding full cash payments, while also delaying delivery for years, leading to numerous protests.[63] In Kafr al-Sheikh in 2010, the governor, Major General Ahmed Zaki Abdin, negotiated with applicants who had already received their units in the town of al-Riad to move to unsold units in a nearby village, so that he could sell their apartments in an open auction, claiming that they could fetch a healthy profit that could be used to fund more housing units.[64] While some applicants agreed, others took the governor to court and managed to get the public prosecutor to freeze the auction—an order Abdin ignored. He would continue a controversial term in office before becoming minister of local development and then head of one of the largest state-owned real estate development companies.

Cronyism and bribery were also widespread in Mubarak's NHP. Regime parliamentarians were in on the lottery, and in one case the mayor of the small town of Bulqas accepted a bribe in return for twelve apartments.[65] For a small bribe, previously reserved units in Gharbiya were reallocated to others who skipped the queue and did not meet the eligibility criteria, leading to protests and a court case.[66]

Given the NHP's shoddy application regime, one would assume it could not get worse. But it was indeed worse with the SHP, at least in its early days. With over 5 million applications made on hastily scribbled pieces of paper between February and June 2011, the ministry and local housing departments must have had their work cut out vetting them. When the project was relaunched in 2014, the advertisements invited previous applicants to "complete reservation documents" as long as they had their receipt (figure 6.5). But that priority was later removed, probably because no one wanted to vet tens of thousands of new applications against the millions already submitted—or simply lost.

The SHP's application regime evolved, with SHMFF setting up a centralized database that flags anyone who has previously received a unit, a government land plot, or a cooperative loan. So far it appears to be monitored, with over one hundred thousand applicants having been refused for noncompliance,[67] and those found to have falsified information sued and their units sequestered.[68] The lottery system has been replaced by a digitized points-based system, relying on pre-entered social parameters with priority established by household size, gender, and marital status. In the event that applicants have the same number of points, the system favors the lower earners.

While no significant complaints have been made about this system, complaints have been made about income investigators hired by the banks to establish credit worthiness demanding bribes to give their green light.[69] These escalated to the extent that it elicited a formal response from the head of the SHMFF, who declared that companies with repeated complaints would be removed.[70] The new digital application system, along with myriad forms and documents required, have played a role in complicating matters for thousands of applicants who have had their applications rejected because of entry errors, or have had to rely on pop-up vendors to fill in their forms in exchange for a fee.[71]

But SHP income stipulations have been legally circumvented altogether. Over forty thousand units have been sold under nonsubsidized schemes to cash payers, while bulk sales have been made to local governorates, who then allocate the units using their own application regimes, which are most likely corrupt.

Numbers versus Needs

It is not clear where the NHP's target of half a million units or the SHP's target of one million units came from. Was the latter simply a doubling of the former, or perhaps an emulation of projects in other countries? Sweden had its Million Program in the 1960s, while Angola's 2008 project with the tagline "My Dream, My Home" also promised a million homes.[72] By contrast, India's Housing for All project has promised 10 million homes in two years, and China adds 2 million government-built homes to the housing stock each year.[73]

All these projects come from what economists have termed the 'supply-side' school: a build-it-and-they-will-come mentality. While there are numerous stories and news reports of endless waiting lists for subsidized housing in Egypt, these have been the result of badly designed projects, rather than an attestation to their success.

Thousands of units are built every year without there being any clear idea of who will end up living in them, contributing heavily to Egypt's housing vacancy rate, which has developed into a phenomenon that housing critic Milad Hanna pithily described in the 1980s as "dwellers without dwellings, and dwellings without dwellers."[74] By 2006, almost a third of homes were counted as vacant, a proportion that held in the 2017 census, which listed almost 12 million homes as empty.[75] Indeed, one study found that a staggering half of recently built government housing was empty[76]—either waiting to be sold, or already sold but kept empty by owners who did not currently need them or could not commute to their homes because there was no means of transport. Mubarak was especially proud of this vacancy after rehousing many victims of the 1992 earthquake within weeks, boasting in a speech, "Many countries were surprised where I got them [the victims] homes, and the US president himself asked me . . . I told him, 'We build.' We are not a rich country where everyone has insurance."[77]

Between 2005 and 2011, Mubarak's NHP managed to build 380,000 units, averaging a little over 60,000 units a year—much higher than production over the previous decade, but missing the target by 25 percent (table 6.1). The government only built around 70 percent of these, with an almost exclusive focus on ownership schemes, essentially abandoning the rental schemes. The private developer Mustathmirin scheme fared much worse, building less than three-quarters of its target despite heavily subsidized land and direct subsidies. The self-build Ibni Baytak scheme was the only one to (barely) exceed its target and make up a full quarter of the NHP.[78]

Perhaps the NHP's most impressive achievement was that, despite not achieving its target number, and high demand in some areas, tens of thousands of units were standing empty on the eve of their patron's demise. In the months leading up to the 2011 uprising, but especially in the security vacuum that succeeded it, thousands of empty government-built homes in at least twenty-one housing estates were stormed and squatted;[79] around 3,600 were NHP units.[80] As squatters almost exclusively targeted public, rather than private homes, their actions leave little doubt that it was as a conscious assertion of their right to housing—not just any housing, that which the government built and excluded them from. As anthropologist Nicholas Simicik Arese observes, an informality used to protest the immorality of formal planning.[81]

So why were all these units empty? There were thousands of completed or nearly completed units that applicants had rejected because of incomplete infrastructure.[82] Others had already been allocated to beneficiaries, but either because of lack of services, transport, security, or possibly speculation, they had not moved into them.[83] The rest had not been sold because people found them too expensive and the application conditions too demanding.[84] In the case of the *qura al-Zahir al-Sahrawi* scheme, fifty-eight villages stood empty because land for reclamation had not been readied, rendering the homes useless for the farmers who had applied for them.[85] This led the Central Audit Authority to investigate the responsible Ministry of Housing agency for misuse of public funds to the tune of LE500 million, in addition to a further LE5 million that was spent on dams to protect two villages that were built in a flash flood zone.[86] Even the Ibni Baytak scheme is sparsely populated a decade after it was built, since infrastructure, services, and security still lag, as we see in chapter 2.

The SHP's penchant for creating vacant housing is even more flagrant than that of the NHP. Like his predecessor, al-Sisi is perceptibly proud of building housing units. He proclaims that "no other country in the world could build the amount of housing we built, not in our region, or the world."[87] Between 2012/13 and 2017/18, around half a million SHP units were built (figure 6.9). This was quite a bit more than the NHP managed in six years with both public and private finance, but was exactly half the number of units that should have been completed by then. Most pertinent is the miniscule scale of the social gain, as less than half of those—190,000 units—were delivered to beneficiaries, and these were not necessarily poor. At current average delivery rates, the remaining 300,000 units could stand empty for years, while thousands of new units continue to be built.

As with the NHP and many other government housing projects, the SHP has built thousands of units for which there is no demand, or more

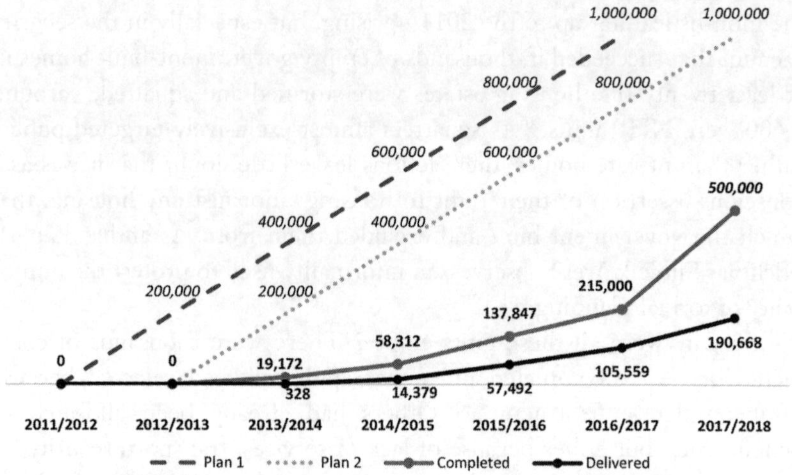

6.9: Comparison between unit targets, completions, and deliveries for the SHP 2011/12-2017/18. (Aggregated. Based on Shawkat, "A Million Units for Whom?")

accurately, not built on the basis of feasibility studies to ascertain whether low-income households would want or could afford relatively expensive three-bedroom apartments in housing blocks. Over half of Egypt is rural, where households tend to prefer family houses over apartment blocks. It has not helped that in seven governorates, which are mostly provincial, over half the units were concentrated in a single new city each, usually a suburb of the provincial capital. These units are only suitable for those already living in the capital, and simply ignore the majority living in towns and villages. Conversely, in some places units did not meet demand, leading to applications being rejected, or where new units were to be built, delays in delivery.

With a large unsold inventory of built units, the Ministry of Housing took extraordinary actions to sell them. One of these was to sell SHP units to higher-earning applicants, basically upper-middle-income earners, by introducing the unsubsidized Hur (Free) SHP scheme, as well as the so-called Distinguished Social Housing/Sakan Misr and the Egyptians' Abroad schemes (table 6.3). Another has been to sell units in bulk to local government, which would use its own mechanisms to sell the units to applicants,[88] most probably higher-income households.

If the SHP was not designed according to market demand, as a social project it could have been designed to respond to social needs, with construction targeted in areas with a high housing affordability burden, for instance. When the number of delivered units is compared to newly formed households that cannot afford housing, the SHP has only been able to address 7 percent of those on average.[89] Even focusing only on the 160,000 households formed every year below the poverty line, the SHP would have served just 16 percent,[90] which was of course theoretical given the affordability burden described earlier.

Budgets and Financing

Both the NHP and the SHP have cost billions of Egyptian pounds to implement, which would not be a bad thing if they served low-income families.

While the NHP centralized both housing program design and management at the national level, local Housing Accounts and the state-owned NUCA financed construction for two-thirds of the original plan, with the Treasury supporting any deficits at the local level, in addition to financing the village housing scheme *qura al-Zahir al-Sahrawi*. The remaining third was to be privately financed, an evolution of the Future Housing's public–private partnership. Private finance was to be divided between private sector developers under the Mustathmirin (Investors) scheme, at 20 percent of the NHP, with the remainder financed by individuals participating in the self-build Ibni Baytak plots.

Details around the financing are sketchy at best, since disaggregated budget data for the agencies involved is not publicly available, and most of the projects' follow-up reports mention only subsidies. Just one report, released in 2012, estimates an overall cost of LE34 billion,[91] which seems surprisingly plausible, though tells us little if we do not investigate further. First, we have to differentiate between investment costs, which were to be recouped by the government agencies after homes were sold, and subsidies, which are treated as nonrepayable grants. Based on the final delivery numbers of public sector ownership units in 2012 and average costs during the project, investments totaled almost LE20 billion, most of which should have been recouped (table 6.4).

The subsidies can be divided into three forms: construction, land, and interest rate. *Construction subsidies* refers to the money paid to government agencies to cover the difference between what they were willing to spend on the units and the unified price the units are sold for. Here, the total costs of the rental units have been considered subsidies because the rents would not have generated enough income to recover costs. If we add on the maximum allowable cash subsidies that were intended to be paid to the individual self-builders and the private developers—though not all applicants in these schemes qualified for them—these total around LE8.2 billion (table 6.4). The land subsidy that covers so-called trunk infrastructure—roads, utility pipes, and cables reaching the sites—cost LE9.2 billion, including half of the cost for the private sector land where the self-builders and investors paid the balance (table 6.4). This does not include the market cost of the land, but that is a whole other kettle of fish. For public sector schemes, land costs are not calculated because only the units are sold without a *hisa fi al-ard* (land portion), as the land remains under the ownership of the government agencies.[92] The private sector brokered an advantageous deal.

Calculating the interest rate subsidy for the NHP has been difficult since there is no available information and state-owned banks were expected to fund it themselves, something the World Bank thought was already very risky.[93] The highly fluctuating interest rates at the time, along with rising inflation, might go some way to explain the financing chaos that occurred mid-project. Overall, subsidies accounted for nearly LE18 billion, but with LE9 billion covered by government land sales.[94]

The figures look big when added up, but in reality it was a very badly managed project by a very stingy government. When considered on a yearly basis, and with the self-allocated cross-subsidization, the cost to the Treasury was around LE1.5 billion per year, which paled in comparison to the contemporary subsidy budget for all of Egypt, which was LE134 billion in 2008/09.[95] Surely the social cost of housing, the largest burden on families after food, should be more than that? In our case there is the added caveat that the initiative does not target those who actually need housing.

With regard to the SHP, between 2012/13 and 2017/18 direct government funds constituted about two-fifths of the LE77.8 billion cost, with the balance funded by revenue from unit sales, an Emirati grant, and a bank loan.[96] Government 'investments,' along with the loan, constitute an 'outstanding' 59 percent of spending that should be recouped once units are sold. But this outrageous price tag—double that of the NHP for roughly the same number of units within a decade—indicates that little, if any, effort has gone into reducing or regulating costs. More pertinently, this inflated spending should have been double that, as LE136.5 billion was originally earmarked for the SHP in the public budget over that time frame. Somewhere in the belly of this project is an answer.

		A. Construction Subsidies		B. Land Subsidies				C. Investments			
Scheme	Completed Units (thousands)	Subsidy per unit LE (thousands)	**Total LE (thousands)**	Land m^2 (thousands)	Cost LE/m^2	**Total LE (thousands)**	Total subsidies (A+B) LE (thousands)	Avg. cost per unit LE (thousands)	**Total LE (thousands)**	Total (A,B,C) LE (thousands)	Average subsidy per unit LE (thousands)
Public Sector Ownership	**235**	20.0	**4,696**	49,310	140	**6,903**	**11,600**	75	**17,611**	**29,210**	49.4
Public Sector Rental	31	61.3	**1,878**	6,432	140	**900**	**2,778**		**1,878**	**4,656**	90.7
Total Public Sector	**265**		**6,574**	55,742	140	**7,804**	**14,378**		**19,489**	**33,867**	
Total Private Sector	**119**	12.5	**1,656**	19,368	70	**1,356**	**3,012**		**0**	**3,012**	25.3
Total	**384**		**8,230**	75,110		**9,160**	**17,390**		**19,489**	**36,879**	

* At an average rule-of-thumb of 20 units per feddan (4,200 square meters.)

6.4: Estimated cost of the NHP.

On the subsidy side, similar to the NHP, there are the three forms of construction, land, and interest rate subsidy. Today the government and the World Bank like to call construction subsidies demand-side subsidies, arguing that they go toward the applicants and not the contractors, making them more transparent,[97] as opposed to supply-side subsidies. While like the NHP, SHP applicants could qualify for up to LE25,000 in cash subsidies toward buying their home, the more recent form differs from the older one in that the subsidies are distributed inversely to income, supposedly benefitting lower earners. Up until 2018, actual subsidies averaged LE17,000 per unit, which with a lower subsidy-to-unit ratio than the NHP, and barely three-quarters of units sold as subsidized, in real terms makes the new units much more expensive to buy than at any time previously. Overall, about LE3.1 billion was credited to the GSF to disburse to applicants between 2013/14 and 2017/18, funded through a $500 million World Bank loan.[98]

But the days of so-called supply-side subsidies would not be banished forever. In 2017, a further LE5 billion in subsidies was added by the government, funded through NUCA to cover differences in cost that were supposedly incurred after the Egyptian pound lost almost half its value in November 2016.

Meanwhile, in 2014, the World Bank loan would also help establish yet another housing agency, the Social Housing Fund (SHF), which would be the main central agency managing housing, much like its short-lived ancestor, the Economic Housing Fund (EHF) of the late 1970s, mentioned in chapter 5.[99] Confusingly, the SHF existed alongside the GSF, sharing a CEO and chair of the board, with the GSF continuing its role of receiving and vetting applications, as well as allocating units and subsidies to those accepted, while the SHF managed the project and its finances until they were merged in 2018 to become the Social Housing and Mortgage Finance Fund (SHMFF).[100]

Where the mortgages had failed in the context of the NHP project because of high compound interest, the Central Bank came to the rescue of the SHP with its Low Income Mortgage Initiative in 2014, lending to commercial banks from reserves at a lower rate than the 7 percent simple interest they are then sold for. (In 2018, market rates averaged 18 percent.) Initially, the interest rate subsidies were written off as an opportunity cost—a virtual calculation of the loss made if the loans were made at market rates. But this novel method almost went the way of the NHP's loan system, when in 2017 it irked the IMF, which had recently bailed Egypt out through a new $12 billion financial restructuring loan, and so has been keeping tabs on Egypt's economic policy. In its first review of the loan, the IMF recommended "that the practice be discontinued or financed from the budget."[101] This sent the SHMFF and the World Bank squabbling over how to finance the interest rate subsidies from other sources, eventually reaching an agreement with the Treasury to foot the LE2.3 billion a year bill for the next twenty years.[102] This figure is expected to double once the remaining quarter of a million units are sold, and quadruple if all one million units are built and sold.

Finally, the cost of servicing the land has not been made public, though if we take a recent tender that estimated LE208 per square meter, that means that the 190,000 units delivered have received LE8.3 billion in land subsidies.[103] In total, besides the interest rate subsidy that so far is not in cash, the SHP has benefited from LE16.4 billion in subsidies up until 2018, or a little over LE86,000 per unit. At an average of LE3.3 billion per year over the five years that the SHP has been operating, it amounts to 10 percent of the national subsidy budget.[104]

Affordable Housing: A Chimera

The observation of Mahmud Riad, Egypt's first housing minister, that "the people living in the slums cannot, in most cases, afford to pay an economic rent for properly built houses"[105] still holds true for government housing, more than eight decades on. Apart from the rentals of the 1950s through the 1970s, affordability of so-called social, national, or economic housing for those in need has remained elusive. Even when it was affordable, the numbers produced have never been enough to match needs. The move toward selling rather than renting units since 1978, as we see in chapter 5, has turned housing into a commodity that higher earners as well as those with the right credentials—government employees, regime cronies—compete over with the poor. This 'social' housing then becomes a market asset that can either be sublet informally or sold to make a profit. Centralizing housing provision has politicized it: branding projects with the names of rulers, timing them for political gain, and targeting segments that are more likely to support the regime. Emphasizing ready-built housing at the expense of an array of possible 'soft' policy solutions, such as rent vouchers, rent regulation, and finance for self-build, has led to what Milad Hanna termed the "sovereignty of the contractors"[106]— projects are designed to give maximum benefit to contractors and not the client. This opaque contracting system circumvents tenders,[107] which would ordinarily ensure the best product for the lowest cost. The result has been vastly inflated housing prices, with large proportions of social housing found to be unaffordable to the poor and subsequently sold unsubsidized to higher earners, some on the condition that they pay in US dollars, just to recoup the costs.

Access to a barely affordable government-built home has only been achieved through squatting in them, or standing in the way of a bulldozer's blade. Since al-Sisi ordered slum "residents be relocated to adequate homes in two years and not three"[108] in May 2016, the 2009 project to upgrade so-called unsafe areas has gone into overdrive. Over 200,000 families identified as living in areas of immediate danger or in inadequate housing have been targeted by the project. But rather than improving where they live—such as by making repairs, extending utilities, or regularizing tenure—the focus has been on demolishing their communities and relocating residents to shiny new mass housing estates that many have been coerced into accepting. Bashayir al-Khayr in Alexandria will be home to 30,000 families sent from all over the city. With over 150,000 people it will be the size of a small city itself, but one crammed into one-fifth of a square kilometer.[109] Residents resettled to the 20,000-unit Asmarat estate in Cairo live under heavy surveillance and are made to pay unaffordable rents, leading many to receive eviction orders for nonpayment. A number of residents received two-year prison sentences for protesting the rents.[110] They faced a double eviction: the first from their original homes, and the second from where they were resettled.

At the other end of the scale, since 2014 the government has been investing billions of Egyptian pounds in building almost a quarter of a million housing units for profit. Over fifty thousand unsold SHP units have been jazzed up and sold for almost double their cost as the Distinguished Social Housing/Sakan Misr project. Another 150,000 units are being built under the Dar Misr brand, a joint project between NUCA and the Armed Forces Engineering Authority, initially launched as middle-level housing that was significantly more expensive than median prices.[111] It has since been facelifted into the Janna Luxury Housing Project with swimming pools and gyms after Sakan Misr prices crept in, with 2018 advertised prices double those of 2014.

It does not stop there. Capital Residence is a 25,000-unit housing development in the New Administrative Capital, a joint venture between

NUCA and the Ministry of Defense.[112] Over 2,000 units were sold in 2018 for prices ranging between LE1.3 and 2.2 million,[113] ten times the value of a median-priced home. The same year, NUCA and the state-owned Housing and Development Bank created City Edge Developments, a company tasked with building and marketing their luxury housing. By year's end, it announced sales of LE11 billion,[114] mostly from five coastal resort skyscrapers on the Mediterranean, where the average price of one square meter sold for the equivalent of an average family's annual earnings.[115]

But this vast arsenal of government construction could go a long way to improve housing for hundreds of thousands of families in need every year. The power of these projects to control housing prices through sheer scale could be used to lower rather than raise house prices. Their profits could help bolster mainstream public finance to fund a range of appropriate and meaningful housing support. Millions of rent vouchers could be made to those that are affordability burdened—households that cannot afford to rent housing where they live—taking advantage of millions of already existing, privately financed housing units that are built where people would actually prefer to live, and not in the middle of the desert. This in turn would be money the landlords could use to improve less than adequate homes: making much-needed building repairs, adding nonexistent infrastructure, and so on.

Instead, the profits of the grand government projects remain locked up in state-owned companies and the government agencies that own them,[116] with shavings scattered here and there, generally only used to finance construction. On the Platinum Jubilee of the Imbaba Worker's estate, Egypt's first large-scale housing project, government-built housing has never been farther from solving the housing problem.

7

HOUSING UNRAVELS

Bayti wa matrahi (my home and the place I belong) is a popular Egyptian phrase that captures how many Egyptians view their homes—not just as a dwelling, but a sociospatial state that can express status, identity, and location. Yet for most Egyptians tenancy of their homes is not guaranteed, putting millions of families at grave risk of being thrown out and their homes reassigned, confiscated, or demolished.

While not all residents living informally are at constant risk of being evicted, as complicity between residents and key officials has bought some amnesty,[1] the layers and complexity of informal tenure have made it easy for government agencies to evict residents from properties whenever deemed necessary and where public backlash would be minimal. For many, the resettlement of over 50,000 Nubian families in the 1960s to build the High Dam is an example of forced eviction in Egypt. However, the country has a more recent history of relocation. An estimated 41,000 families were resettled between 1997 and 2013, due to so-called slum and unsafe area development projects alone.[2] A large portion of these relocations amount to forced eviction, as little or no participation took place and over half were relocated to housing outside the city.[3] These statistics do not include other forms of eviction, such as those related to expropriation orders, eviction orders for squatting on state-owned land, and eviction court rulings where formal tenure has fallen into informality.

Between 2013 and 2015, thousands of families had their homes along the border with Gaza demolished and were forced to relocate from Rafah in North Sinai with little or no compensation because of the government's so-called war on terror.[4] Thousands more have fled the region because of armed fighting.

The patterns in the demolishment of homes show that housing policy is surreptitiously set up to force most Egyptians into informality, or semi-formality—a twilight zone where residents are not really sure if they are breaking the law, but are nevertheless sure they are exercising their right to a home.

In addition to state-led eviction or relocation, thousands of people have been forcibly evicted by other citizens, which is itself possible because of the absence of the state. Over the last decade, one million Old Rent (rent-controlled) tenancies have been dissolved. While many had run their course, some renters were displaced by local developers gentrifying older neighborhoods. In the best cases, these residents were given compensation to vacate their apartments.[5] In the worst cases, they were victims of building collapse, given that a third of building collapses are blamed on dilapidated, unmaintained buildings and 15 percent on premeditated structural damage.[6]

But why is forced eviction so common in Egypt? Primarily, it is a product of informal tenure, where most Egyptians live in a gray spectrum without clear legal tenure of ownership, lease, rent, or in-kind use, as this chapter will show. But it is also because of lax and arbitrary enforcement of the rule of law by the state, exacerbated by the fact that many government agencies claim jurisdiction on a large portion of urban land and seek to capitalize on ballooning land prices courtesy of a deregulated property market. In addition, various laws lead to the expropriation of private property without adequately protecting the rights of owners.[7]

This situation has inevitably led Egypt to rank 77 out of 128 countries on the Global Property Rights Index,[8] an index that ranks performance based on a number of factors, including rule of law, political stability, control of corruption, and judicial independence. On rule of law alone, as ranked by the World Justice Project, Egypt comes close to the bottom, at 110 out 113 countries.[9]

Ownership may be the original form of tenancy for a unit, but it is not the only form. Rent is the second most popular tenancy in Egypt, and tenants face similar problems to owners, as most do not have registered contracts—a legal requirement to guarantee rights are upheld in cases of dispute—since landlords seek to evade income tax. It gets even more complicated where informal units are rented—a double informality—as how would the second form of tenancy (rent) of an originally informal tenancy (ownership) be ratified?

Things get murkier still. Possibly millions of families are living as squatters, without any form of documentation that legally proves their tenancy. There are verbal contracts outlining the in-kind use of rooms by *bawwabin* (porters), as well as the informal subletting of rooms on rooftops or basements out of sight of absentee landlords.[10] Complicated *waqf ahli* (religious trust) leases run out without the tenants vacating the units. There are descendants of tenants living in *masha'a* buildings—common ownership—where decades of inheritance have complicated ownership. There are also tenants of older public housing, especially emergency shelter, where original beneficiaries have informally sublet or sold their units, or where legal wording of contracts is vague. And of course there are plain and simple squatters who have built shacks on public or private land, mostly in desert outskirts of cities, who with time and stability have rebuilt the shacks into concrete buildings. Then there is the more recent postrevolution squatting where thousands of families have moved into vacant blocks of subsidized housing.

This chapter is where all the threads of informality that wove throughout the previous chapters converge. It shows how a spectrum of informality exists in all forms of tenure—owner-built, government-built, or rented homes—and at different levels of the housing provision process from land use to construction. There are five main components to housing that can be either formal or informal, with several degrees in between. In a general order of events, these are land tenure, land use, construction, unit tenure, and unit use.

Builders, owners, and tenants of homes that have one or more informal components have probably done a risk-benefit analysis before committing to their home, as each of these five components carries different weights of legal risk that may cut costs or make housing more affordable. There are many cases where people have unwittingly landed an informal home, or more intriguingly, where the formality has simply eroded over time. Somewhere along the line, government agencies picked up on this informality—or did they also create it?

As the budget deficit ballooned to 13 percent of GDP in 2013—easing to 9.5 percent in 2017[11]—the government has been further institutionalizing and developing its asset management tools, in a bid to plug this deficit and pay back foreign loans that have surpassed $100 billion. The Committee to Exploit Unused State Assets has been working to build a central database of land administered by the various government agencies, showing size, location, and value, as well as laying plans to invest this land.[12] Whatever existed on that land will be removed to make way for these new investments. Among the examples documenting the spectrum of housing informality in Egypt is an alarming number of cases where government agencies have developed tools to exploit the informal tenure of many communities. This has mostly been in the interest of profiting from the rent gap—the difference in cost between evicting residents and the market value of the land.[13] While this rent gap is capitalized on where gentrification occurs—by hiking up prices of previously less desirable properties after sprucing them up with cafés and art galleries—in Egypt it has been the endemic phenomenon of informal tenure that has facilitated the exploitation of the rent gap.

Self-build on Squatted Land

The essential element of every construction project is land. In Egypt, land can either be formally acquired by buying a registered plot or informally secured by squatting. Sometimes things are not so clear. A large proportion of homes have dubious tenancy through inherited deeds, usually in historic neighborhoods or in the majority of villages where a multitude of land reform laws and interagency corruption have rendered once formal tenure obscure.

Starting with squatting, which includes most urban shack dwellers and many rural communities across Egypt, the land on which their houses are built has been adversely possessed through *wad' al-yad*—literally claiming by hand, and known widely as adverse possession. While abolished as a legal form of tenure on state-owned land in 1957, the law did not abolish *wad' al-yad* on private land if it is not contested within a fifteen-year period.[14] In addition, every couple of decades or so since then, exceptional legislation has been passed to formalize *wad' al-yad*, though under particular conditions.

One of these laws, 148/2006, allowed for the "sale or lease of state-owned land under *wad' al-yad* for whoever built on it or reclaimed it and cultivated it as smallholdings at a maximum of one hundred feddans for desert land and ten feddans in the old agricultural lands prior to the enactment of the law." But the legislation left it open to each government agency to apply the law's provisions as it saw fit—what claims it would or would not accept and how much it would charge for selling or leasing the land ex post facto to the current tenants.[15]

Ultimately it is not clear how many households benefited from Law 148/2006 or have been able to completely formalize their tenure, with complete paperwork, payments, and a registered title of ownership or lease. There is also evidence that authorities abused their power and set formalization fees too high.

In one telling example, residents of al-Salamoni, a five-hundred-house hamlet in Suhag that lies on the desert fringe of the agricultural basin, were initially happy with the new law as they would finally be able to own the land they had been living on for decades.[16] In 2008, the rate at which the local council offered to formally sell them the land was between LE50 and LE60 per square meter, which was affordable considering that they had been paying ground rents of LE1.25 per square meter as *'awayid* (land returns tax) over the past forty years. *'Awayid* are not legal leases but rather the old real estate tax which many local councils levy on *wad' al-yad* land. While most Egyptians believe this to be a kind of formal recognition, legally the payment of *'awayid* only proves residence and not tenure, as it does not afford any rights to the land and can be revoked without notice. This is apart from the fact that its value can also change without notice.

In 2011, the local council hiked the formalization price to between LE200 and LE300 per square meter, which was unaffordable for most of the residents who had not yet bought the land. The local council also hiked the *'awayid* to LE10 per square meter, possibly in an effort to force residents to buy the land. A group of residents took the council to court, where the dispute could take years to resolve.

The methods used to tackle adverse possession evolved into a bespoke Committee to Recover State Land (CRSL), formed in 2016. It was initially established to inventory state land that was subject to *wad' al-yad* between 2006 and 2016.[17] But in 2017, using an updated regularization law, it metamorphosed into a machine to act not just against adverse possessors of land, but illegal changes in land use and lessors in arrears. The committee levied regularization fees against anyone it could prove did not have clear land title, or in the event of failure to pay, it would sequester the land.[18] Within eighteen months, the committee announced it had demolished transgressions on 32,619 acres of urban land—out of a total of 41,428 acres—through eleven 'demolition waves,' while it reported recovering 1.2 million acres of agricultural land out of a total of 2 million acres.[19] It is not clear how much of this was land recovered from adverse possessors and how much was because of illegal change of land use in private hands, as the terms *istirdad* (recovery) and *izalat* (removal) of *al-ta'addiyat* (transgressions) are used interchangeably. There were the 'transgressions' that it would not tolerate, as opposed to the 295,000 applications it had accepted during that time to regularize either adverse possession or change of land use by June 2018, the deadline stipulated by law.[20] A certain amount of that land had been grabbed by well-connected institutions, such as the Rigal Amn al-Mustaqbal (Future Security Men) Cooperative, which boasts 12,000 police officers and judges as its members,[21] and alone adversely possessed an incredible 27,000 acres of desert.[22] Individuals and poor communities were the main losers.

Ramlit Bulaq in Cairo is one of many urban communities where residents have squatted on privately owned land (figure 7.1). The area had been an industrial site that belonged to the al-Kafrawi and 'Izzawi families, who allowed workers in their factories to live on a portion of the land where their mansion was located. Over the years, the landlords abandoned the land and sold the factory, and Bulaq became a prime site overlooking the Nile. There were 500 families in Ramlit Bulaq in 2014, living in one- or two-story homes that ranged from shacks to concrete and brick buildings, most with electricity, some with running water, and all on leaky septic tanks.

Although the residents have been there for decades, much of which has been uncontested as the law requires the formalization of adverse possession, the squatters never took their informal—though not illegal—tenancy to court to formalize it. There are many reasons why. It might have been lack of awareness and a belief that their claim was automatically recognized. It is also possible that most could not afford the time or money to bring their case to court, for if straightforward cases took years, how long would complex cases such as squatting take? In any case, their tenure is in a gray zone. It does not afford them full rights to their homes or to infrastructure, and indeed the Bulaq municipality has not allowed municipal water or sanitation networks into the area, and even blocked a local charity from wanting to offer assistance in this regard.[23]

This gray zone was exploited with Cairo Governor Decree 8993/2011 for the temporary expropriation of Ramlit Bulaq. The expropriation was based on a map of vulnerable communities detailing the formality of land ownership, one that Hosni Mubarak's government had been using to relocate residents of these areas on the pretext of saving them from dangerous conditions. The National Map of Unsafe Areas, produced in 2009 by the

Informal Settlements Development Facility (ISDF), identified 404 'unsafe' areas, home to 212,000 families. Intriguingly, the map identified the tenure of the land the unsafe areas were on—private land or state-owned land. Over half the total number of families living in unsafe areas, 120,000, were living on state-owned land.

Another intriguing fact was that the amendment of Law 10/1990 on Expropriation of Private Land for Public Benefit—eminent domain in the United States and compulsory purchase in the United Kingdom—meant that areas designated as unsafe but where the ownership was private could be expropriated as projects of public benefit. Therefore even the remaining 92,000 private units could be expropriated for development.

Much like the American 'urban renewal' schemes during the second half of the twentieth century, famously critiqued by urban activist Jane Jacobs in her book *The Death and Life of Great American Cities*, many ISDF-designated unsafe areas have been the subject of state-led gentrification. Enter the Cairo 2050/2052 plan to gentrify the more lucrative parts of Cairo, drawn up by the government think tank, the General Organization for Physical Planning (GOPP) and the Cairo governorate. This mega plan sought to capitalize on the state-induced property boom of the 2000s, when land prices of so-called prime locations on the riverfront in the heart of Cairo went up 44 percent a year over the course of a decade.[24] The Urban Development Plan for Rod al-Farag,[25] part of the Cairo 2050/2052 plan, included the "demolition of unsafe shacks" and the relocation of residents in three "slum nodes"—including 'Ashwa'iyat Nile Towers (referring to Ramlit Bulaq)—to housing estates in the new cities outside Cairo, or payment of compensation.[26] According to a former head of the ISDF, the Ramlit Bulaq project could net them LE600 million.[27]

But how did it become 'unsafe' in the first place? Well it seems that the Cairo governorate, along with some unscrupulous speculators, have long had their eye on Ramlit Bulaq. On one hand, the governorate has banned the installation of water and sewage networks, citing it as an informal area,[28] a tactic that has worked to displace some residents, but also to negatively affect the price of real estate in the area. With time, it started to decay, though the decay was also helped by speculators buying out residents, but first forcing them to demolish their own homes and leaving the mounds of rubble in place—partly to prevent them from moving in again but also to accelerate the decay of the community and make Ramlit Bulaq less and less inhabitable.

In parallel to aiding the physical decay of Ramlit Bulaq were other acts of coercion. In August 2012, a police officer stationed at the Nile City Towers adjacent to Ramlit Bulaq shot and killed an unarmed resident, inciting riots that ended in the mass arrest of fifty-one men from the area in a dawn raid the next morning.[29] The court ruling in 2013 annulling the expropriation order of Ramlit Bulaq cited a number of incidents since 1997 that were used to terrorize the residents into selling out to the corporation that owns the adjacent luxury towers for unfairly low prices.[30] This included not opening an investigation into the shooting and killing of 'Amr al-Buni in the towers by the police officer, as well as a number of recorded complaints made by residents about another officer based at the towers for kidnapping children from Ramlit Bulaq and framing them for crimes they did not commit. The court concluded that the Cairo governorate had been complicit with the tower owners in attempting to evict the residents and use the land for commercial purposes.

Had it not been for a keen-eyed lawyer who noticed the sequestration decree in the *Official Gazette*, an appeal would not have been lodged.[31] The appeal was eventually won, mostly on technical grounds, whereby the Cairo governorate was found not to have completed the formal steps to sequester the land.[32] Had it done so, the appeal would unlikely have succeeded. This move helped give temporary respite to the residents, who had already engaged with an urban activist during their case and worked together on a participatory development plan outlining their views on how they wanted to upgrade the area and ultimately formalize their tenure.[33] Throughout the design of the plan, a number of meetings were held with the ISDF, as well as Nile City representatives. The plan was subsequently presented to the ISDF in January 2016, but was never adopted.

The court case also recognized the Ramlit Bulaq residents' claim to the land, stating, "The papers presented to court prove ownership by the residents of the land and the buildings . . . for more than seventy years for some of them and fifty years for others."[34] These residents remain far from having registered title to their homes. In November 2017, Cairo Governor Decree 5725/2017 was issued to replan thirty 'unsafe' areas. Replanning is a legal circumvention of expropriation, allowing some fig leaf of participation—and number one on the list of areas was Ramlit Bulaq. By 2018, the squatted mansion and a large number of homes were cleared and turned into parking areas for the adjacent towers (figure 7.1), paving the way for the eviction of the rest of the Ramla.

7.1: The 'Izzawi mansion, inundated by the shacks of Ramlit Bulaq, Cairo. February 2015. Aerial images in 2018 show that the mansion and many homes have been demolished. (Photograph by Yahia Shawkat.)

Self-build on Private Land

The source of most tenure informality in Egypt is the change of land use from agricultural to urban, which is illegal, rather than squatting as may be the case in other countries. It is change in land use that actually defines the majority of *'ashwa'iyat*. Although land is in private hands, it is standard practice in most countries that land use or zoning laws define how owners may use their land, whether for residential, industrial, agricultural, or other purposes.

The process of converting Egypt's 'black land' from agricultural to urban use began in earnest in the mid-twentieth century, both formally—such as Madinat al-Awqaf, which is now the bustling neighborhood of Mohandiseen in Cairo—and informally (figure 7.2). In terms of the informal, most urban literature points the finger at a mix of population growth and the drying up of rental units as Old Rent (rent control) laws effectively ended private sector build-to-rent (chapter 3), leading to skyrocketing prices for ownership units. Petrodollars pouring in from Egyptians working in the Gulf and seeking to make their mark were used to fund the private building boom in rural areas. In fact, as we see in chapter 2, the government has pursued a highly methodical practice since the 1950s, whereby it has left millions to provide themselves with homes through self-build, only to identify them as illegal and then allow amnesties in exchange for fees and votes—a coerced clientelism.

Ultimately, older self-built communities have been incorporated into the 'formal' city, and one would innocently assume that police and fire stations, postal codes, and government schools were a form of recognition. But almost no ex post facto building permits have been issued leaving millions living in a gray zone of tenure.

A Ministry of Housing agency estimated that there were 3 million informal homes in 2018.[35] Would the government enforce the law and demolish millions of units, or would it formalize them? Since 2015, a law has been in the works to reconcile *(tasaluh)* most of these illegal buildings in return for hefty fines. At the same time, some government agencies moved to demolish some of the newer informal buildings, though these were mostly on state-owned land, as mentioned in the previous section. By April 2019,

7.2: Private agricultural land that is informally subdivided and built on. The nine-story block is clearly not a family home. Mansuriya Canal, Giza. April 2012. (Photograph by Yahia Shawkat.)

the Construction Violations Reconciliation Law 17/2019 was passed, with parliament expecting a ridiculous windfall revenue of LE300 billion from regularizing the millions of informal homes built on private land.[36] As this comes at the time of writing, it remains to be seen what this unprecedented step will do, as many owners will surely not be able to pay, and will thus face demolition of their homes, or they will simply remain informal.

The informal modification of land use is not a phenomenon particular to the poor. In the early 2000s, individuals and developers bought tens of thousands of acres of desert land on the Cairo–Alexandria and the Cairo–Ismailiya highways designated for agricultural land reclamation. Rather than intensive farms, suburban homes and compounds with lawns and private swimming pools sprouted (figure 7.3).[37] The government only started to pay attention after things got way out of hand, and in 2008 the Ministry of Agriculture decided to levy fines of LE100,000 per acre of all land that was developed in contravention of the designated land use—that is, homes larger than 2.5 percent of the land plot area, swimming pools, and lawns—in exchange for formalizing the developments.[38] In the event that the fee was not paid, the developer would be put into administration by the government and the assets sold to pay off the fine. Since then, however, the government has not been comprehensively acting upon these warnings, and by early 2016 a mere LE204 million in fines had been collected out of an estimated LE67 billion that government clerks wrote up, as developers or individuals, many of whom are well connected, refused to pay.[39] The Suleimaniya Golf development alone had been levied fines worth LE2.3 billion (figure 7.3).[40]

This was when the government started to change tack, first through the aforementioned CRSL, and then by reassigning the land from the Ministry of Agriculture to its own developer, the New Urban Communities Authority (NUCA). Residents on the Cairo–Alexandria highway woke up one day to find themselves part of the sprawling 32,000 acre New Sphinx City.[41] For one thing, NUCA had the mandate to develop urban land and sell it for a good profit, and therefore the incentive to take action against owners, either by levying fines for changing the land use from agricultural to urban, or in the event they could not pay, sequestering an area equaling the value of the fine.[42] It also had the money to do this. None of these things were true for the Ministry of Agriculture.

As opposed to the previous examples, where land was not formally sanctioned for construction, people bought land the authorities designated for

7.3: Aerial image showing sanctioned agriculture reclamation (top right), in addition to borderline low-density second homes on large plots (bottom right), and an illegal higher-density neighborhood that is part of the Suleimaniya Golf development (top left) on the Cairo–Alexandria highway, later designated New Sphinx City. (Image dated February 2016, © 2018 Digital Globe/ ©2018 GOOGLE.)

urban use and applied for a building permit. But the permit they obtained did not give them the building they expected. Many who intend to build according to the rules end up not doing so, put off by outdated maps, unqualified engineers, and outrageous fees.[43] Others have become experts at squeezing out every last inch of real estate they can to build on. That is why many Egyptian cities have largely mismatched skylines where buildings on a single street are of varying heights, the precise number of illegal extra floors determined by how unscrupulous or politically connected the building owners are.

In one subdivision in Cairo, a group of developers built an extra floor or two more than they were supposed to, as well as building more than the permitted footprint, leaving barely any space between the buildings. They were banking on the reconciliation law being passed, and then simply paying the fines, but in February 2015, the local district moved to demolish the extra floors (figure 7.4). While some demolitions are final and the whole floor is cleared, others are done for show, as we see in

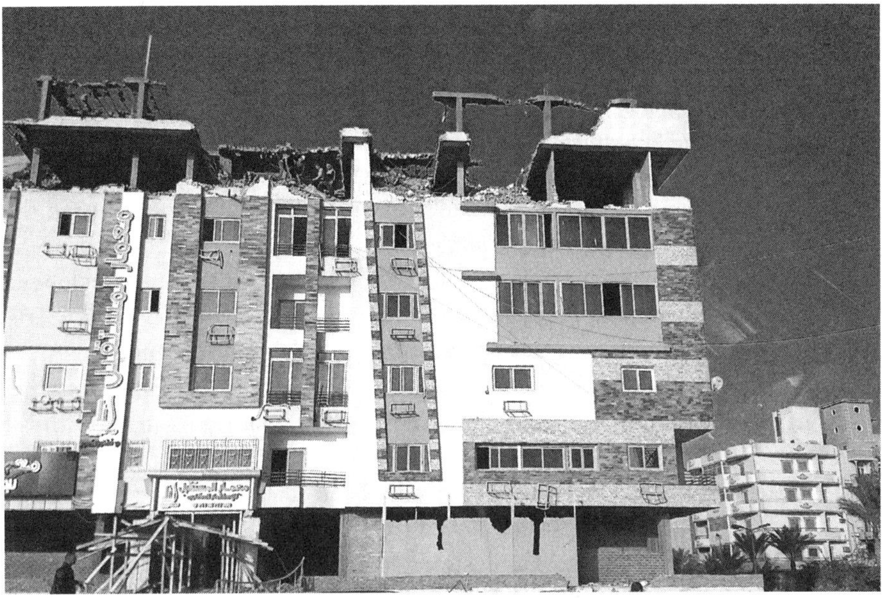

7.4: Demolition of two illegal floors in al-Hadaba al-Wusta, Muqattam, Cairo, February 2015. (Photograph by Yahia Shawkat.)

chapter 2. In these cases, developers have paid off the authorities, who need to record that the demolition actually happened.[44] Tens of thousands of demolition decrees lie in municipal drawers unimplemented, especially once buildings are occupied.[45]

*'Izba*s and Villages

In 1997, around 6 million fellahin living on land that was under rent control laws passed during the agrarian reform of the 1950s faced the threat of being made both landless and homeless.[46] Law 96/1992, passed five years prior and implemented in 1997, was part of a raft of government-induced 'free market policy' liberalizations in the agricultural sector that included abolishment of bartering, predefined pricing for products, and food production subsidies, as parliament supported the government in aligning "with the evolution of global economic policy."[47] The law came into deadly effect. Between 1997 and 2004, at least 344 fellahin were killed, 2,357 injured, and 3,330 arrested while resisting the handover of their land and homes.[48] Most of the fellahin could not afford the higher land rents, which increased thirtyfold overnight, and they were thus evicted from the land.[49] Although Article 4 of the land tenancy law stipulated that fellahin living in houses on rented land and who did not own another home could not be evicted until the government provided alternative housing within the same municipal area, one million new homes were certainly not provided by the time the law came into effect in 1997.

Most tenants were not just resisting the loss of their livelihoods, but also the loss of their homes. Amid the euphoria of agrarian reform in the 1950s, the situation of the fellahin's homes in the *'izba*s was not made clear. The land on which a majority of these homes was built either still belonged to the landowner as part of the land they retained, or became the property of the government agencies administering the land. After land rents were liberalized, many landowners sought force in evicting the fellahin from the *'izba* homes.[50] If that did not work, resistant fellahin were slapped with jail sentences on the basis of unpaid fines for squatting in the very homes the government had enshrined in law for their protection.[51] It was not just the old landowning families that moved to evict the fellahin, but government agencies that owned or administered land under the land reform laws as well, namely the Agrarian Reform Agency (ARA) and the Awqaf (Religious Endowments Authority).

Ultimately, Law 96/1992 created a new chapter in the destabilization of housing for millions of Egyptians, where an uncertain number were evicted and made homeless. Less than 2 percent of tenant families were given alternative housing, all in the remote new villages of *qura al-kharigin*.[52] Some, though, have continued to live in their *'izba* houses. In an *'izba* in Sharqiya, two-thirds of residents were able to negotiate affordable terms for buying their houses from the landowners, while the rest have continued to squat in their homes under an uneasy amnesty after attempts at forceful eviction by the landowners failed.[53] In 'Izbit Fuda in Daqahliya, over seventy of the ninety mud-brick houses were rebuilt in redbrick and concrete low-rises by the late 2000s, but only after the pasha died and they were made owners of a portion of the land they cultivated by one of his heirs.[54] An untold number of tenants living on *'izba*s under government agency ownership have been able to pay an annual property tax *('awayid)*, though on contracts affording little if any rights.[55]

But some government agencies have also acted to evict the fellahin. As urban development spread informally over greenfield, large portions of Awqaf-administered agricultural land became prime land for real estate development, making it lucrative to evict the farmers and develop or sell the land. The farmers of 'Izbit al-'Arab, for example, gained the right to own their land as an outcome of agrarian reform policies in the Arab socialist era of the 1950s, when large private landholdings were sequestered and much of it redistributed as smallholdings. This included land held under trust by the Awqaf.[56]

The ARA, formed in the 1950s, redistributed Khedive Isma'il's waqf in Alexandria to smallholders, registering most of the land with the Real Estate Tax Authority but not the Real Estate Registry, as was the norm.[57] Within a decade of the Awqaf's dissolution in 1952, it was re-established with Law 80/1971 stipulating that the ARA should reassign all land back to its jurisdiction. Two years later another legislative act, 42/1973, amended this provision, stipulating that only land that was not redistributed to smallholders would be reassigned back to the Awqaf. However, the Awqaf ignored the 1973 amendment and brought most of the Isma'il waqf back under its de facto jurisdiction in 1975 when it revoked the farmers' ARA rent-to-own contracts, replacing them with fixed-term rental contracts.[58] Today the Awqaf is both de jure and de facto landlord over four thousand hamlets,[59] or about 15 percent of Egypt's rural communities, where roughly 1.5 million families live, many without clear formal tenure.

In 'Izbit al-'Arab, farmers typically rent out an acre for LE2,000 annually, netting the Awqaf a mere LE600,000 (from the 300-acre Muthalath parcel it does not legally own, part of the Isma'il waqf). But in a dubious partnership between the Awqaf and the Alexandria governorate,[60] the governorate would receive a third of the Muthalath in exchange for reassigning the land as part of the city limits, evicting the residents, demolishing any buildings on the land, and servicing the new subdivisions with infrastructure. This would leave the Awqaf with a handsome LE6 billion profit.[61] It also inventoried all of its land as part of the recent asset management spree, and was able to boost state revenue by selling off assets worth LE1.2 billion in one auction alone.[62]

At the heart of the Awqaf's capitalization on its informally assigned assets, it seems to have relied primarily on a complacent or complicit ARA, which did not fully register the redistributed smallholdings in the 1960s, as well as exploiting the many layers of legislative amendments that govern land reform. But legal maneuverings were not enough to evict the Muthalath residents, and so illegal methods of eviction came next. Some farmers alleged that the Awqaf filled in a canal and diverted raw sewage to a number of land parcels, ruining the existing crops and any chance for new crops to grow.[63] They also accused the Awqaf of hiring thugs to live in shacks and prevent the farmers from reopening the canal it had filled in to starve their crops.[64] A cluster of families protested the sale of their land by the Awqaf to a number of housing cooperatives set up by employees of state agencies. This community mobilization against the evictions was met with a brutal response. In 2009, Hasan Shindy, a leading figure in the effort, was found murdered in the fields with a warning etched on his clothes.[65]

There is also a huge rent gap in Muthalath al-Montazah. Some residents who finally agreed to sell their land to the Awqaf did so for LE143 per square meter, while the Awqaf had sold similar plots at auction for LE3,000 per square meter.[66] Intriguingly, real estate developers operating in the area sell land for about LE10,000 per square meter, suggesting that some auctions by government agencies are rigged to be undervalued in favor of the private developers that buy the land from them.

There was no letting up of the Awqaf's attempts to pressure the residents to leave. In December 2014, they moved to demolish eleven houses, compelling the residents to protest and threaten that 1,200 of them would go on hunger strike if the Awqaf did not halt its demolitions.[67] It is not clear how much time they have before another demolition, as a special Committee to Inventory the Awqaf's Assets was established by the president in July 2016 to inventory and value the Awqaf's assets and take action regarding any land that has been encroached on.[68]

Ownership and Government Housing

While it is largely an open-and-shut case that units built on squatted land—entailing illegal land use or illegal construction—have informal tenure, that of legally built units is also informal, or at best semiformal. The epitome of formal tenure, whether ownership or rent, is registration of contracts at the Real Estate Registry and the Notary Public. A 1998 study found that the ownership of about 90 percent of units in Egypt were unregistered and the situation of most was such that they could never be registered.[69]

The study stated that as a consequence of decades of informality, formal legal tenure was not sought mostly because of complex and protracted steps to register property, which could include seventy-seven bureaucratic procedures and take from six to fourteen years to complete. Costs of registration are also high. Although the government has brought down the cost of registration from 2 percent of the cost of a property to a flat fee that should range from LE500 to LE2,000, depending on the size of the property, the Real Estate Registration offices have used loopholes to boost the fee in relation to the number of co-owners.[70] In 2013, they started to collect unpaid capital gains tax of 2 percent from the new owners, which should have been paid by the sellers, discouraging many from registering. These costs do not include lawyers' fees, other bureaucratic procedures needed to complete the paperwork, and of course bribes.

Ultimately, while full registration at the Real Estate Registration office provides the most secure contract, most Egyptians tend to use three other forms of legal, though not always fraud-proof, avenues to formally transfer title. One can endorse the contract in court through contract signature confirmation *(sihhat tawqi')*, register a petition for the execution of a contract *(da'wat sihha wa nafaz)* if the seller refuses to endorse the contract after sale, or register the sale at the Notary Public via power of attorney *(tawqil)* that transfers rights of use and sale to the buyer.[71] In Egypt, even preliminary and unregistered sale contracts are recognized by law,[72] where in the event of a dispute, the burden of proof lies with the party that is not in physical possession of the property.

Decaying historic city cores, old city centers, and downtowns have seen a large proportion of residents lose the continuity of title. Legal battles ensue, with claimants hanging signs and banners on doorways, over balconies, or painting on walls, stating that the property is under their sole ownership (figure 7.5). One of the main reasons for this is the complex and corrupt dissolution of property held under religious trust *(waqf)*. A government agency called the Awqaf administers two types of property called *waqfs*—*waqf khayri* (charitable trust), which is property donated permanently as *waqf*, and *waqf ahli*, which is property put under temporary administration by the Awqaf for a set number of years, but that it does not own, during which its returns would fund secular activities such as schooling for a member of the donor family. In 1952, around eleven thousand *awqaf ahli* were disbanded with the dissolution of the Awqaf by the new socialist government and were supposed to be returned to their owners.[73] This process was mired by government corruption and complicated by Islamic inheritance laws, along with the fact that most of the urban *waqfs* had many, usually poorer, tenants who would face eviction by the multiple owners.[74]

Indeed, many of the houses in al-Gumruk neighborhood in Alexandria are without clear tenure. One dilapidated house on Gama'i alley, off the wide al-Nasr Avenue, is home to a shoemaker and his family.[75] They claim it was a *tikiya*, a traditional Muslim private hostel sponsored by rich families that would host Sufi pilgrims to a nearby shrine, as well as the homeless.

7.5: Top banner proclaims ownership of entire building by Mona Elias Nashed as per a registered contract and a court ruling. Bottom banner proclaims partial ownership of someone else according to a preliminary contract. Port Said, January 2016. (Photograph by Yahia Shawkat.)

When I asked why they had not sold out to local developers shoehorning multistory blocks in the narrow-alleyed district,[76] they said the blessings *(baraka)* of Sidi ʻAbd al-Latif, whose shrine is adjacent to the *tikiya*, were priceless. However, the Gamaʻi house originally belonged to the namesake family and has been at the center of legal battles between the descendants and the Awqaf for years.[77]

In 2008, only 15.2 percent of New Rent (market rent) contracts were registered or endorsed.[78] This was out of 94 percent that had written contracts in the first place (for more on rent see chapter 3). An untold number of those with contracts have—to their knowledge or unbeknown to them—inadequate or illegal contracts that may waive their tenure rights.

So-called hosting *(istidafa)* contracts provide no legal coverage and do not stipulate any exchange of money between the parties. They are used widely in thousands of social housing apartments as a loophole because owners are not allowed to rent them out, as legislation restricts the rent or sale of subsidized government housing by beneficiaries.[79] Paying tenants can be evicted at any time, and may end up losing a lot of money, as in practice the value of the entire duration is paid up front.

Illegal evictions are known to happen, as are illegal occupations where tenants refuse to pay or continue to occupy a unit after the end of the contract. One case of mass eviction of private tenants on the part of individuals was recorded in February 2011, when hundreds, if not thousands, of tenants in the Nahda housing estate northeast of Cairo were evicted by their private landlords during the police vacuum in the wake of the January 2011 revolution, fearing that local government would notice they had been renting out their apartments illegally.[80]

As with ownership, there are formal long-term rent contracts that have eroded to informality over time. Old public housing, originally rented out in the 1950s and 1960s, was offered for sale to their tenants in Egypt's own right-to-buy scheme in the late 1970s. But utterly confusing legal wording obscured exactly which public housing would be sold to their tenants. Article 1 of Prime Ministerial Decree 110/1978 specified that units "rented out for below the official rent, at LE1 per room for economic housing, and LE1.5 per room [bedrooms and hall] for middle housing" could be sold. Unsurprisingly, the more than 140,000 housing units the governorates had built over the course of a quarter of a century had differing rental values,[81] according to the year they were rented, their location, and the amount of rent reduction stipulated by the various pieces of rent control legislation passed over the years.

Tenants would take governors to court, spending the next decade or two battling over what their exact rent was, and whether or not they could buy the units they rented. Some courts ruled that the decree meant that rental values should not be lower than the stated value, while others ruled that anything higher did not qualify to be owned.[82] In the end, no one knows how many old units were sold to their tenants, how many remained public property, and how many lingered in legal limbo for near perpetuity. In this limbo, a considerable number of tenants stopped paying rent, sublet the apartments, died and the heirs continued living in the units without formalizing their situation, or sold them using semiformal contracts.

In 2015, municipal authorities in Port Said started tallying the residents of old public housing as part of a project to demolish the buildings on the pretext they were unsalvageable, in order to build new, profitable blocks.[83] The tallies were used to decide who had formal tenure and would be evicted and rehoused in new public housing, and who would be evicted without any compensation. A reading of the official tally forms shows that many residents who did not have clear rights (for example, they were inheritors, informal buyers, or shack dwellers on the roofs of the block) were allowed to be rehoused under temporary agreements as long as their informal situation was reconciled with the authorities.[84] The forms did not detail the conditions of reconciliation.

There is also quasi-government housing where tenure is even more complex. The workers' colonies *(musta'marat)* were built by mostly private business in the 1940s, as we see in chapter 5. In the 1960s, large businesses were nationalized, and their assets thus became government property.

Musta'marat al-Mahalla was one such colony. It is a unique place with pitched roof, single-story houses dating to the 1940s, along with a number of 1970s five-story apartment blocks scattered between them. The low-density buildings interspersed with gardens and tree-lined streets are a stark contrast to the crowded city just beyond its walls. The original settlement was an early public–private partnership between the government, which supplied the land, and the Mahalla Spinning and Weaving Company (MSWC), which financed the construction.[85] It would act as emergency shelter to house communities displaced as a result of the Second World War, but then be used by the company after the war ended. The apartment blocks were built in 1977 as part of an expansion plan, this time using the company's housing fund established in the 1960s as part of an employee profit share scheme, whereby 5 percent would be earmarked for housing.[86] Today it is an impossible task to prove who owns the units.

Ever since Law 203/1991 came on the back of structural adjustment policies pushed through by the IMF and World Bank, the government has been trying to privatize state-owned companies, sometimes at bargain rates. While the law restructured publicly held companies for privatization, the first attempt to privatize MSWC in 2004 failed due to workers' protest.[87] A decline in production and a rise in debt, brought on by a lack of investment in the company, in addition to the aforementioned scramble to sell state-owned assets, have recently prompted the Holding Company for Cotton Spinning and Weaving (HCCSW), which owns MSWC, to boost revenue through international restructuring consultants and inventorying its assets.[88] Privatizing MSWC with hundreds of people living on its assets was not an ideal situation to say the least, which may explain why it has demolished the homes it has been able to vacate, as opposed to reassigning them to new employees. But if MSWC does not own the land, how would it profit? In 2009, it emerged in the press that MSWC and the Gharbiya governorate had a planned joint development to build a 5,448-unit commercial housing project in place of the *musta'mara*,[89] a scheme that could be valued at LE1.6 billion.

To grease the rails for the evictions of the *musta'mara* residents, MSWC exploited complacent district courts, complex tenure arrangements with the Gharbiya governorate, and missing information tying the workers' housing fund to the apartments. It has also refused to repair old water piping that polluted the drinking water as a further measure to evict the residents, forcing them to rely on a well built by a charity.[90]

Through local pressure and the help of a rights organization, in 2014 al-Mahalla Pensioners' Union was able to get the MSWC to agree to stop filing new eviction orders until negotiations with the union on how workers were going to be compensated were completed. Additionally, Article 78 of the 2014 Constitution guarantees the right to adequate housing, which extends to the provision of alternative housing in cases of eviction. Despite all this, the courts did not accept the appeals filed against the old eviction orders, or against the ground rents.[91] As MSWC is one of almost two hundred public sector companies that are up for privatization, many of which own or administer employee housing, the future does not look promising for their residents.

A Manufactured Informality

Informality of homes in Egypt is not going away any time soon, given that both complex factors and strong vested interests in the status quo are at play. The first factor concerns how the official structure that is supposed to govern the formality of homes, as well as regulate land and unit use, is corrupt, inept, and unrepresentative of the communities it is meant to serve. Local government in Egypt is officially called local administration, as it is made up of appointed positions, the governor, city and district heads, as well as a Local Executive Council.[92] The elected Local Popular Councils (LPCs), which served mostly as a consultative body with almost no powers over the appointed executives, were dissolved in 2011, and have yet to be reelected eight years on.

The second factor is a socially inequitable housing policy that has moved to deregulate the property market, resulting in huge inflation of land and house prices that far outstrip any rise in income. Half of the population cannot afford to buy or rent the average home,[93] and those who have the means to self-build cannot easily find suitable and affordable formal serviced land.[94] The government's yo-yoing policy toward informal urbanization looks set to continue, with contradictory messages of allowing formal infrastructure connections, mooting a formalization law for years, and moving to demolish swaths of informal construction.

The third factor is the government's asset management hunt since 2015, as it looks to plug its budget deficit by selling off property it owns or claims that it does. With an executive that has historically played a strong role in legislation,[95] and a legislature that has shown little resistance, new precedents in exploiting and privatizing land to which the government has laid claim is a certainty.

This diabolical mix of factors makes it impossible to foresee steps to recognize the informal tenure of millions of Egyptians with legally vague tenure, and with it mitigate the housing crisis. In fact, there is all the incentive to perpetuate, expand, and exploit the informal status quo.

EPILOGUE: BACK TO HOMES

One might be forgiven for seeing the state of housing in Egypt today as a postapocalyptic scene, except that the apocalypse is not over, and the housing crisis is in full swing. While scores of homeless people do not fill the streets, this is because Egypt criminalized vagrancy decades ago, instead breeding an invisible homeless population, where millions live in less than adequate housing as the average properly built home is unaffordable to over half of Egyptians—whether to buy or rent.[1] There are 1.3 million households living in overcrowded conditions, while 3.2 percent of Egyptians live in fear of their homes collapsing.[2] Until we see what the new reconciliation law—passed in early 2019—will do in terms of legalizing informally built housing, at least 70 percent of families do not have secure tenure.[3] Untold thousands, as we saw in chapter 7, are at immediate risk of eviction, through unfair legal practice, as well as extralegal and at times violent tactics, while tens of thousands more face expulsion if rent control is abolished. While the government pours billions of Egyptian pounds into so-called social housing, it excludes the poor and vulnerable who need it most. Meanwhile, official policy is actively commodifying housing, as the government is also the largest for-profit housing developer in Egypt. International financial agencies are also to blame for their part in the housing crisis, through financing policies that have for the most part served the interests of a global financial market, instead of putting the poor first, as some of them have claimed.

Given this bleak state of affairs, as well as the lack of any political will to drastically change the situation, it would be "hopelessly utopian"—as David Madden and Peter Marcuse conclude in their investigation into the state of housing in the United States[4]—to imagine housing for everyone in

Egypt. But they also leave a window open to dream, asking if it is "plausible to imagine universal and unconditional housing, in sociable and environmentally sustainable communities, as a matter of right rather than a commodified privilege?"

Indeed, the theoretical framework for a right to housing already exists in Egypt. Article 78 of the Constitution enshrines such a right, stipulating that the state draw up a national housing plan. The plan has actually been written, by the capable hands of urban development specialists David Sims and Hazem Abdelfattah, though it is still under wraps. Maybe the Egypt Housing Strategy, as it is called, has proved too progressive for the government, pragmatically increasing its role as regulator and decreasing its role as provider. Some of the strategy's components are not progressive enough, as they do not directly tackle the commodification of housing. Egypt Vision 2030, the national sustainable development plan, is going full steam ahead. Its Urban Development Pillar mentions a 'gap' between supply and demand[5] that needs to be addressed. The government has also promised to work toward the United Nations Sustainable Development Goal 11.1 that calls for ensuring access for all to adequate, safe, and affordable housing by 2030. The UN Special Rapporteur on Adequate Housing even had some positive things to say about the housing situation in Egypt after a rare visit in late 2018, welcoming the constitutional right to housing and being impressed by the number of social housing units being built.[6] The rapporteur did, however, stress the importance of a consultative process for the housing plan that is informed by human rights principles.

While it seems lucrative for the government to have the status quo remain as it is, an alternative reality is to have housing go back to being about homes that generate revenue for the government, albeit in a different way, while also playing a social role.

Decommodify Housing

The effect of any policies or projects to help make housing more affordable would be washed away as soon as they are enacted if housing continues to be a lucrative commodity. Short of wishing for the real estate bubble to burst and house prices to tumble, the exaggerated effects of the boom-and-bust real estate and construction economy are toxic for all involved. The first people laid off in a recession are the foundation of the construction industry itself: the workers, who lead a precarious existence on the meager wages they are paid. Their sheer numbers can send unemployment and poverty soaring, wiping portions of growth from the economy, not to mention increasing personal hardship. Next come workers in all the supporting industries, from building materials to finishes, after which the businesses themselves start to fold, and the economy shrinks some more.

The risky business of investing means that all producers in the chain hedge against the risks involved by hiking up their profit margins to cover the lean years. This of course leads to higher prices and lack of compensation for workers when they are laid off. In especially bad years, banks foreclose on bankrupt construction and real estate companies, and then bemoan the busted market and the depressed value of the assets they have just acquired.[7]

After the storm passes, the costs and time needed to rebuild businesses and put the expertise back together are phenomenal. In a market that caters to a wide economic spectrum of buyers, growth may be smaller, but it is sustained, risks are reduced, and everyone has the potential to benefit.

There are many mechanisms for decommodification. The government needs to lead by example, and the first thing it should do is put a moratorium on all policies that commodify and financialize housing, namely the drive to internationalize the housing market through the policy of exporting real estate. Restructuring of the capital gains tax on real estate sales to penalize speculators (quick sales) and incentivize owner-occupiers is a quick and sure way to cool down the market, with the added benefit of raking in some money for the government, and perhaps substitute revenue it loses once it divests from real estate. The real estate tax also needs to be restructured so that it is more progressive, with a low load on modest owner-occupiers, and a heavy load on large properties, vacation homes, and multiple-property owners. It should also be earmarked for local services—similar to council taxes in the United Kingdom—so that people benefit from it and are less likely to view it as just another tax, and resist paying it. Ultimately, the over-investment in real estate needs to be redirected, and what better way than encouraging and incentivizing investment in industry?

Rent Reform

As rent control unravels—whether under its own cycle of decay, as a result of articles in the legislation being struck down as unconstitutional, or the government and parliament responding to calls for decontrol—the fallout of almost 1.5 million households being made homeless in a short span of time is, to put it mildly, significant. It is not clear where the 100,000 families who left rent-controlled homes every year between 2006 and 2017 have gone. In the liberalized rental market, regulated by a seventy-year-old law, there is little chance that they or current New Rent tenants can find affordable rents.

Given that millions of homes already exist and are standing vacant, it seems logical to tackle this dimension first. Priority should be given to penning a new, balanced rental law that outlaws discriminatory practices and upholds the rights of both landlords and tenants in a pragmatic manner. As we have seen, excessive control scares away potential landlords and breeds circumvention when not enforced. More progressive ways of enforcing fair rentals must thus be sought. Official support is needed for dispute resolution as a first instance, without recourse to courts, as the court system is currently overwhelmed. Building on the existing culture of customary law (*'urf*), civil society organizations could be encouraged to provide dispute resolution services, awareness on landlord and tenant rights and obligations, and help with drafting fair contracts. Charities can be better managed to step in and fund tenants in arrears or contribute to funding deposits. A renewed trust between parties would go a long way to restoring this fundamental avenue to a home.

Social Housing Reform

Another delinquent in need of some discipline is the government housing regime. Let us assume there is the will for change. The first step would be to break off all real estate and housing production from the Ministry of Housing and transfer it to the Ministry of Investment, or the newly founded sovereign wealth fund as a public investment interest that generates revenue for the Social Housing Fund. The massive scale of government housing production can also go a long way to regulating market prices and helping cool them down. This would leave the Housing Ministry with the role of regulator for both private and public business, focusing on the social interest with much less of a conflict of interest.

With a direct line of credit, and free from the politics of real estate, social housing might then become a fully fledged program that tackles all forms of deprivation from adequate housing, rather than just building flawed housing. The first instance of support would be rent vouchers made out to affordability-burdened households that cannot afford market rents. In the event rents are still too high, the government could initiate a program to manage the rental of private property under long-term rents, in exchange for peace of mind for landlords that rents would be paid and they would be able to recover their property from noncomplying tenants. Support should also be made to owners of homes in need of repair or utilities, in the form of grants or low-interest loans. A third component would be the promotion of secure tenure, without exclusively focusing on ownership titles, which have their limitations,[8] by offering other options through measures such as communal or cooperative ownership, usufruct/lease, and basic recognition/amnesty from demolition, and with it, the risk of eviction.

Utilizing Vacant Units

Before any talk of building new homes, something should be done about those millions already standing empty. The aforementioned suggestions for reform of real estate and of rent would help bring some of those homes into use. But these vacant homes should be studied in more detail. For one thing, some might not be of the appropriate size or require investments to modify or complete. Others are abandoned because of structural issues and need to be rebuilt or extensively repaired. Here the Social Housing Fund might help with providing easy credit and expertise. But there are also thousands of homes that have more complex legal issues, from inheritance and contestation to informality and fraud, which special judicial commissions—and possibly some legal reform—might untangle. There are of course wholly inadequate homes that no one wants, whether those built in ultradense neighborhoods, or at the other end of the scale, government-built housing in the middle of nowhere. These could be repurposed as movie sets, or stand as testimonies to what "should not be done."

Encouraging the Social Production of Habitat

With over two-fifths of urban dwellers and almost all rural dwellers living in homes they have built, and no sign of the practice fading, self-building should be officially encouraged and supported to evolve away from agricultural greenfield and onto brownfield or desert land. Decentralizing urban planning and focusing on much smaller and more relevant new communities could provide formal serviced land where it is needed at profitable rates to the government agencies involved. Restructuring housing cooperative finance to target community-based home building, rather than large anonymous corporation-like cooperatives, would go a long way in providing financial support where it is needed.

Back to Homes

Overall, the key issue is to denormalize the housing crisis, which exists for a reason, and therefore can be addressed. Millions of people have proven their resilience in coping with the crisis. Communities have banded together to help one another, whether to build on squatted land, tap into utilities, or pay for late rent. These everyday heroics should not be forgotten, and in fact should be studied and supported. While waiting for government bureaucracy to catch up, much can be done by social entrepreneurs, philanthropists, activists, and even international agencies to remedy some of the symptoms of the crisis. The conversation has started, and to paraphrase Madden and Marcuse,[9] housing should start to be less about real estate and more about homes.

NOTES

Chapter 1

1 Thanks to Salma Khamis for helping compile a list of films on housing issues.
2 Raafat, "The Zamalek Legend 1860–1940."
3 Riad, "Tahdid al-manatiq al-sina'iya wa insha' masakin al-'ummal."
4 Nasser, "Khitab al-ra'is Gamal 'Abd al-Nasser fi al-mu'tamar al-sha'bi bi-midan al-Jumhuriya bi-l-Qahira ma' al-ra'is Sukarno bi munasabat al-'id al-thalith li-thawrat Yulyu." Nasser also used the terms "homes problem," and "housing problem," during the same speech in a sign that official discourse was still undecided. The references used in laws were consistent. Nasser's efforts in public housing are discussed in chapter 5.
5 Rent Reduction Law 55/1958, Explanatory Note; Law 29/1966, Explanatory Note. Parliament has been very much an extension of government in Egypt since the 1950s, and so ministers can be considered lawmakers. See for example Waterbury, *The Egypt of Nasser and Sadat: The Political Economy of Two Regimes*, 365. One indication of this is the absence of parliamentary reports accompanying laws passed through the 1950s and 1960s. While parliament played a bigger role from the 1970s onward, most laws were prepared by the government and discussed in parliament with little changes made.
6 See for example, Gorman, *Historians, State and Politics in Twentieth Century Egypt: Contesting the Nation*.
7 Abu-Lughod, *Cairo: 1001 Years of the City Victorious*, 136.
8 Shakur, Mehanna, and Hopkins, "War and Forced Migration in Egypt."
9 Minister of Interior Decree, 819/1969.
10 *Muhaggarin* stayed in apartments built for employees of the Ideal company in Hadayek al-Qubba and in the military Huckstep Camp (known colloquially as Haykstep). See Shakur, Mehanna, and Hopkins, "War and Forced Migration in Egypt." See also Minister of War Decree 264/1969.
11 Shakur, Mehanna, and Hopkins.

12 Nasser, "Khitab al-ra'is Gamal 'Abd al-Nasser amam al-hay'a al-barlamaniya li-l-ittihad al-ishtiraki 16/5/1965."

13 Hanna, "Real Estate Rights in Urban Egypt: The Changing Sociopolitical Winds."

14 Building permit costs were raised tenfold by Building Law 656/1954.

15 Building and Demolition Law 344/1956.

16 Illegal Subdivision Amnesty Law 29/1966, Explanatory Note.

17 Informal Subdivision Amnesty Law 135/1981, Joint Parliamentary Committee Report.

18 Sadat, "Message by President Anwar El Sadat to the Habitat Conference in the City of Vancouver, June 6th, 1976."

19 Sadat, "Kalimat al-ra'is Muhammad Anwar al-Sadat ila al-sha'b fi munasabat irsa' hajar asas madinat 10 Ramadan fi 29 Mayu 1977."

20 Sadat, "Kalimat al-ra'is Muhammad Anwar al-Sadat fi al-'id al-thani li-l-thawra al-khadra' fi 29 yanayir 1981."

21 Economic Housing Fund Law 107/1976, Explanatory Note.

22 Economic Housing Fund Law 107/1976, Joint Parliamentary Committee Report.

23 Housing Law 49/1977, Explanatory Note and Joint Parliamentary Committee Report.

24 Prime Ministerial Decree 197/1979.

25 New Urban Communities Law 59/1979, Joint Parliamentary Committee Report.

26 Some critics doubt these extremely high figures. They can be partly explained by a relaxation of the building code, which allowed permits for construction that would not have been accepted previously, thus soaking in a large portion of the already existing capacity for informal construction, and not necessarily reflecting a new appetite for construction. See the section on methodology.

27 Bayat and Denis, "Who Is Afraid of Ashwaiyyat?"

28 While the 1976 census enumerated what it termed as 'owned' *(milk)*, the 1986 census differentiated between 'owned' *(milk)* and 'bought' *(tamlik)*. I have projected back from the three successive censuses the proportion of 'bought,' which was barely evident in urban households. 'Owned' also includes properties gained through inheritance or buying an entire building, though it can be assumed that these make up a much smaller incidence than building. For definitions of the census terms see CAPMAS, "al-Ti'dad al-'am 1986 al-mujallad al-awwal—al-juz' al-thani: khasa'is al-sukkan wa-l-zuruf al-sakaniya."

29 We can see how the census enumerates substandard/squatted housing in a table correlating home type with tenure. 'Rooms within units' (subdivided homes) and 'standalone room or more' show up in each of the tenure

categories except 'bought.' 'Shack and tent' do not show up as 'furnished rent' or 'bought,' and neither do 'courtyard and tomb,' as well as being the only substandard housing not showing up as 'owned.' See CAPMAS, 62.

30 Mubarak, "Khitab al-ra'is Muhammad Hosni Mubarak fi al-ijtima' al-mushtarak li-majlisay al-sha'b wa-l-shura."

31 Unknown, "Mubarak yatlub hallan jazriyan wa 'ajilan li-mushkilat al-iskan."

32 Mubarak, "Nus kalimat al-ra'is Muhammad Hosni Mubarak fi iftitah mu'tamar Misr sanat 2000."

33 Unknown, "Hal mushkilat al-iskan yabda' hadha al-'am."

34 Dawoud, "al-Kafrawi: hal mushkilat al-iskan ba'd 3 sanawat."

35 Mitchell, "No Factories, No Problems."

36 Fawzy, "Wazir al-iskan fi hadith sakhin."

37 New Rent Law 4/1996, Joint Parliamentary Committee Report.

38 *al-Ahram*, "Mubarak haris 'ala tawfir al-khadamat li-l-muwatinin wa hal mushkilat iskan mahdudi al-dakhl."

39 Mubarak, "Khitab al-ra'is Muhammad Hosni Mubarak fi iftitah al-dawra al-barlamaniya al-jadida."

40 Mubarak, "Kalimat al-ra'is Muhammad Hosni Mubarak fi al-liqa' al-sha'bi bi-khitam al-hamla al-intikhabiya."

41 *Sada al-balad*, "*Sada al-balad* yanfarid bi-nashr tafasil mashru' al-thalath alaf wihda sakaniya al-khassa bi-mashru' al-quwwat al-musallaha bi-Dahshur."

42 Ministry of Housing and Urban Communities, "al-Wathiqa al-marji'iya li-istratijiyat wa siyasat al-iskan fi Misr 2012–2027 (unpublished report)," 11.

43 *al-Ahram*, "al-Sisi yutliq mubadarat al-milyun wihda sakaniya li-l-shabab."

44 *al-Ahram*, "Wazir al-iskan fi nadwat *al-Ahram*: infirag azmat al-iskan khilal 4 sanawat." It is noteworthy that while the article's title quoted the minister as saying 'housing crisis,' in the text, both the interviewer and the minister exclusively use the term 'housing problem.'

45 Shawkat, "Property Market Deregulation and Informal Tenure in Egypt."

46 The data gathered for this graph is far from perfect, with Turkey and European countries counting building permits, the United States counting completed units, while data for China was inferred from square meterage under construction (divided by an implied average of 100 meters for one unit), and India from news sources.

47 For some unfortunate reason, the 2017 census stopped differentiating between owned *(milk)* and bought *(tamlik)*, and so figures have been forecasted from the three previous censuses.

48 For 1960/61–1975, see Joint Housing Team, "Immediate Action Proposals for Housing in Egypt," 3. For 1976–1983/84, see Hanna, *Le logement en Égypte*, Tableau I. For 1984/85–1995/96 see World Bank, "Egypt—Analysis of Housing Supply Mechanisms," 86.

49 The 1973 Statistical Yearbook quotes 32,000 homes built by the public sector for LE22 million, in addition to 1,300 homes built by cooperatives using LE2.5 million in government loans. See CAPMAS, "al-Kitab al-ihsa'i al-sanawi li-jumhuriyat Misr al-'arabiya 1952–1973," 144.

50 CAPMAS, "al-Kitab al-ihsa'i al-sanawi li-jumhuriyat Misr al-'arabiya 1952–1980," 149.

51 For example, one famous study on informality in Egypt quotes 800,000 public housing units built between 1952 and 1978, rather than 248,552, if the 1973 yearbook quote was used in addition to the later sources. See de Soto, "Dead Capital and the Poor in Egypt," 9.

52 Barrada, Wheaton, and Annez, "Public Policy and the Economics of Housing. Appendix A: Public Policy and the 'Shortage' of Housing in Egypt."

53 Joint Housing Team, "Immediate Action Proposals for Housing in Egypt," 2.

54 CAPMAS, "al-Kitab al-ihsa'i al-sanawi li-jumhuriyat Misr al-'arabiya 1952–1973," 148.

55 CAPMAS, "al-Ti'tad al-'am li-l-sukkan wa-l-iskan wa-l-munsha'at 'am 1996: al-nata'ij al-niha'iya li-ti'dad al-mabani li-ijmali al-jumhuriya," 209; CAPMAS, "al-Ti'tad al-'am li-l-sukkan wa-l-iskan wa-l-munsha'at 2006: al-nata'ij al-niha'iya li-ti'dad al-mabani 2006 li-ijmali al-jumhuriya," 136; CAPMAS, "al-Nata'ij al-niha'iya li-l-ti'dad al-'am li-l-sukkan wa-l-iskan wa-l-munsha'at li-'am 2017: al-sukkan wa-l-zuruf al-sakaniya," 255.

56 Hanna, *al-Iskan wa-l-masyada: al-mushkila wa-l-hal*, 246–47.

57 The housing critic and former head of the parliamentary housing committee doubted high figures for formal private sector housing production in the 1976–1986 period. See Hanna, *Le logement en Égypte*.

Chapter 2

1 Dorman, "The Politics of Neglect: The Egyptian State in Cairo, 1974–98," 45–46.

2 On a global level, there is the seminal Turner, *Housing by People: Towards Autonomy in Building Environments*. For Egypt, there are many works that provide vignettes and case studies, though focusing on informal self-build. See for example, Kadi, *L'urbanisation Spontanée Au Caire*.; Soliman, *A Possible Way Out: Formalizing Housing Informality in Egyptian Cities*.; Kipper and Fischer, *Cairo's Informal Areas between Urban Challenges and Hidden Potentials*; Sims, *Understanding Cairo: The Logic of a City Out of Control*, chapter 4

3 CAPMAS, "Annual Bulletin of Labour Force 2017," 29.

4 For those in construction in Cairo and the big cities, it is impossible to get any work done in the two weeks after Eid (formally a three-day holiday), as workers head back to their villages to build for themselves or others.

5 Interview, G.A., Sheikh 'Awwad village, South Sinai, April 17, 2012.

6 Cement and some other materials cannot be stored for long, but one owner-builder was able to buy the steel rebars she needed, one of the costliest single purchases after land, whenever she saved enough money, because prices were always rising. Interview, O.R., a resident of Helwan, Cairo, January 6, 2018. This is also echoed in el-Jesri, "The Other Side of the Tracks: Ezbet Arab Abu Regeila."

7 Based on a multiyear study of three informally self-built areas in Greater Cairo. World Bank, "Egypt—Analysis of Housing Supply Mechanisms," 61. It is worth noting that this report benefited from "significant inputs" from Mustafa Madbuli, then director of the technical office of the Ministry of Housing's think tank, the General Organization for Physical Planning, and the section on informal construction is based on a study he co-prepared. World Bank, v. At the time of writing, Madbuli is Egypt's prime minister and minister of housing, utilities, and urban communities.

8 The roof including two rooms cost LE60,000 in 2006, while another LE60,000 was spent extending it to a finished three-bedroom apartment. That same year, a formal finished apartment in the same building was selling for LE180,000. Interview, A.S., a resident of Gisr al-Suez, Cairo, January 5, 2018.

9 World Bank, "Egypt—Analysis of Housing Supply Mechanisms," 59.

10 In the Maspero Triangle in Cairo, which was recently demolished by the government, over three-quarters of residents worked in the neighborhood. Madd, "Maspero Parallel Participatory Project," 132.

11 Tipple, "Transforming Government-Built Housing: Lessons from Developing Countries."

12 This is evident in many works cited in this chapter, but for a succinct example see Shehayeb, "Advantages of Living in Informal Areas."

13 For a thorough and sober insight into one self-built community that spanned fifteen years, see Deboulet, "The Dictatorship of the Straight Line and the Myth of Social Disorder: Revisiting Informality in Cairo."

14 Bavelaar, "Waqi' al-bahth 'an maskan mula'im."

15 Interview, O.A., Manshiyat Nasir, Cairo, September 27, 2012.

16 These could range from lawyers, local councilors, and MPs, to contractors with well-practiced maneuvers, such as building over the weekend or at night. See Sims, *Understanding Cairo: The Logic of a City Out of Control*, 126. In some cases, there may be organized crime families. See Tawakol, "Speculative Informal Housing Provision and Its Sociospatial Impacts on Greater Cairo Areas: A Case Study on 'El-Matareya,'" 70.

17 Bribes may add 20 to 30 percent to construction costs. World Bank, "Egypt—Analysis of Housing Supply Mechanisms," 61.

18 Deboulet, "The Dictatorship of the Straight Line and the Myth of Social Disorder: Revisiting Informality in Cairo."

19 Ibrahim, "Whose Customs? The Role of Customary Reconciliation in Sectarian Disputes and State Responsibility," 49–50 and Annex.

20 Egypt recently ranked last in the region in a rule of law index, ranking 110 out of 113 countries worldwide. World Justice Project, "Rule of Law Index 2017–2018: Egypt." Housing informality is further explored in chapter 7.

21 "Id wahda li-l-qada' 'ala al-balatgiya fi Ibni Baytak." This was especially so in Sixth of October City where forty thousand plots (almost half the entire project) were laid out.

22 *al-Ahram*, "Ra'is jihaz madinat Sitta Uktubar al-jadida: al-intiha' min 'adad kabir min mashru'at al-marafiq bi-mantiqat Ibni Baytak."

23 Egypt News, "Kalimat ra'is al-Sisi fi mu'tamar Misr al-tanmiya al-mustidama," from time code 11:05.

24 Al-Aees, "Bedouin Protection Money Raises Average Cost of Real Estate Projects by 15-20%."

25 These figures refer to the year 1891. Selim, *Unfinished Places*, 80. This is also an excellent historical analysis of urban planning in Cairo.

26 The Arab Quarter in Port Said housed mostly Egyptian menial workers and laborers, who according to the 1882 census, numbered 10,963 people. It was considered a slum until a disastrous fire led to major replanning in 1884, entailing the sale of micro plots to residents to rebuild their homes according to rules set by the Common Domain. See Piaton, "Architecture Patronale Dans l'Isthme de Suez (1859–1956)."

27 Public Works Order 549/1889, Article 5.

28 Public Works Order 549/1889, Articles 9, 14, and 15.

29 Law 22/1909, Article 8.

30 Mitchell, *Rule of Experts: Egypt, Techno-Politics, Modernity*, 188.

31 For example, Laws 69/1933 and 118/1950 regulating the *'izba*s, Law 51/1940 regulating buildings, and Law 52/1940 regulating subdivisions.

32 Hammad, *Industrial Sexuality: Gender, Urbanization, and Social Transformation in Egypt*, 114–17.

33 Volait, "Town Planning Schemes for Cairo Conceived by Egyptian Planners in the 'Liberal Experiment' Period."

34 Volait, "Town Planning Schemes for Cairo Conceived by Egyptian Planners in the 'Liberal Experiment' Period."

35 Farag, "Mantiqat Qanat al-Suways."

36 'Abd al-Gawwad, "Mushkilat al-masakin fi Misr wa 'ilajiha."

37 From 1940 to March 9, 1955. Law 259/1956, Article 1. The date of amnesty would later be extended to June 20, 1956 according to Law 32/1958.

38 Law 259/1956, Explanatory Note.

39 Law 29/1966, and Minister of Housing Decrees 826/1967 and 47/1968.

40 Kadi, *L'urbanisation Spontanée Au Caire*, 266.

41 Presidential Decree 549/1976.

42 Law 147/1957.
43 Law 135/1981, Explanatory Note.
44 Building Regulation Law 106/1976, Explanatory Note.
45 Joint Housing and Community Upgrading Team, "Housing and Community Upgrading for Low-Income Egyptians," 2.
46 Law 107/1976, Article 22.
47 Aulas, "Sadat's Egypt: A Balance Sheet."
48 The Housing and Community Upgrading for Low-Income Egyptians Project was described as one of the largest projects sponsored by USAID as part of American support to Egypt after the peace treaty with Israel. It included both in situ upgrading and new housing components. See Taher, "Foreign Aid and Power Relations: The Government of Egypt, USAID and Housing in Helwan," 180–81. It came to be known colloquially as *al-mashru' al-amriki* (the American project). For more on the project, see Joint Housing and Community Upgrading Team, "Housing and Community Upgrading for Low-Income Egyptians."
49 Taher, "Foreign Aid and Power Relations: The Government of Egypt, USAID and Housing in Helwan," 179.
50 Aga Khan Award for Architecture, "Ismaïliyya Development Projects," 177.
51 Aga Khan Award for Architecture, 179.
52 Matteucci, "Long-Term Evaluation of an Urban Development Project: The Case of Hai El Salam."
53 Interview with David Sims, an urban expert who was present at the meeting with the governor, Cairo, December 3, 2019.
54 Kadi, *L'urbanisation Spontanée Au Caire*, 244–45.
55 Ghannam, *Remaking the Modern*, 37.
56 Ghannam, *Remaking the Modern*, 38. See also Cairo Governor Decree 97/1979 concerning demolition of 'Ishash al-Turguman, and Presidential Decree 229/1981 concerning demolition of 'Arab al-Muhammadi.
57 Ghannam, *Remaking the Modern*, 38.
58 Law 27/1956. While there have been many slum clearance plans of entire neighborhoods based on this law since it was issued, especially in Cairo, none of them were ever implemented apart from limited demolitions to widen streets and squares. For more on the decades-old masterplans to replan Bulaq, see Selim, *Unfinished Places*.
59 El-Tohamy, "Mubarak Builds Power Base on Favorable Public Opinion . . . and Vows to Put Muzzle on Egypt's Corrupt 'Fat Cats.'"
60 *The New York Times*, "Sadat's Half Brother Is Sentenced to Jail."
61 Interview with Hagg Salah Abu Ahmad, the *kahul*, or fall guy who claims he was part of the Sadat family operation, and whose name was on all land contracts. See Shadow Ministry of Housing, *Qissat mantiqat 'Izbat al-Haggana/ al-kilo arba'a wa-nuss, al-Qahira*.
62 Shadow Ministry of Housing.

63 Lippman, "Pyramids Loom Off the 18th Green."
64 El-Sanga, "Egypt Demolishes Vacation Homes."
65 Law 30/1983 amending articles of Building Law 106/1976, Joint Committee Report.
66 Urban Planning Law 3/1982, Joint Committee Report.
67 Law 3/1982, Article 67.
68 Laws 30/1983, 54/1984, and 99/1986.
69 Law 31/1984, rules for assigning private state land, Explanatory Note, and Prime Ministerial Decree 857/1985, Executive Regulations.
70 For a detailed account see Tadamun, "'Izbit Khayrallah and the Struggle for Land: Security of Land Tenure."
71 Tadamun, "'Izbit Khayrallah and the Struggle for Land: Security of Land Tenure."
72 Cairo Governor Decree 75/1990.
73 Cairo Governor Decree 75/1990, Committee Meeting Minutes.
74 Bayat, *Life as Politics: How Ordinary People Change the Middle East*, 45–46.
75 Sims, Sejourne, and El Shorbagi, "The Case of Cairo, Egypt."
76 Ministry of Interior, "Musdarat al-Qita'."
77 Minister of Supply Decree 178/2017, Article 4.
78 Sejourne, "Inhabitants' Daily Practices to Obtain Legal Status for Their Homes and Security of Tenure: Egypt."
79 The 2006 census counted 576,322 homes as not connected to the formal grid, a large proportion of which could be surmised to be using illegal electrical connections as suggested by news reports on the lodging of cases against illegal users numbering tens of thousands. For example, see *Masrawy*, "Dabt 227 alf qadiyat sariqat tayyar kahruba'i 'abr al-tawsilat ghayr al-qanuniya."
80 *Mumarsa* is the legal term for negotiated bids for contracts that do not involve auction or tender, and with regard to electricity are used to describe the voluntary reporting of illegal tapping. Electricity Law 87/2015, Article 71. Employees of the electricity companies also face penalties for participating in illegal connections.
81 There is no direct translation, as *mumarsa* is a legal term used to describe the disposal (sale, rent, lease) of government property for a predefined value that is defined by neither auction nor tender. With regard to electricity, it is used to describe the voluntary reporting of illegal tapping. Electricity Law 87/2015, Article 71. Employees of the electricity companies also face penalties for participating in illegal connections.
82 Interview, A.S., a resident of Gisr al-Suez, Cairo, January 5, 2018; Interview, S.R., Shabramant, Giza, April 10, 2012.
83 *al-Wafd*, "Mumarasat al-kahraba' tuhaddid nisf sukkan Shubra al-Khayma bi-l-habs."
84 *Sawt al-umma*, "Qari' yurwi tajribatih ma' mabahith al-kahraba'.'" Some

residents, unable to afford the fines or bribes, confine themselves to their neighborhoods, where they believe it would be impossible for police to arrest them. Interview, R.M., a resident of Basatin, Cairo, December 28, 2017.

85 Law 25/1992, Joint Committee Report.

86 Law 25/1992, Articles 13b and 17b.

87 Law 25/1992, Article 31.

88 United Nations Department of Humanitarian Affairs, "Egypt—Earthquake Oct 1992 UN DHA Situation Reports 1–9."

89 For a detailed account of the stigmatization of the residents of informal areas in the 1990s, with a focus on Imbaba, see Singerman, "The Siege of Imbaba, Egypt's Internal 'Other,' and the Criminalization of Politics."

90 CAPMAS, "Dirasat al-manatiq al-'ashwa'iya fi Misr."

91 For example, the large districts of al-Matariya and Dar al-Salam in Cairo. Cairo Governor Decrees 422/2000 and 1248/2000.

92 CAPMAS, "Dirasat al-manatiq al-'ashwa'iya fi Misr."

93 For example, the Mawardy area in Cairo. Cairo Governor Decree 671/2001.

94 The minister of electricity was joined by the ministers of culture, local administration, housing and utilities, scientific research, and planning. Prime Ministerial Decree 1484/1996 regulating the Committee of the National Project to Upgrade Slums.

95 Vice Military Commander Decrees 1/1996 and 7/1996. Since Egypt has been under emergency law almost continoulsy since the 1950s, the Prime Minister exploited his exceptional powers to "preserve life, public health and public order, and to confront the building collapse phenomenon."

96 Presidential Decree 2/2004.

97 *al-Ahram*, "Ra'i *al-Ahram*: tatwir al-manatiq al-'ashwa'iya awlawiya muhima."

98 For example, see Ministry of Electricity and Energy, "Egypt Electricity Holding Company Annual Report 2006/2007," 38.

99 Cabinet approval 129, dated September 26, 2005. Ministry of Electricity and Energy, "Egypt Electricity Holding Company Annual Report 2006/2007."

100 Dated November 1, 2005. Ministry of Electricity and Energy.

101 Law 138/2006, in addition to Prime Ministerial Decree 1626/2006, Executive Bylaws and Minister of Housing Decree 232/2006, Standards.

102 Ministry of Electricity and Energy, "Egypt Electricity Holding Company Annual Report 2010/2011," 40.

103 Between 1993 and 2011. Ministry of Electricity and Energy, 40.

104 Mubarak, "Mubarak's Speech in the Final Session of the Fourth Congress of the National Democratic Party (official translation)."

105 Charbel, "What Fate Awaits Ezbet El-Haggana?"

106 Sims, *Understanding Cairo: The Logic of a City Out of Control*, 119.

107 For a revealing case study of these, see Tawakol, "Speculative Informal Housing Provision and Its Sociospatial Impacts on Greater Cairo Areas: A Case

Study on 'El-Matareya.'"

108 *Ruz al-Yusuf*, "Tajaddud al-sira' bayn rijal al-a'mal wa-l-mashahir wa muhafiz al-Qahira 'ala Ard al-Haggana."

109 *al-Shuruk*, "Nazif yusdir qararan fawriyan bi-waqf qararat izalat amlak 'ailat al-Sallab."

110 *al-Shuruk*, Al-Sallab would keep his properties but would be made to pay LE10 million in fines. *Al-Ahram al-misa'i*, "al-Sallab yarfa' al-raya al-bayda'."

111 Shawkat, "The Duweika Disaster Ten Years On—Part 1: Disaster and Aftermath."

112 Presidential Decree 305/2008. The speed with which the ISDF was established may be partly based on preparations already under way to set up another fund to repair and rebuild housing in danger of collapse as stipulated in the Unified Building Law 119/2008 (Article 97), but which never materialized.

113 The areas were divided into four descending grades in terms of priority: 1) life-threatening, 2) unsuitable shelter, 3) health risks, 4) informal tenure, see Khalifa, "Redefining Slums in Egypt." These were mostly shacks and many were already identified in the National Project to Upgrade Slums.

114 CAPMAS, "Dirasat al-manatiq al-'ashwa'iya fi Misr."

115 It is not easy to measure progress in this project as new areas are added, or number of units within areas increase, despite a number of projects being realized. This estimate is based on the difference between the housing units in the original 2009 report and one based on data in 2014 that showed 58 areas developed, comprising 29,600 housing units. See UNDP, "Egypt's Progress towards Millennium Development Goals," 37. Other reports present different data, depending on the years compared.

116 These figures only cover slum clearance and upgrading, and do not include evictions of squats or expropriation. Shawkat, *al-'Adala al-ijtima'iya wa-l-'umran—kharitat Misr*, 82–83.

117 *al-Shuruk*, "Shafiq: taqnin awda' al-mu'tadin 'ala al-aradi al-zira'iya (bas di akhir marra)."

118 Ministry of Electricity and Energy, "Egypt Electricity Holding Company Annual Report 2011/2012," 38.

119 Ministry of Electricity and Energy, 38.

120 Shadow Ministry of Housing, EIPR, and TTC, "Why Do Buildings Collapse in Egypt?"

121 Shadow Ministry of Housing, "Taqrir 'an karithat 'umarat hayy al-Gumruk bi-l-Iskandariya 1/2."

122 Abdel-Mohsen, "Maadi Demolition Campaign Turns Fatal."

123 *al-Ahram*, "al-Sisi yukshif li-l-*Ahram* 'an al-khutut al-'arida li-barnamijihi al-intikhabi."

124 The head of the Ministry of Housing's Office for Technical Oversight of Buildings estimates that 2.9 million new informal units were built between

2011 and 2018, which is plausible when compared to average annual production over the last decade. See *al-Akhbar*, "Taftish al-iskan: 2 million wa 900 alf 'aqar mukhalif fi Misr."

125 Prime Ministerial Decree 886/2016, and Minister of Electricity Decrees 254/2016 and 462/2016 outlining detailed procedures.

126 Prime Ministerial Decree 231/2017.

127 Egypt State Information Service, "Sisi: Nobody Above Right & Law."

128 Afify, "Battle over the Nile."

129 *Al-Monitor*, "Following Deadly Clashes, Nile Island Residents Keep Up Fight against Evictions."

130 El-Mahdawy, "'Nobody Is Leaving Their Homes.'"

131 Ibrahim, "Infirad: al-raqaba al-idariya tuhaqiq fi waqa'i' al-hadm bi-qura al-Sahil al-Shamali."

132 *al-Ahram*, "*al-Ahram* yahsul 'ala nass qanun al-tasaluh fi ba'd mukhalafat al-bina.'"

133 Prime Ministerial Decree 1631/2019.

134 Almoghazy, "Forced Informality: When Housing Rights and Building Laws Collide."

135 Shawkat, "Property Market Deregulation and Informal Tenure in Egypt."

136 Foucault, *Security, Territory, Population: Lectures at the College de France 1977–78*, 99.

Chapter 3

1 Hanna, "Real Estate Rights in Urban Egypt: The Changing Sociopolitical Winds."

2 Cooper, *Cairo in the War: 1939-45*.

3 Law 55/1958, Explanatory Note.

4 Nasser, "Kalimat al-ra'is Gamal 'Abd al-Nasser wa-ta'qibatuh fi munaqashat al-lajna al-tahdiriya li-l-mu'tamar al-watani li-l-quwa al-sha'biya—al-jalsa al-thaniya."

5 Law 46/1962, Explanatory Note.

6 Three years after Law 46/1962 was passed, twenty-five thousand contracts in Cairo alone were still pending review. Law 7/1965, Explanatory Note.

7 Comment by Mustafa Abu Zayd Fahmy, a law professor and member of the ASU's Policy Committee, later justice minister and public prosecutor under Sadat. See Arab Socialist Union, "al-Jalsa al-sadisat 'ashar li-l-lajna al-markaziya li-l-ittihad al-ishtiraki al-'arabi."

8 In one party committee meeting, ASU member Mashur Ahmad Mashur highlighted how members of a valuation committee in Banha had inflated the rental value of units they owned that were incongruously part of a housing cooperative. Arab Socialist Union, "al-Jalsa al-thalithat 'ashar li-l-lajna al-markaziya li-l-ittihad al-ishtiraki al-'arabi."

9 Law 7/1965, Explanatory Note.

10 Ministry of Foreign Affairs, "Letter from the Ministry of Foreign Affairs to al-Shark Insurance Company."

11 Hanna, "Real Estate Rights in Urban Egypt: The Changing Sociopolitical Winds."

12 Law 121/1947, Article 6 stated that any payments exceeding or in addition to the legal rent should be reimbursed, though no penalty was imposed on those who did not comply.

13 In a debate with academics, two participants complained to Nasser that they had spent months looking for a place to rent and could not afford the LE300 *khiliw rigl* on their LE27 salaries, the same as the down payment toward buying a new government apartment, which they also could not afford. See Nasser, "Munaqashat al-ra'is Gamal 'Abd al Nasser min Jami'at Iskandiriya ma' al-mab'uthin"; Nasser, "Munaqashat al-ra'is Gamal 'Abd al-Nasser min Jami'at Iskandiriya ma' al-mab'uthin—al-yawm al-thani."

14 Nasser, "Munaqashat al-ra'is Gamal 'Abd al-Nasser min Jami'at Iskandiriya ma' al-mab'uthin—al-yawm al-thani."

15 Comment by 'Abd al-Gabir 'Allam of the parliamentary committee for economic affairs. Arab Socialist Union, "al-Jalsa al-rabi'at 'ashar li-l-lajna al-markaziya li-l-ittihad al-ishtiraki al-'arabi."

16 Interview, A.M., an Old Rent tenant in Cairo, January 5, 2018.

17 'Allam stated that the report cited only the original ruling on December 1, 1968, which was in a landlord's favor, but which was overturned on appeal on January 14, 1969, about three weeks before the report was published. Arab Socialist Union, "al-Jalsa al-rabi'at 'ashar li-l-lajna al-markaziya li-l-ittihad al-ishtiraki al-'arabi."

18 Arab Socialist Union, "al-Jalsa al-khamisat 'ashar li-l-lajna al-markaziya li-l-ittihad al-ishtiraki al-'arabi." A freezing order *(wad' al-'aqar taht al-hirasa)* meant the asset was frozen and administered by a state-appointed guardian until the courts issued a final verdict.

19 Arab Socialist Union, "al-Jalsa al-sadisat 'ashar li-l-lajna al-markaziya li-l-ittihad al-ishtiraki al-'arabi."

20 Arab Socialist Union, "al-Jalsa al-sadisat 'ashar li-l-lajna al-markaziya li-l-ittihad al-ishtiraki al-'arabi."

21 *al-Ahram*, "Shakawi khiliw al-rigl: ihalatha ila al-muda'i al-ishtiraki."

22 Brown, *The Rule of Law in the Arab World Courts in Egypt and the Gulf*, 109–111.

23 Vice Military Commander Order 4/1976, Explanatory Note.

24 Amin, *Egypt's Economic Predicament: A Study in the Interaction of External Pressure, Political Folly, and Social Tension in Egypt, 1960-1990*, 47–48.

25 Vice Military Commander Order 4/1976.

26 Al-Sharqawi, "Madha yatlub al-mullak wa-l-musta'jirun wa-rijal al-qanun min al-qanun al-jadid li-l-iskan . . . ?"

27 Hanna, "Real Estate Rights in Urban Egypt: The Changing Sociopolitical Winds."
28 Law 49/1977, Joint Parliamentary Committee Report.
29 Law 49/1977, Joint Parliamentary Committee Report.
30 Law 49/1977, Joint Parliamentary Committee Report.
31 This was a highly complicated measure whereby owners could propose to the local housing department how their investments were distributed according to the level of units they aimed to build—economic, middle, upper middle, or luxury, as defined by another set of laws that regulated the sale of subsidized building materials to all levels except luxury. The 10 percent of investment value would then be calculated based on each level the building comprised.
32 Sadat, "Kalimat al-ra'is Muhammad Anwar al-Sadat ila rijal al-sahafa wa-l-i'lam fi 26 Junyu 1977."
33 Mayo, Garnett, and Ramez, "Informal Housing in Egypt," 187.
34 Mayo, Garnett, and Ramez, "Informal Housing in Egypt," 187.
35 A provision was added that the penalty would be dropped if it were reported by the offending tenants or middlemen, but not the owners.
36 Mayo, Garnett, and Ramez, "Informal Housing in Egypt," 173.
37 Mayo, Garnett, and Ramez, "Informal Housing in Egypt," 165 and 173.
38 Law 136/1981, Joint Parliamentary Committee Report.
39 *al-Ahram*, "Qurud bi fayda 3% li tarmim al-manazil al-qadima."
40 It is not clear how this figure was reached, and may include demolitions to build structurally sound buildings. Joint Housing and Community Upgrading Team, "Housing and Community Upgrading for Low-Income Egyptians," 2–3.
41 Hanna, "Real Estate Rights in Urban Egypt: The Changing Sociopolitical Winds."
42 Law 136/1981, Housing Committee Report.
43 Law 136/1981, Joint Parliamentary Committee Report.
44 In the early 1980s, one tenant accepted a contract of LE150 per month in Cairo, ten times the median gross rents in the city in 1981. A.M., an Old Rent tenant in Cairo, January 5, 2018; Mayo, Garnett, and Ramez, "Informal Housing in Egypt," 175.
45 Law 136/1981, Joint Parliamentary Committee Report.
46 Mayo, Garnett, and Ramez, "Informal Housing in Egypt," 187–88.
47 Ten of the eighty-eight articles in Law 49/1977 and eight of the twenty articles in Law 136/1981 have been ruled partially or wholly unconstitutional. See recent printed editions of the laws to reflect these rulings.
48 Mayo, Garnett, and Ramez, "Informal Housing in Egypt," 188.
49 Law 65/1971 concerning the investment of Arab funds and free zones, later replaced by Law 43/1974 concerning the investment of Arab and foreign funds and free zones, and other successive laws.

50 At least seven minister of housing decrees were issued between 1978 and 1985 extending rent control to dozens of villages in Giza, chief of which were Bashtil (Law 188/1978) and al-Baragil (Law 162/1984), which later became two of Giza's largest informal areas.

51 Taher, "Foreign Aid and Power Relations: The Government of Egypt, USAID and Housing in Helwan," 191–93.

52 Court of Cassation, Appeal 2638/58, October 26, 1989.

53 Monthly rent was LE30. Interview, A.H., an Old Rent tenant in Cairo, April 3, 2018.

54 Lakeland Ledger, "Building Collapses Kill 26 in Egypt."

55 United Nations Department of Humanitarian Affairs, "Egypt—Earthquake Oct 1992 UN DHA Situation Reports 1–9."

56 Law 4/1996, Joint Parliamentary Committee Report.

57 Law 4/1996, Explanatory Note.

58 Ghallab and 'Abd al-Mun'im, "Maglis al-sha'b yuwafiq 'ala tahrir al-ijar fi al-maskin al-jadida wa-l-khaliya."

59 Ghallab and 'Abd al-Mun'im.

60 Joint Housing Team, "Immediate Action Proposals for Housing in Egypt," 59.

61 Barrada, Wheaton, and Annez, "Public Policy and the Economics of Housing. Appendix B: A Proposal for Improving the Legal Relationship Between Tenant and Landlord in Egypt."

62 Law 4/1996. Joint Parliamentary Committee Report.

63 Egyptian Businessmen's Association, "Egyptian Businessmen's Association Website—Home Page."

64 Law 131/1948, Article 147.

65 Sims, Kamal, and Solomon, "Housing Study for Urban Egypt," 44.

66 Sims, Kamal, and Solomon, "Housing Study for Urban Egypt," 43.

67 Sims, Kamal, and Solomon, "Housing Study for Urban Egypt," 42.

68 Shukrallah, "Despite Cost, 'New Rent' Leaves Tenants Wanting." The fifty-nine-year limit is also the longest lease allowable by law.

69 Sims, Kamal, and Solomon, "Housing Study for Urban Egypt," 42.

70 Al-Saqqar, "Ba'd tatbiquh bi-saba' sanawat: al-ikhla' . . . mushkilat qanun al-ijarat al-jadid!"

71 Shukrallah, "Despite Cost, 'New Rent' Leaves Tenants Wanting."

72 Abotawila, "Understanding Egyptian Social Housing Squatting Phenomenon Post January 2011: The Production of Space in Elmouhtalla," 59–62.

73 For example: OLX, "Rental Ad—Furnished Apartment for Foreigners Only in St. 85 Sarayat."

74 While vacancies are indeed a phenomenon, there are many methodological issues that lead to overestimation. Sims, *Understanding Cairo: The Logic of a City Out of Control*, 165–66. In 2017, one million units were abandoned because of structural damage, and four million were unfinished. Another

four million had yet to be occupied, and the rest were empty because owners had another home or were abroad. CAPMAS, "al-Nata'ij al-niha'iya li-l-ti'dad al-'am li-l-sukkan wa-l-iskan wa-l-munsha'at li 'am 2017: al-sukkan wa-l-zuruf al-sakaniya." Even if we cancel out half the vacancies due to overestimations, as well as unusable units, this still leaves more than four million units empty, enough to house all of the 600,000 households formed annually for the next seven years.

75 Al-Banna, "Laysa bi-l-qanun wahdahuh."

76 Shawkat, "Egypt State of Rent 2017."

77 Shawkat, "Egypt State of Rent 2017."

78 In Cairo, the incidence of *khiliw* was around 9 percent. See Mayo, Garnett, and Ramez, "Informal Housing in Egypt," 173.

79 These were the coming to power of the Free Officers (law passed in 1952), Egypt's Union with Syria (1958), announcement of socialist laws and the dissolution of the union (1961), widespread complaints of a housing shortage when the government took 'our cement' to build the High Dam (1965), and after the 1967 defeat and the influx of *muhaggarin* (war displaced) (1969). See Hanna, "Real Estate Rights in Urban Egypt: The Changing Sociopolitical Winds."

80 Egypt ranked 110 out of 113 countries in a recent rule of law index. See World Justice Project, "Rule of Law Index 2017–2018: Egypt."

81 *Al-Masri al-yawm*, "Mushajaratan bil-l-Qalubiya bi-sabab al-khilaf 'ala shiqqatayn."

82 *Al-Yawm al-sabi'*, "Habs 14 shakhsan tashajaru bi-l-asliha al-nariya bi-sabab al-ijar al-qadim fi a-Marg."

83 Shadow Ministry of Housing, EIPR, and TTC, "Why Do Buildings Collapse in Egypt?"

84 For example, see investigative report by el-Shimi, "10 Nabrawy Street, in Danger Again, Points to Web of Interests behind Demolitions."

85 *Ahram Online*, "'Amendment of Egypt's Old Rent Law Not Expected Soon,' Says Senior MP."

86 *Ahram Online*, "'Amendment of Egypt's Old Rent Law Not Expected Soon,' Says Senior MP.

Chapter 4

1 Fahmy, *All the Pasha's Men: Mehmed Ali, His Army, and the Making of Modern Egypt*, 100–101; Mitchell, *Rule of Experts: Egypt, Techno-Politics, Modernity*, 59–60.

2 Mitchell, *Rule of Experts: Egypt, Techno-Politics, Modernity*, 61–62.

3 Mitchell, *Rule of Experts: Egypt, Techno-Politics, Modernity*, 62 and 66-67.

4 *Al-Masri al-yawm*, "Gaddafi Met with Tribal Representatives in Sinai and Visits Beheira Today."

5 Sonbol, *The New Mamluks: Egyptian Society and Modern Feudalism*, 93.

6 It is rather telling that a political historian, rather than an urban historian, first wrote about the history of model villages in Egypt. Mitchell, *Rule of Experts: Egypt, Techno-Politics, Modernity*, 69.
7 Burchardt, *Paradise Lost: Rural Idyll and Social Change Since 1800*, 58–59.
8 Hekekyan's father was an interpreter for Prince Mohamed 'Ali, and in 1917 was able to get him a state-sponsored scholarship to Stonyhurst College in Lancashire, England, to study English and Latin, after which he studied industrial and civil engineering. He was called back to Egypt in 1931. Mostafa, 'Asr Hekekyan, 74–75.
9 Tadamun, "'Izbit Awlad 'Allam."
10 Abaza, *The Cotton Plantation Remembered: An Egyptian Family Story*, 139; Abaza, 129–30. The use of the term *'izba* became synonymous with both estate and hamlet. Abaza, 129–30.
11 Abaza, *The Cotton Plantation Remembered: An Egyptian Family Story*, 130.
12 Abaza, *The Cotton Plantation Remembered: An Egyptian Family Story*, 127-128.
13 Abaza, *The Cotton Plantation Remembered: An Egyptian Family Story*, 132.
14 Mitchell, *Rule of Experts: Egypt, Techno-Politics, Modernity*, 71.
15 Ayrout, *The Egyptian Peasant*, 117.
16 Mitchell, *Rule of Experts: Egypt, Techno-Politics, Modernity*, 70.
17 Saad, "Peasants' Perceptions of Recent Egyptian History," 67.
18 Ayrout, *The Egyptian Peasant*, 18.
19 For example, Khedival order of February 11, 1885, Laws 22/1909 and 69/1933 setting standards for the creation of *'izba*s, Laws 46/1942 and 62/1947 on improving health in villages (amended in 1956), and Law 118/1950 stipulating minimum standards for new *'izba*s.
20 This was 12 percent of the population. See Mitchell, *Rule of Experts: Egypt, Techno-Politics, Modernity*, 71.
21 By 1952 there were eleven thousand owners of land parcels over fifty feddans in area. CAPMAS, "al-Kitab al-ihsa'i al-sanawi li-jumhuriyat Misr al-'arabiya 1952–1973," 60. Many of the sources quoted in this section mention fifteen thousand to seventeen thousand estates at the time. But the government statistics for the period only mention the number of landowners, where one owner could own more than one estate, while each estate could have more than one *'izba* (hamlet), especially the larger ones.
22 Beinin, *Workers and Peasants in the Modern Middle East*, 119.
23 A typhus epidemic would infect 110,000 people between 1940 and 1945, killing 20,000. A malaria epidemic in 1942 to 1944 infected almost one million people and killed 200,000. A few years later, in 1947, a cholera epidemic would kill two-thirds of the 33,000 people it infected. Kohn, *Encyclopedia of Plague and Pestilence: From Ancient Times to the Present*, 96–97 and 100.
24 Mitchell, *Rule of Experts: Egypt, Techno-Politics, Modernity*, 188.
25 Burchardt, *Paradise Lost: Rural Idyll and Social Change Since 1800*, 60.

26 Al-Said, *Tarikh al-haraka al-shuyu'iya al-misriya min 1940–50—al-mujalad al-thalith: tarikh al-munathamat al-yasariya al-misriya*, 58.

27 Azzam, "The Development of Urban and Rural Housing in Egypt," 152–54.

28 Azzam, "The Development of Urban and Rural Housing in Egypt," 150-151.

29 Azzam, "The Development of Urban and Rural Housing in Egypt," 150–51.

30 'Abd al-Gawwad, "al-Maskan al-sihhi li-l-fallah." Many of the 1947 *Majallat al-'imara* articles cited in this chapter were part of a special edition of the magazine dedicated to papers presented as part of the Healthy and Economic Homes section at the Third Arab Engineering Conference held in Damascus in September 1947. See 'Abd al-Gawwad, "al-Mu'tamar al-handasi al-thalith."

31 'Abd al-Gawwad, "al-Maskan al-sihhi li-l-fallah."

32 Nur, "Islah al-qarya al-misriya."

33 Nur, "Islah al-qarya al-misriya."

34 'Abd al-Gawwad, "al-Maskan al-sihhi li-l-fallah"; Azzam, "The Development of Urban and Rural Housing in Egypt," 167.

35 Karim, "*Islah al-qarya, bayn al-qarya al-namuzajiya wa-qaryat al-intiqal.*"

36 Karim, "*Islah al-qarya, bayn al-qarya al-namuzajiya wa-qaryat al-intiqal.*"

37 Karim, "*Islah al-qarya, bayn al-qarya al-namuzajiya wa-qaryat al-intiqal.*"

38 Herleth, "The Good Life."

39 Hoeven, "Woonschool."

40 'Abd al-Gawwad, "al-Maskan al-sihhi li-l-fallah." A number of migrants' villages were built in the 1930s and 1940s in different parts of Egypt. Some others are covered in chapter 5.

41 Letter from al-Marg MP Ahmad 'Ali Ibrahim to the executive director of the government's Informal Settlements Development Facility dated April 24, 2017. See *Barlamani*, "Na'ib al-Marg Ahmad 'Ali: tadbir al-i'timad al-mali li-naql 'ishash al-Andalus wa tir'at Birlant bi-mantiqat al-'Assara."

42 Mitchell, *Rule of Experts: Egypt, Techno-Politics, Modernity*, 188–89. Fathy would build New Gurna in Luxor in 1945, the Lu'lu'at al-Sahara *'izba* on Hafez 'Afifi's estate in Giza in 1950, the New Bariz model village in the New Valley in 1967, and the Dar al-Islam village in New Mexico, United States in 1981.

43 Timothy Mitchell provides a detailed critique of New Gurna titled "Making the Nation." See Mitchell, *Rule of Experts: Egypt, Techno-Politics, Modernity*, 187–95.

44 UNESCO, "Safeguarding Project of Hassan Fathy's New Gourna Village, Preliminary Phase Document."

45 UNESCO, "Safeguarding Project of Hassan Fathy's New Gourna Village, Preliminary Phase Document."

46 UNESCO, "Safeguarding Project of Hassan Fathy's New Gourna Village, Preliminary Phase Document."

47 Mas'ud, "al-Muwatin al-namuzaji."

48 Mas'ud, "al-Muwatin al-namuzaji."

49 Mitchell, Rule of Experts: Egypt, Techno-Politics, Modernity, 40.

50 There were five other criteria, including that beneficiaries come from a rural family or one that cultivates land. Minister of Finance Decree 7/1947.

51 Laws 67/1948 and 83/1949 earmarking LE132,900 and LE45,235 from the budget reserves respectively for these loans.

52 Article by the director of the Department of State Property based on a paper presented at the Third Arab Engineering Conference. See Abudah, "Tatwir manzil al-fallah."

53 Abudah. The exact numbers are based on United States National Archives, "Record Group 59, Departmnet of State, Central Files, Egypt.," 874.16/2-1951 and 5–1851. In: Mitchell, *Rule of Experts: Egypt, Techno-Politics, Modernity*, 311.

54 According to Abudah, there were initially four new villages: al-Muhammadiya, al-Ibrahimiya al-Qibliya, al-Ibrahimiya al-Bahariya, and al-'Abassiya (based on names of previous rulers Muhammad 'Ali, Ibrahim and 'Abbas, respectively). Al-Muhammadiya was the main village of the four, though renamed two years later to Manshiyat Faruq al-Awwal after King Faruq as per Minister of Interior Decree of March 23, 1950, and then reverted back to al-Muhammadiya most probably after the monarchy was abolished in 1952. Based on recent maps, there were another five villages built also bearing royal names: al-Sa'idiya al-Bahariya, al-Sa'idiya al-Qibliya, al-Isma'iliya 3, al-Tawfiqiya, and al-Fu'adiya (named after the khedives Said, Isma'il, and Tawfiq, and King Fouad, Faruq's father respectively). Al-Fu'adiya was renamed Taftish Thani, also possibly after the 1952 regime change, and known on different maps as al-Muhandisin and al-'Umara. See IDSC, "Dalil al-taqsim al-idari li-l-muhafzat hatta mustawa al-shiyakha wa-l-qarya."

55 Beinin, Workers and Peasants in the Modern Middle East, 119.

56 CAPMAS, "al-Zimam wa-l-masahat al-munzari'a fi jumhuriyat Misr al-'arabiya 'am 1970," 78.

57 Mainly Laws 178/1952, 152/1957, 127/1961, 44/1962, and 15/1963.

58 Springborg, "State-Society Relations in Egypt: The Debate over Owner-Tenant Relations."

59 USAID, "A.I.D. Project Impact Evaluation Report No. 43, The Egyptian American Rural Improvement Service, A Point Four Project, 1952–63," 2.

60 Alterman, *Egypt and American Foreign Assistance 1952–1956: Hopes Dashed*, 79.

61 Nasser, "Khitab al-ra'is Gamal 'Abd al-Nasser fi Bur Sa'id fi zikra yawm al-nasr."

62 Wahdan, *Planning Egypt's New Settlements: The Politics of Spatial Inequities*, 26.

63 Alterman, *Egypt and American Foreign Assistance 1952–1956: Hopes Dashed*, 82.

64 Mu'assasat Mudiriyat al-Tahrir. *Muzakkira marfu'a ila majlis al-wuzara' 'an al-hisab al-khitami fi 30 junyu 1954 li mu'assasat mudiriyat al-tahrir min majlis*

idarat al-mu'assasa.

65 Mu'assasat Mudiriyat al-Tahrir.

66 Nasser, "Khitab al-ra'is Gamal 'Abd al-Nasser fi jami'at al-Qahira bi-munasabat 'id al-wihda."

67 Azzam, "The Development of Urban and Rural Housing in Egypt," 154.

68 Azzam, "The Development of Urban and Rural Housing in Egypt," 154.

69 Tadros, "The Human Aspects of Rural Resettlement Schemes in Egypt."

70 Downs, "Revolutionary Egypt Reclaims the Land, November 27, 1954."

71 Yunis, *Nida' sha'b: tarikh naqdi li-l-idiyulujiya al-nasiriya*, 160–61.

72 These were designed by the Department of Social Affairs' Dress, Customs and Traditions Committee. See Yunis, 160–61.

73 Alterman, *Egypt and American Foreign Assistance 1952–1956: Hopes Dashed*, 79.

74 el-Shakry, "Cairo as Capital of Socialist Revolution?"

75 *al-Ahram*, "Usus jadida li-l-tarbiya bi-mudiriyat al-Tahrir," September 11, 1955 in Yunis, *Nida' sha'b: tarikh naqdi li-l-idiyulujiya al-nasiriya*, 163.

76 Tadros, "The Human Aspects of Rural Resettlement Schemes in Egypt."

77 Criteria of the Migration, Settlement, and Community Development Department in 1960. See Tadros.

78 Tadros, "The Human Aspects of Rural Resettlement Schemes in Egypt."

79 el-Shakry, "Cairo as Capital of Socialist Revolution?"

80 Downs, "Revolutionary Egypt Reclaims the Land, November 27, 1954."

81 Hopkins et al., *Participation and Community in the Egyptian New Lands: The Case of South Tahrir*, 67.

82 The first eighty-eight homes were distributed to war veterans, workers who worked on the project, and fishermen from Maryut. See Voll, "Egyptian Land Reclamation since the Revolution."

83 Tadros, "The Human Aspects of Rural Resettlement Schemes in Egypt."

84 For Mudiriyat al-Tahir, see village names in Marakaz Kom Hamada in Beheira governorate list of main villages in the censuses of 1960, 1966, 1976, 1986, and 1996, as well as a recent official list of place names. For the New Valley, see village names for Markaz Baris in the New Valley, IDSC, "Dalil al-taqsim al-idari li-l-muhafzat hatta mustawa al-shiyakha wa-l-qarya."

85 al-Rafe'i, *Muqaddimat Thawrat 23 Yulyu Sanat 1952*, 105. She is somewhat of a mythologized character of Egyptian resistance to British colonialism, as she also appears as the "first martyr" of the 1919 Revolution in other accounts. For example: Abouelnaga, *Women in Revolutionary Egypt: Gender and the New Geographics of Identity*, 112.

86 al-Rafe'i, *Muqaddimat Thawrat 23 Yulyu Sanat 1952*, 106–7.

87 Yunis, *Nida' sha'b: tarikh naqdi li-l-idiyulujiya al-nasiriya*, 74–75.

88 Yunis, *Nida' sha'b: tarikh naqdi li-l-idiyulujiya al-nasiriya*, 74–75.

89 Naguib, *Kalimati li-l-tarikh*, 181–82.

90 This was a former soldier and early settler of South Tahrir describing his

relationship to Hassanein. Hopkins et al., *Participation and Community in the Egyptian New Lands: The Case of South Tahrir*, 67.

91 Al-Salamoni, *al-Jil al-ladhi wajah 'Abd al-Nasser wa-l-Sadat*, 242.

92 Ibrahim, "Hikayat barlamaniya: inqilab al-dubbat al-ahrar taht qubbat al-barlaman."

93 Springborg, "Patrimonialism and Policy Making in Egypt: Nasser and Sadat and the Tenure Policy for Reclaimed Lands."

94 Springborg, "Patrimonialism and Policy Making in Egypt: Nasser and Sadat and the Tenure Policy for Reclaimed Lands."

95 Wahdan, *Planning Egypt's New Settlements: The Politics of Spatial Inequities*, 23–24.

96 Hopkins et al., *Participation and Community in the Egyptian New Lands: The Case of South Tahrir*, 38.

97 USAID, "A.I.D. Project Impact Evaluation Report No. 43, The Egyptian American Rural Improvement Service, A Point Four Project, 1952–63," 15.

98 Hopkins et al., *Participation and Community in the Egyptian New Lands: The Case of South Tahrir*, 54–55.

99 USAID, "A.I.D. Project Impact Evaluation Report No. 43, The Egyptian American Rural Improvement Service, A Point Four Project, 1952–63," 10.

100 USAID, "A.I.D. Project Impact Evaluation Report No. 43, The Egyptian American Rural Improvement Service, A Point Four Project, 1952–63," 10.

101 USAID, "A.I.D. Project Impact Evaluation Report No. 43, The Egyptian American Rural Improvement Service, A Point Four Project, 1952–63," 18.

102 Hopkins et al., *Participation and Community in the Egyptian New Lands: The Case of South Tahrir*, 64.

103 Tadros, "The Human Aspects of Rural Resettlement Schemes in Egypt"; USAID, "A.I.D. Project Impact Evaluation Report No. 43, The Egyptian American Rural Improvement Service, A Point Four Project, 1952–63," H–2.

104 Tadros, "The Human Aspects of Rural Resettlement Schemes in Egypt."

105 Tadros, "The Human Aspects of Rural Resettlement Schemes in Egypt."

106 Scudder, "Evaluative Research on Human Settlements." In: Tadros, "The Human Aspects of Rural Resettlement Schemes in Egypt."

107 Adriansen, "Land Reclamation in Egypt: A Study of Life in the New Lands."

108 Voll, "Egyptian Land Reclamation since the Revolution." The Mubarak graduates' villages accepted evictees of the 1992 tenancy counter-reform from 1997 onward (see later in the chapter).

109 Springborg, "Patrimonialism and Policy Making in Egypt: Nasser and Sadat and the Tenure Policy for Reclaimed Lands."

110 Wahdan, *Planning Egypt's New Settlements: The Politics of Spatial Inequities*, 37.

111 al-Ahram, "al-Sadat a'ta isharat al-bad' li-awwal mugamma' zira'i sina'i fi al-sahra'."

112 al-Ahram, "al-Sadat a'ta isharat al-bad' li-awwal mugamma' zira'i sina'i fi

al-sahra'."

113 al-Ahram, "al-Sadat a'ta isharat al-bad' li-awwal mugamma' zira'i sina'i fi al-sahra'."

114 World Bank, "New Land Development Project (West Nubariya)," 21.

115 World Bank, "New Land Development Project (West Nubariya)," 50.

116 al-Ahram, "Dhahabt ila za'im al-mu'arada fi Shirbin mu'akkidan 'ala mafhum jadid li-l-hayat al-hizbiya." Despite newspaper headlines and commemorations marking December 25 as the day Sadat launched the project, the cornerstone would actually be laid on the next day, while actual construction work had started some time prior to this.

117 al-Ahram, "Dhahabt ila za'im al-mu'arada fi Shirbin mu'akkidan 'ala mafhum jadid li-l-hayat al-hizbiya."

118 al-Ahram, "Mahgragan hubb wa wafa' wa asala fi Mit Abul Kom." In addition to the houses, a school, a sports center and other public buildings were constructed.

119 Adriansen, "Land Reclamation in Egypt: A Study of Life in the New Lands."

120 Adriansen. Criteria similar to the New Lands project were maintained, including that applicants should be under thirty years old, male (project managers believed women would be absentee landlords), have no police record, and not be employed by the government (or have relinquished their positions).

121 Springborg, "State-Society Relations in Egypt: The Debate over Owner-Tenant Relations." For more on the evictions, see chapter 7.

122 The government gave priority to evictees, though only 16,727 families were resettled there by 2003. See Adriansen, "Land Reclamation in Egypt: A Study of Life in the New Lands."

123 Adriansen, "Land Reclamation in Egypt: A Study of Life in the New Lands."

124 Sims, *Egypt's Desert Dreams: Development or Disaster*, 49.

125 *al-Sharq al-awsat*, "Mubarak ya'id fi jawla intikhabiya bi-l-Nubariya bi-istislah milyun faddan wa manh qurud 100 alf jinih li-kul usra"; Ministry of Housing, Utilities, and Urban Development, "Mashru' qura al-Zahir al-Sahrawi."

126 Egypt State Information Service, "1.5 Million Feddan Project."

127 Using Google Earth, I have been able to find around forty Zahir Sahrawi villages: a number of the *kharigin* villages are partly empty, with a large one in Suhag and another in Farafra completely abandoned; nine new villages around Lake Nasser in Aswan, where mostly only the walls were built; seven empty new villages as part of the Sahl al-Tina area of the North Sinai Agricultural Development Plan (NSADP), of which six have about fifty houses, while one, al-Amal, has four hundred; two of the five Darb al-Arba'in villages south of the Baris Oasis in the New Valley stand empty, while a third is fighting sand dune inundation.

128 According to a report by the Ministry of Agriculture and Land Reclamation (MALR), 69,962 beneficiaries received land from the project between 1987

and 2003. See Adriansen, "Land Reclamation in Egypt: A Study of Life in the New Lands." Each beneficiary is estimated to be a household of five individuals. This is of course an upper level estimate that assumes all beneficiaries remained there with their families, as we will see later. The rest of the MALR table gives figures for projects from 1952, but they only focus on graduates and so have not been used.

129 Based on the 1960 and 2006 censuses. See CAPMAS, "Egypt in Figures 2016."

130 Five of the eleven occupied homes in the village of New Basaisa in Ras Sedr, North Sinai, housed single male landowners. See Mahdy, "Dynamics of Development in Rural Egypt to New Desert Communities: The Case of the Basaisa."

131 Sims, *Egypt's Desert Dreams: Development or Disaster*, 84.

132 Sims, *Egypt's Desert Dreams: Development or Disaster*, 95-96. Also chapter 3 for a comprehensive account of the failures of the land reclamation schemes under Sadat and Mubarak.

133 Adriansen, "Land Reclamation in Egypt: A Study of Life in the New Lands."

134 Adriansen, "Land Reclamation in Egypt: A Study of Life in the New Lands."

135 *al-Ahram*, "Qura sahl al-husayniya hajarha 80% min al-shabab!"

136 *al-Ahram*, "Bi sabab al-baltaja wa-l-sariqat: shabab al-kharijin yahjarun qaryat Siddiq al-Minshawi bi-Suhaj."

137 *al-Yawm al-sabi'*, "Musa wa-l-Khidr: qaryatan mansiyyatan bila khadamat bi-l-Fayyum"; *al-Ahram*, "Qaryata Musa wa-l-Khidr kharij nitaq al-khidma"; *Ruz al-yusuf*, "Rihlat 'adhab min jahannam ila qura al-Anbiya' bi-l-Fayyum."

138 *al-Masri al-yawm*, "Qura al-Minya al-namuzajiya: buyut ashbah."

139 *al-Ahram*, "al-Ashbah taskun qaryat al-Zahir al-Sahrawi bi-l-Mahamid."

140 *al-Masri al-yawm*, "al-Muhasabat: ihdar 500 milyun jinih fi al-Zahir al-Sahrawi."

141 Shawkat and Hendawy, "Myths and Facts of Urban Planning in Egypt."

142 al-Ahram, "Tawqi' 'aqd ta'sis sharikat al-Ismailiya-Misr li-l-Tanmiya al-Zira'iya," 3. The other shareholders were Banque Misr, the Nasser Social Bank, the Suez Canal Authority pension fund (all state-owned), two businessmen and "a group of Ismailia citizens."

143 Sims, *Egypt's Desert Dreams: Development or Disaster*, 95–96.

144 Hanna, *al-Iskan wal-siyasa*, 80.

145 Sims, *Egypt's Desert Dreams: Development or Disaster*, 95.

146 This was through USAID and the now defunct DANIDA. See Adriansen, "Land Reclamation in Egypt: A Study of Life in the New Lands."

147 JICA, "The Feasibility Study on the North Sinai Integrated Rural Development Project (Phase II) in the Arab Republic of Egypt—Final Report"; Kuwait Fund, "Completion Of Development Of 400,000 Faddan In North Sinai."

148 Deputy, "Designed to Deceive: President Hosni Mubarak's Toshka Project," 65.
149 Sims, *Egypt's Desert Dreams: Development or Disaster*, 84.
150 Sims, *Egypt's Desert Dreams: Development or Disaster*, 86.
151 Deputy, "Designed to Deceive: President Hosni Mubarak's Toshka Project," 87–89.
152 KADCO, "KADCO Egypt."
153 Amwal al-Ghad, "Saudi Al Rajhi Co. to Pump $135mn in Egypt's Toshka until 2020"; al-Dahra Egypt, "al-Dahra Holding."
154 Arafat and El Nour, "How Egypt's Water Feeds the Gulf."
155 South Valley Development Company, "Nubdha 'an mashru'at sharikat junub al-wadi."
156 Ministry of Defense and Military Production, "al-Sharika al-Wataniya li-Istislah wa-Zira'at al-Aradi al-Sahrawiya bi-Sharq al-'Uwaynat"; al-Awqaf Authority, "al-Istithmar al-zira'i."
157 *al-Yawm al-sabi'*, "al-Quwwat al-musallahha tahtal al-markaz al-awwal fi istislah aradi Sharq al-'Uwaynat."
158 Egypt Countryside Development Company, "al-Mashru' al-qawmi li-tanmaiyat al-milyun wa nisf faddan: al-tarh al-awwal li-sighar al-muzari'in wa-l-shabab"; Egypt Countryside Development Company, "al-Mashru' al-qawmi li-tanmiyat al-milyun wa nisf faddan: al-tarh al-awwal, da'wa li-l-mustathmirin li-l-taqaddum li-l-ta'hil."
159 New Urban Communities Authority, "Madinat Tushka al-Jadida."
160 They were not in *mabani li-l-sakan* (homes), but *mabani 'amma* (general buildings, defined as nonpermanent housing such as hostels, hotels, prisons, or hospitals). See CAPMAS, "al-Ti'tad al-'am li-l-sukkan wa-l-iskan wa-l-munsha'at 2006: al-nata'ij al-niha'iya li-ti'dad al-mabani 2006 li-ijmali al-jumhuriya."
161 A theory developed by James C. Scott, where he examined how states attempted to "arrange" the population in order to simplify taxation, conscription, and demobilization. Scott, *Seeing Like a State: How Certain Schemes to Improve the Human Condition Have Failed*, 2.
162 A tally based on searching the archive of the online news site *Akhbar al-Wadi al-Jadid* for the years 2013 through 2017.
163 *Akhbar al-Wadi al-Jadid*, "Musalsal jadid min al-ihmal wa istighlal al-atfal: wafat al-tifl Mubarak athna' jam' al-batatis bi-l-'Uwaynat."
164 *Akhbar al-Wadi al-Jadid*, "*Akhbar al-Wadi al-Jadid* tukshif ma'sat 'imalat al-atfal fi sharq al-'Uwaynat."

Chapter 5

1 The government had size and quality standards for four levels of housing: economic, middle, upper middle, and luxury. See Minister of Housing and

Reconstruction Decree 237/1977.

2 Mubarak, *al-Khitat al-tawfiqiya al-jadida li-Misr al-Qahira wa-muduniha wa-biladiha al-qadima wa-l-shahira* (20 volumes), vol. 8, 26 and vol. 15, 46.

3 The Helwan housing project was part of a new spa city built in 1870. See Volait, "Réforme Sociale et Habitat Populaire: Acteurs et Formes (1848–1964)."

4 Unless otherwise noted, all information in this section is from Volait.

5 See for example Khedival Decree of November 9, 1904, expropriating land to build houses and stables for the Irrigation Department in Minya, and Khedival Decree of January 10, 1907, expropriating land in Assiut to build housing for the Railway Department.

6 Mas'ud, "al-Maskan al-sihhi min al-nahiya al-takhtitiya wa-l-iqtisadiya."

7 Riad, "Alexandria."

8 The agreement of July 9, 1907 between the Heliopolis Company and the Government of Egypt was to build four hundred housing units and rent them out at predefined rates for fifty years. See Law 123/1955.

9 Ilbert, "Heliopolis: Colonial Enterprise and Town Planning Success."

10 Made on January 30, 1921, the agreement was to supply six hundred units at predefined rents for thirty years. See Law 123/1955.

11 A government loan covering two-thirds of the costs was made available to the company in exchange for supplying the units. Once the units were delivered, the municipal government would also take over infrastructure, as well as street operation and maintenance, ordinarily the responsibility of the company. Volait, "Réforme Sociale et Habitat Populaire: Acteurs et Formes (1848–1964)."

12 Piaton, "Architecture Patronale Dans l'Isthme de Suez (1859–1956)."

13 Ilbert, "Heliopolis: Colonial Enterprise and Town Planning Success."

14 The garden city movement was primarily founded by Ebenezer Howard, and his book *To-Morrow: A Peaceful Path to Real Reform*, which promoted the merging of rural and urban ideals to plan almost utopian self-sustaining neighborhoods.

15 Piaton, "Architecture Patronale Dans l'Isthme de Suez (1859–1956)."

16 Harlow, *Paper Chase: The Amenities of Stamp Collecting*, 217.

17 Piaton, "Architecture Patronale Dans l'Isthme de Suez (1859–1956)."

18 Piaton, "Architecture Patronale Dans l'Isthme de Suez (1859–1956)."

19 Fanon, *The Wretched of the Earth*, 3–6.

20 Almoghazy, "A Tied Life: The Rise and Fall of Company Town Housing in Egypt."

21 Volait, *Egypt (1914–2014): Global Architecture Before Globalization*.

22 Pallini and Scaccabarozzi, "British Planning Schemes for Alexandria and Its Region, 1834–1958."

23 Ashour, *al-Mi'mariyin al-misriyin al-ruwad khilal al-fatra al-libiraliya bayn thawratay 1919 wa 1952*, 356 and 438.

24 The government financed LE110,000 of the LE1.5 million cost, which also included social services and a cinema. See Volait, "Réforme Sociale et Habitat Populaire: Acteurs et Formes (1848–1964)." For a rare aerial view of the workers' town, see Hawas, "The Industrial Centres," 92.

25 Ashour, *al-Mi'mariyin al-misriyin al-ruwad khilal al-fatra al-libiraliya bayn thawratay*, 395.

26 Examples are New Lanark in 1799 and the more elaborate Copley in 1849. See Burchardt, *Paradise Lost: Rural Idyll and Social Change Since 1800*, 61–62.

27 Tignor, *State, Private Enterprise and Economic Change in Egypt, 1918–1952*, 223.

28 For an in-depth account of factory town life in the 1930s and 1940s see Hammad, *Industrial Sexuality: Gender, Urbanization, and Social Transformation in Egypt*, 114–15.

29 Hammad, *Industrial Sexuality: Gender, Urbanization, and Social Transformation in Egypt*, 113.

30 Egypt gained nominal independence from Britain in 1922.

31 Tignor, *State, Private Enterprise and Economic Change in Egypt, 1918–1952*, 143.

32 Around 550 houses were available, and assuming both husband and wife worked that would be 1,100 workers. Meanwhile dorms housed 1,500 single workers, making a total of 2,600 workers. The total workforce was 27,000. Hammad, *Industrial Sexuality: Gender, Urbanization, and Social Transformation in Egypt*, 54.

33 Hammad, *Industrial Sexuality: Gender, Urbanization, and Social Transformation in Egypt*, 54.

34 Ashour, *al-Mi'mariyin al-misriyin al-ruwad khilal al-fatra al-libiraliya bayn thawratay*, 187.

35 Mas'ud, "al-Maskan al-sihhi min al-nahiya al-takhtitiya wa-l-iqtisadiya."

36 Riad, "Tahdid al-manatiq al-sina'iya wa insha' masakin al-'ummal."

37 Most probably the city government of Red Vienna, so-called because it was led by a social democratic government from the 1920s.

38 His calculations were based on homes costing LE150 to build including price of land and utilities, and thus requiring an 8 percent annual yield to cover the costs, translating to a monthly rent of LE1. This rate would breach the 20 percent that he saw as the affordable limit, where LE5 per month was higher than the average wage. Subsidies would result in a reduction to a 4 percent annual yield.

39 Sixteen of the thirty-five presentations were part of the Economic and Healthy Homes section, five of which were on Egypt alone, and most were printed in a special edition of *Majallat al-'imara* magazine (1947, vol. 7, nos. 5 and 6).

40 Riad, "Tahdid al-manatiq al-sina'iya wa insha' masakin al-'ummal."

41 See chapter 4 and Mas'ud, "al-Muwatin al-namuzaji."

42 Mas'ud, "al-Maskan al-sihhi min al-nahiya al-takhtitiya wa-l-iqtisadiya."

43 Mas'ud, "al-Maskan al-sihhi min al-nahiya al-takhtitiya wa-l-iqtisadiya."

44 Applicants were expected to have been in government employment for a minimum of ten years, married with children, to not own a home in Cairo, to be working close to the estate, and be members of the estate's cooperative. Priority was given to workers of the al-Amiriya Press, then the al-Amiriya Workshops, followed by those specified by ministerial decree. The rent contract stated that a worker could be evicted if they were fired, violated moral codes, broke the terms of the contract, or the government needed the unit back. See Ministry of Social Affairs Decree 7/1950.

45 Calculations were based on a LE13.3 monthly wage and the assumption that it was affordable for 15 percent of the wage to be spent on rent. The government would aim to recoup 5 percent annually of the LE4 million in construction maintenance and management costs over forty years (with land and utilities provided for free). That would mean that affordable monthly rents would be set at LE2, while at-cost rent would be LE2.8, with the difference borne by the government for forty years. See Mas'ud, "al-Maskan al-sihhi min al-nahiya al-takhtitiya wa-l-iqtisadiya."

46 Karim, "Madinat Faruq al-Awwal bi-wadi Kom Ombo."

47 Their report was titled, "Mashru' li-tawfir al-sakan li-l-tabaqat al-mahdudat al-dakhl fi Misr." See Volait, "Réforme Sociale et Habitat Populaire: Acteurs et Formes (1848–1964)."

48 Royal Decree of August 17, 1950 appointing a general director for Department of Popular Homes *(idarat al-masakin al-sha'biya)*.

49 Azzam, "The Development of Urban and Rural Housing in Egypt," 102.

50 Marsum of June 15, 1953.

51 Azzam, "The Development of Urban and Rural Housing in Egypt," 103.

52 Permanent Committee for Public Services, "Majlis al-khadamat fi 'am al-taqrir 'an al-majlis fi 'amahu al-awwal," 2.

53 The sites were the garden of Muhammad 'Ali Palace in Shubra, Telal Zeinhom, and Helwan in Cairo, Shubra al-Khayma in Qalubiya, and the Tosson Palace gardens in Mahmudiya in Alexandria. See Permanent Committee for Public Services, 2.

54 He announced that a total of LE20.8 million was spent over the last three years on construction, support for owners and tenants, and housing cooperatives to build 289 homes (most probably as loans). Of the 4,310 popular homes built, 1,460 were in Hilmiyat al-Zaytun and 2,200 in Imbaba (1,000 units of which were built before 1952), and 650 in Helwan. See Nasser, "Khitab al-ra'is Gamal 'Abd al-Nasser fi al-mu'tamar al-sha'bi bi-Midan al-Jumhuriya bi-l-Qahira ma' al-ra'is Sukarno bi munasabat al-'id al-thalith li-thawrat Yulyu."

55 Government employees in provincial capitals were a main target, with two hundred units planned for them in Qena, Kafr al-Sheikh, and Banha. Seven

hundred units were planned for employees and workers of a weather station in Belbeis, another 2,800 for railroad employees, and 7,500 were planned for workers across Egypt, 1,000 of which had broken ground in Zeinhom in Cairo, with another 4,000 planned for Shubra, Helwan, and Imbaba.

56 Azzam, "The Development of Urban and Rural Housing in Egypt," 107. See also Law 177/1956 allowing funding for Abu Za'bal housing expansion, and Minister of Municipal and Village Affairs Decree 168/1961 allowing for the expropriation of land in al-Mahalla al-Kubra to build popular homes.

57 Bishop, "Talking Shop: Egyptian Engineers and Soviet Specialists at the Aswan High Dam," 174.

58 Nasser, "Kalimat al-ra'is Gamal 'Abd al-Nasser fi iftitah majlis al-umma."

59 Zabbal, "al-Qahira tujadid shababiha: al-ta'mir fiha 'ala qadam wa-saq."

60 Mossallam, "Hikayat Sha'b—Stories of Peoplehood: Nasserism, Popular Politics and Songs in Egypt, 1956–1973," 95.

61 Nasser, "Kalimat al-ra'is Gamal 'Abd al-Nasser fi iftitah majlis al-umma."

62 Wahab, "Problems of Nubian Migration."

63 The government held a 20 percent stake, while social insurance and savings funds, along with twenty still-private banks and insurance companies, contributed the remainder. See Law 601/1953 allowing government investment in company to build popular homes, Explanatory Note, and Marsum of May 20, 1954 establishing Development and Popular Homes Company SAE.

64 Prime Ministerial Decree 14/1954 assigning 106,000 square meters of state land in Abbasiya, Cairo to housing, and Minister of Social Affairs Decree 9/1954 expropriating 65 acres in Hilmiyat al-Zaytun, Cairo.

65 These included a housing estate for military officers in Abbasiya, Cairo, another in Belbeis Airforce Base, Sharqiya, and a few blocks for government employees in Kafr al-Sheikh. See Azzam, "The Development of Urban and Rural Housing in Egypt," 107–108, and 110. See also Laws 602/1954 and 71/1955 and Minister of Finance Decree 136/1955.

66 Between 1954 and 1961, 6,612 homes were built, dropping to a mere 712 between 1961 and 1967. See Rageh, *al-'Umran al-misri*, 2:113–14.

67 CAPMAS, "al-Kitab al-ihsa'i al-sanawi li-jumhuriyat Misr al-'arabiya 1952–1976," 143.

68 Volait, "Réforme Sociale et Habitat Populaire: Acteurs et Formes (1848–1964)."

69 Law 123/1955.

70 Awqaf City was originally conceived as an upper-class district of villas and residential apartment blocks planned on agricultural land on Cairo's west bank in the 1940s as a joint venture between the Ministries of Awqaf (Religious Endowments) and Public Works on royal property *(amlak amiriya)*, as well as two large *waqf*s belonging to Sinan Pasha and Muhammad Said Pasha. Royal land subsequently became state land when the monarchy was annulled

and a republic established in 1952. See Marsum of October 3, 1940 and Marsum of October 9, 1944 establishing Madinat al-Awqaf land subdivision.

71 Nasser, "Khitab al-ra'is Gamal 'Abd al-Nasser fi al-mu'tamar al-sha'bi bi-Midan al-Jumhuriya bi-l-Qahira ma' al-ra'is Sukarno bi-munasabat al-'id al-thalith li-thawrat Yulyu." See also Minister of Municipal and Village Affairs Decree 1057/1955.

72 Nasser. See also Hanna, "Real Estate Rights in Urban Egypt: The Changing Sociopolitical Winds."

73 El-Bahrawy, "A House of No Importance," 42.

74 Mansha'at 23 Yulyu (July 23 Estate) and Mansha'at al-Nasr li-dubbat al-saf (al-Nasr Estate for Army Officers). See Presidential Decree 31/1970.

75 CAPMAS, "al-Kitab al-ihsa'i al-sanawi li-jumhuriyat Misr al-'arabiya 1952–1976," 143.

76 In an ASU meeting in 1970, Housing Minister Hussein Mustafa stated that 70 percent of total investments would be for economic units (where the government would cover all costs), 25 percent for middle units, and 5 percent for upper middle (where the government would have an unspecified share). However, this may only point to how the government distributed investments in its own projects, as the same document shows that the 1970/71 budget outlined a total of 26,000 housing units would be built, with the government building 8,000 of them, or about 31 percent, which is less than half of what the housing minister stated they would be building. See ASU, "al-Jalsa al-hadiya wa-l-'ishrun li-l-lajna al-markaziya li-l-ittihad al-ishtiraki al-'arabi."

77 In a party discussion, Nasser stated that the government had stopped building for the poor after the 1967 defeat, while middle housing that was more expensive to rent out stood vacant, and that this fuelled the 'counter-revolution.' See ASU, "al-Jalsa al-hadiyat 'ashar li-l-lajna al-markaziya li-l-ittihad al-ishtiraki al-'arabi."

78 Hanna, "Real Estate Rights in Urban Egypt: The Changing Sociopolitical Winds."

79 al-Ahram, "Madha tam ba'd khamas asabi' min bad' tandidh mashru' Nasser li-l-Iskan?," 3.

80 Nasser, "Kalimat al-ra'is Gamal 'Abd al-Nasser fi al-ihtifal bi-tawzi' al-masakin al-sha'biya fi Hilmiyyat al-Zaytun."

81 Nasser, "Kalimat al-ra'is Gamal 'Abd al-Nasser fi al-ihtifal bi-tawzi' al-masakin al-sha'biya fi Hilmiyyat al-Zaytun."

82 Nasser, "Kalimat al-ra'is Gamal 'Abd al-Nasser fi al-ihtifal bi-tawzi' al-masakin al-sha'biya fi Hallab."

83 While the diary is not dated, I have assumed it was written sometime in 1961, as it is positioned among a collection of documents from that year, and details in the entry describe future organizations that were established in 1961 or later. Nasser, "Mufakira bi-qalam al-ra'is 'an takwin majlis a'la li-l-difa' wa

khitta li tahrir Filastin wa-l-iskan wa-l-'ilaj wa-l-ta'min al-sihhi wa-l-sina'a."
84 Nasser, "Mufakira bi-qalam al-ra'is 'an takwin majlis a'la li-l-difa' wa khitta li tahrir Filastin wa-l-iskan wa-l-'ilaj wa-l-ta'min al-sihhi wa-l-sina'a."
85 Waterbury, *The Egypt of Nasser and Sadat: The Political Economy of Two Regimes*, 339. A year later, Nasser's political party, the Arab Socialist Union (ASU), was founded.
86 Presidential Decree 1674/1973, naming Osman as minister for reconstruction, was issued on October 27. Presidential Decree 5/1974 formally regulated the new ministry, but less than six months later Sadat would merge it with the Ministry of Housing, creating a super Ministry of Housing and Reconstruction under Osman (Presidential Decrees 72/1975 and 336/1975).
87 According to a contemporary report, 85 percent of Suez and 20 percent of both Ismailiya and Port Said were destroyed or damaged beyond repair, while the town of Qantara, was completely destroyed. See Antar, "Suez Reborn."
88 Law 62/1974, Explanatory Note, presented by Osman to Sadat.
89 Although Osman's Arab Contractors was nationalized under Nasser, he kept his position as chairperson under Presidential Decree 1228/1964, while supervision was given to the minister of housing under Presidential Decree 4415/1965. Sadat's presidential decrees forming the Ministry of Reconstruction brought the company under Osman's "direct supervision" and did not specify Osman's resignation as chairperson.
90 Data is sketchy depending on the source. A MoHR table cited 4,864 reconstruction units built in 1974, and 20,000 in 1975. Ministry of Housing and Reconstruction in Joint Housing Team, "Immediate Action Proposals for Housing in Egypt—Statistical Appendix," 51. A 1977 news report cited 55,000 units repaired by then, and 17,000 rebuilt. Antar, "Suez Reborn." By contrast an *al-Ahram* news report cited 121,500 economic and emergency units built between 1974–77. *Al-Ahram*, "Injazat al-ta'mir bi Sina wa-l-qanah. In all likelihood this figure includes repaired units as well as single room barrack-style temporary housing that may have been built for workers.
91 'Abd al-Tawwab, "Bila rutush: sakin al-hugra al-safih yamshi kul yawm 3 kilu li-aqrab hanafiyat miya'."
92 Arab Television, "Hadith al-ra'is Muhammad Anwar al-Sadat ila al-tilifisyun al-'arabi fi 24 Yulyu 1977."
93 There is massive coverage of his multiday trips to the canal cities on the Anwar Sadat Digital Archive—Bibliotheca Alexandrina. See, for example, *al-Ahram*, "al-Sadat adda salat al-'id ma' abna' al-Suez wa salat al-jum'a fi al-Isma'iliya"; *al-Ahram*, "Mashakiluna mashakil ta'mir wa taqaddum."
94 Ghannam, *Remaking the Modern*, 37–38.
95 Ghannam, *Remaking the Modern*, 2.
96 'Ishash al-Turguman was just one of five neighborhoods slated for demolition in the Bulaq and Rud al-Farag districts (the others being Maspero, Ma'arouf,

Ramlit Bulaq, and Hikr Abu Duma) to be replaced by a gleaming new so-called Central Business District (CBD). For a thorough examination of the history of attempts to reshape Bulaq see Selim, *Unfinished Places*, 122–23.

97 Another 2,865 units were slated for completion by 1979 in al-Zawya al-Hamra and Ain Shams for resettlement purposes. *al-Ahram*, "al-Sakan al-nadir!"

98 *al-Ahram*, "al-Sakan al-nadir!"

99 Ghannam, *Remaking the Modern*, 39.

100 Sadat, "Kalimat al-ra'is Muhammad Anwar al-Sadat ila 'ummal al-naql fi 18 Yunyu 1977."

101 Law 49/1977 (Article 72) allowed for the sale of rented government housing and Prime Ministerial Decree 110/1978 established the conditions of sale to tenants, as well as to new beneficiaries. The sale of canal zone housing would be regulated by Prime Ministerial Decree 109/1978 (and government-owned workers' housing would be sold under different conditions in the 1990s).

102 Boughton, *Municipal Dreams: The Rise and Fall of Council Housing*, 170–71.

103 Law 107/1976, Explanatory Note. The fund was established in 1976 to finance the discrepancy between local government funds and the planned housing construction that was decided at national level. It was also allowed to capture revenue from sale or rent of all local government property, bonds, exceptional height permit fees, state budget, grants, loans, and construction fines. See Law 107/1976 and MoHR Decree 466/1976, Executive bylaws.

104 The reconstruction housing in the canal cities and Sinai would be sold under similar conditions, though with revenue going to the governorates. See Prime Ministerial Decree 109/1978.

105 These income requirements were imposed on those who were administratively evicted (residents of condemned buildings) and newlyweds, allocated 25 percent each of the new housing in every governorate. The remaining half did not have to meet income requirements—these were relocated government employees, military personnel, and those chosen at the governor's discretion, who were allocated 15 percent, 10 percent, and 25 percent of new housing in every governorate respectively. See Prime Ministerial Decree 110/1978.

106 Court of Cassation Appeal 4705/71, March 6, 2013. The original case was lodged in 1990. The documents have redacted the names of the plaintiffs, making it impossible to know who lodged the court case, disgruntled applicants or a righteous government whistle blower.

107 Sadat, "Kalimat al-ra'is Muhammad Anwar al-Sadat ila al-sha'b fi munasabat irsa' hajar asas madinat 10 Ramadan fi 29 Mayu 1977."

108 Barrada, Wheaton, and Annez, "Public Policy and the Economics of Housing. Appendix A: Public Policy and the 'Shortage' of Housing in Egypt."

109 Hanna, *al-Iskan wa-l-masyada: al-mushkila wa-l-hal*, 65–71.

110 These were Sadat City (a failed new capital), 15 May (his 'corrective'

revolution in 1971), Sixth of October (date of the October War of 1973), Tenth of Ramadan (October War according to the Hijri calendar), 'Ubur (crossing of the Suez Canal), and Badr (codename for the October War operation to cross the canal, also the name of an early Islamic battle).

111 *al-Ahram*, "Tarh 3,000 shiqqa li-l-tamlik fi madinat al-'ashir min Ramadan."

112 Presidential Decree 275/1978 and Law 59/1979.

113 Law 43/1979 regulating local government, and Presidential Decree 487/1979 establishing the MoRNC Housing Fund (RNCHF).

Chapter 6

1 Mubarak, "Nus kalimat al-ra'is Muhammad Hosni Mubarak fi iftitah mu'tamar Misr sanat 2000."

2 Ettouney, "Low Income Family Housing: Notes on Egypt's Experience."

3 Ettouney.

4 Ettouney and Abdel-Kader, "Users' Participation in Low Cost Housing Projects: Post Occupancy Evaluation." At the time the government had set size and quality standards for four levels of housing: economic, middle, upper middle, and luxury. Minister of Housing and Reconstruction Decree 237/1977. Low Cost would later be added to these levels in the Statistical Yearbooks.

5 Interest was 6 percent, and installments were designed to be no more than 25 percent of the income that low-income groups were identified as earning, Ettouney and Abdel-Kader.

6 Mitchell, "No Factories, No Problems."

7 Public Sector Companies Law 203/1991, Article 30.

8 From 4 to 21.5 percent. *Al-Ahaly*, "Madinat al-ahlam yahjurha al-shabab wa mi'at al-usar ta'jaz 'an al-daf'."

9 World Bank, "Egypt—Analysis of Housing Supply Mechanisms," 25. It is worth noting that this report benefited from "significant inputs" provided by Mustafa Madbuli who was then director of the technical office of the Ministry of Housing's think tank the General Organization for Physical Planning, World Bank, v. At the time of writing, Madbuli is Egypt's prime minister and minister of housing, utilities, and urban communities.

10 These were a cooperative housing loan of LE15,000 to be paid back over forty years at 6 percent interest, in addition to a loan of LE4,500 at 8 percent interest that would be paid back over fifteen years. World Bank, "Egypt—Analysis of Housing Supply Mechanisms," 26.

11 *al-Ahram*, "600 sadadu muqaddam al-hajz fi mashru' Mubarak li-iskan al-shabab." See chapter 5 for more on these agencies.

12 World Bank, "Egypt—Analysis of Housing Supply Mechanisms," 25.

13 Sims, *Understanding Cairo: The Logic of a City Out of Control*, 158.

14 This was out of a target of 70,000 units. See New Urban Communities Authority, "Iskan al-shabab wa-l-mustaqbal."

15 *al-Ahram*, "Suzanne Mubarak tua'kid fi hafl taslim 'uqud takhsis shuqaq iskan al-mustaqbal." Given that all the housing was located in the new cities, NUCA also supplied the infrastructure and land for free.

16 A LE14,000 cooperative loan at an interest rate of 5 percent.

17 *al-Ahram*, "Wazir al-ta'mir wa-l-iskan: 22 al-hali . . . bad' al-hajz fi iskan al-mustaqbal."

18 *al-Ahram*, "Suzanne Mubarak tua'kid fi hafl taslim 'uqud takhsis shuqaq iskan al-mustaqbal."

19 Masakin Zeinhom and al-Dweiqa al-Jadida are the largest and more famous of Suzanne Mubarak's estates. There were also smaller estates in 'Ain Helwan, 'Izbit Haridi, and al-Aguza. All were located in Cairo. See *al-Ahram*, "Suzanne Mubarak khilal ziyaratha li-mashru' al-tanmaiya al-mujtama'iya bi-l-Dweiqa."

20 Shehayeb Consult, "Housing Relocation in Cairo"; *al-Dustur al-asli*, "Sukkan al-iwa': min wa'd bi-l-iqama fi masakin mu'aqatta il al-nisyan li-akthar min 30 sana."

21 Mubarak, "Kalimat al-ra'is Muhammad Hosni Mubarak fi al-liqa' al-sha'bi bi-khitam al-hamla al-intikhabiya."

22 World Bank, "Egypt—Next Step Recommendations for Affordable Housing Policy and the National Housing Program," 5–6.

23 A total of 5,181 feddans (21.8 million square meters) were earmarked for the scheme. The plan was to sell at least 50 percent of the land at LE70 per square meter—about half the LE140 it cost the government to service with roads and trunk infrastructure—while the rest of the land not used for NHP units was to be sold at LE333, which was still below market prices. Developers buying plots over 200 feddans got further discounts, for example the Orascom Housing Communities, a joint venture between the Egyptian Orascom Developments and the United States-based real estate developers Blue Ridge Partners and Equity International, bought 2,000 feddans for LE10 per square meter in Sixth of October City to build Haram City. See World Bank, "Egypt—A Framework for Housing Policy Reform in Urban Areas in Egypt," 58.

24 By 2005, a mortgage market had failed to appear although a USAID-funded project to establish a "well-functioning housing finance system" had led to Egypt's first mortgage law (148/2001) and the establishment of the Mortgage Finance Authority (MFA). See Nathan Associates, "Mortgage Market Reform in Egypt—Final Report."

25 The United Nations Development Program (UNDP), the Canadian International Development Agency (CIDA), and the Canada Housing Mortgage Corporation were also funding the National Urban Observatory, a government agency that was supposed to gather real estate data on a regular basis, but only produced one report. See MoHUUC, "State of the Built Environment and Housing Indicators in Seven Egyptian Cities—Comprehensive Report."

26 World Bank, "Egypt—A Framework for Housing Policy Reform in Urban

Areas in Egypt," iii.

27 USAID, "Egypt Affordable Home Production Program (AHPP)"; World Bank, "Egypt—Next Step Recommendations for Affordable Housing Policy and the National Housing Program."

28 Al-Mahdi, "Against Marginalization: Youth, Class, and Revolution."

29 El Maghraby, "H.E. Ahmed El Maghraby, Minister of Housing, Utilities, and Urban Development—Speech at the AmCham Egypt Conference: Real Estate: Where Is it Heading?"

30 World Bank, "Projects: Affordable Mortgage Finance DPL."

31 *al-Ahram al-misa'i*, "Mashru' jadid li-bina' milyun wihda."

32 *al-Yawm al-sabi'*, "Bi-l-suwar, tajamhur al-alaf amam al-iskan li-hajz wihdat sakaniya."

33 *al-Ahram*, "Taqadam laha 5.5 milyun muwatin: al-iskan tatrah 35 alf wihda sakaniya jadida fi 19 muhafza."

34 Ministry of Housing, Utilities and Urban Development, "Kurrasat shurut musabaqat i'dad al-namazig al-mi'mariya wa-l-tasmim al-'umrani li mawaqi' al-iskan dimn barnamij al-dawla li-l-iskan al-ijtima'i."

35 Buna, "al-Mashru' al-fa'iz' bi-l-musabaqa al-qawmiya li-l-iskan."

36 *Al-Ahram*, "al-Sisi yutliq mubadarat al-milyun wihda sakaniya li-l-shabab."

37 Arabtec Holding, "Arabtec Signs Historic Agreement with Egypt's Defence Ministry to Develop and Construct One Million Housing Units in Egypt—Official Press Release."

38 Barnard, "Arabtec's Egypt Housing Deal Still Under Discussion, Says Chairman."

39 *al-Masri al-yawm*, "Mai 'Abd al-Hamid ra'is sanduq al-iskan al-ijtima'i wa-l-tamwil al-'aqari: 120 alf 'amil yatasalamun wihdatihim fi 2019."

40 Al-Sisi, "Kalimat al-ra'is 'Abd al-Fattah al-Sisi khilal al-ihtifaliya bi-murur 60 'aman 'ala ta'mim qanat al-suways wa murur 'am 'ala iftitah al-qanah al-jadida."

41 Egypt News, "Madbuli yu'akkid hal mushkilat al-iskan jazriyan khilal 3 sanawat."

42 10 Tooba, "Built Environment Deprivation Index." Affordability.

43 From the late 1970s, cooperative housing loans with subsidized interest were granted, based on unit size and specifications, and not income.

44 The low-income threshold for single person households was set at LE1,000 and LE1,750 in 2005 and 2008 respectively. See Mortgage Law 148/2001 (Article 6) and Prime Ministerial Decrees 456/2005 and 1864/2008. Some schemes continued using the 2005 levels up until 2013.

45 In 2010, only three years after the first units were delivered, seventeen thousand families had started defaulting on loan payments, *Ruz al-yusuf*, "I'fa' 17 alf muta'aththir fi al-Qawm li-l-Iskan min fawa'id al-ta'khir."

46 Unit prices doubled by 2012 to LE105,000, while the cash subsidy rose to

LE35,000, still leaving LE70,000 to be covered by the applicants, in effect doubling the minimum income to qualify for the loans. *Al-Bursa*, "al-Iskandariya tatrah 2,500 faddan li-iqamat mashru' istithmari mutakamil."

47 A beneficiary of the Tamlik scheme said he had to pay the entire amount upfront in cash because he did not have a formal job. Shawkat, "Mubarak's Promise. Social Justice and the National Housing Programme: Affordable Homes or Political Gain?"

48 *al-Masri al-yawm*, "al-Iskan tukhassis mashru' bayt al-'a'ila li-l-niqabat wa-l-hay'at al-hukumiya hifazan 'ala al-mustawa al-ijtima'i."

49 This is according to a price schedule for the Degla Gardens development dated August 2010.

50 For a detailed study of the project, see Nazmi, "Ru'ya taqyimiya li-mashru' Ibni Baytak."

51 Permits and utility connections cost LE4,150, structural shell LE35,000, exterior finishing LE30,000, and interior finishing LE16,000, Nazmi.

52 Exceptions from maximum income stipulations for families of police and army personnel injured or killed on duty were introduced in 2017. See CBE, "Circular Dated October 8, 2017 Regarding Raising Mortgage Fund and Casualties and Families of Martyrs of Army and Police."

53 *al-Ahram*, "La ahad fawq al-qanun."

54 Social Housing and Mortgage Finance Fund, "Performance Report Fiscal Year 2017/2018," 4; SHF/GSF, "Taqrir al-ada' 'an nash'at sanduq al-tamwil al-'aqari wa-l-iskan al-ijtima'i hatta tarikh 30 Yunyu 2017," 20.

55 CAPMAS, "Annual Bulletin of Labour Force 2017."

56 Shukrallah and Shawkat, "Analysis: Government Policy Commodifies Housing."

57 *al-Bawaba News*, "Ra'is sanduq al-tamwil al-'aqari tatahaddath li-l-*Bawaba News*."

58 There were numerous protests by applicants calling for a rerun of the lottery, which some authorities agreed to. *Al-Yawm al-sabi'*, "Muhafiz al-Wadi al-Jadid yujri i'ada qur'at shuqaq al-awqaf ghadan." The private developer schemes were left to enforce the application conditions themselves—for units that were already too expensive for low-income applicants.

59 This was applied from phase four of the NHP, from 2010 onward. *al-Ahram al-misa'i*, "al-Damin yaghtal hilm al-shabab fi shiqqa."

60 *al-Ahram al-misa'i*, "al-Damin yaghtal hilm al-shabab fi shiqqa."

61 *al-Dustur al-asli*, "al-Na'ib al-'am yahthar tarh al-wihdat al-sakaniya bi-l-iskan al-qawmi fi mazad 'alani."

62 *al-Dustur al-asli*, "al-Na'ib al-'am yahthar tarh al-wihdat al-sakaniya bi-l-iskan al-qawmi fi mazad 'alani."

63 ONA, "Tawaquf harakat qitarat al-Sa'id bi-Bani Sueif bi-sabab al-ihtijaj 'ala 'adam taslim shuqaq al-iskan"; *al-Dustur al-asli*, "Sukkan al-iwa': min wa'd

bi-l-iqama fi masakin mu'aqatta ila al-nisyan li-akthar min 30 sana."

64 *al-Ahram*, "12 da'wa qada'iya did muhafiz Kafr al-Sheikh."

65 These were applied for by one NDP parliamentarian in the names of her four adult children, members of her extended family, and close aides. *Al-Masri al-yawm*, "al-Qabd 'ala ra'is majlis madina fi al-Daqahliya taqada rashwa li-tashil al-istila' 'ala shuqaq iskan Mubarak."

66 *al-Misryun*, "740 usra tataqaddam bi-shakwa did muhafiz al-Gharbiya li-'adam tasallumhum al-shuqaq."

67 *al-Masri al-yawm*, "Mai 'Abd al-Hamid ra'is sanduq al-iskan al-ijtima'i wa-l-tamwil al-'aqari: 120 alf 'amil yatasallamun wihdatihim fi 2019."

68 *al-Masri al-yawm*, "Ra'is sanduqay al-tamwil al-'aqari wa-l-iskan al-ijtima'i: ziyadat as'ar al-i'lanat al-jadida."

69 *al-Naba'*, "Manshur bi-Facebook yakshif sulukan khatiran min muwazaf isti'lam shuqaq al-iskan al-ijtima'i."

70 *al-Yawm al-sabi'*, "al-Tamwil al-'aqari: yatim istib'ad sharikat al-isti'lam hal tikrar shakawa al-muwatinin."

71 *al-Wafd*, "35 alf muwatin sajjalu bayyinatihum khata' fi al-i'lan al-tasi' li-l-iskan al-ijtima'i."

72 Hall and Vidén, "The Million Homes Programme"; Croese, "State-Led Housing Delivery as an Instrument of Developmental Patrimonialism."

73 Makkar, "4 Years of Modi Govt"; *Reuters*, "China Plans Two Million New Units of Public Housing for 2017."

74 *Masakin bidun sukkan, wa sukkan bidun masakin.* Hanna, *al-Iskan wa-l-masyada: al-mushkila wa-l-hal*, 7.

75 While vacancy is indeed a phenomenon, there are many methodological issues. See Sims 2010. In 2017, one million units were abandoned because of structural damage, and four million were unfinished. Another four million had yet to be occupied, and the rest were empty because owners had another home or were abroad. CAPMAS, "al-Nata'ij al-niha'iya li-l-ti'dad al-'am li-l-sukkan wa-l-iskan wa-l-munsha'at li-'am 2017: al-sukkan wa-l-zuruf al-sakaniya."

76 Sims, *Understanding Cairo: The Logic of a City Out of Control*, 159–60.

77 Mubarak, "Khitab al-ra'is Mubarak fi al-ihtifal bi-'id al-'ummal."

78 This is based on an assumption of one unit per plot, though there must have been many more units. One study of 2,200 plots found that almost two-thirds had built the maximum of three floors. Nazmi, "Ru'ya taqyimiya li-mashru' Ibni Baytak."

79 Abotawila, "Understanding Egyptian Social Housing Squatting Phenomenon Post January 2011: The Production of Space in Elmouhtalla," 19. Simcik Arese, "Urbanism as Craft: Practicing Informality and Property in Cairo's Gated Suburbs, from Theft to Virtue."

80 Shawkat, "Mubarak's Promise. Social Justice and the National Housing Programme: Affordable Homes or Political Gain?"

81 Simcik Arese, "Urbanism as Craft: Practicing Informality and Property in Cairo's Gated Suburbs, from Theft to Virtue."

82 In 2013, eight years after the NHP had begun, the housing minister stated that 21,000 units still had no infrastructure. *Al-Masri al-yawm*, "Mihlib: 21 alf wihda sakaniya munafadha bi-l-muhafazat bi-l-mashru' al-qawmi al-sabiq dun marafiq."

83 A field visit to an area the scheme completed three years earlier showed that a portion of the 5,400 completed units were delivered to beneficiaries, and middlemen had already set up shop and were renting and trading them, while an even smaller portion appeared to be inhabited. Shawkat, "Mubarak's Promise. Social Justice and the National Housing Programme: Affordable Homes or Political Gain?"

84 During the NHP's first year, the minister of housing was forced to extend the application deadline by four months due to low demand. *Al-Masri al-yawm*, "Mad hajz wihdat al-mashru' al-qawmi li-l-iskan ila Ughustus al-muqbil."

85 *al-Masri al-yawm*, "Qura al-Minya al-namuzajiya. Buyut ashbah"; *al-Masri al-yawm*, "al-Muhasabat: ihdar 500 milyun jinih fi al-Zahir al-Sahrawi." See Chapter 4 for more on them.

86 *al-Masri al-yawm*, "al-Muhasabat: ihdar 500 milyun jinih fi al-Zahir al-Sahrawi."

87 *al-Mal*, "al-Sisi: mafish dawla bi-l-'alam tiqdar ta'mil zayina 'adad wihdat iskan."

88 At least 3,000 units have been sold to the South Sinai governorate, and 588 in Ras Gharib to the Red Sea governorate to use as compensation for victims of flash flooding. See New Urban Communities Authority, "Wazir al-iskan wa-muhafiz janub Sina' yuwaqi'an brutukulan li-bay' 3 alaf wihda sakaniya bi-l-iskan al-ijtima'i li-l-muhafaza li-tawzi'iha 'ala muwatiniha"; *al-Masri al-yawm*, "588 wihda sakaniya li-l-mutadaririn min al-siyul bi Ras Gharib."

89 Shawkat, "A Million Units for Whom?"

90 Shawkat, "A Million Units for Whom?"

91 Ministry of Housing, Utilities, and Urban Development, "al-Mashru' al-qawmi li-l-iskan," 3.

92 This is a legal term called *bidun hissa fi al-ard* (without a share in the land) and is a form of indefinite lease, where 'owners' own only the bricks and mortar as long as the building is standing. It is widely used by government agencies, while private sellers can also stipulate it, either because they are reselling former government housing, or because there is a problem registering the land. See chapter 7 for more on informality.

93 World Bank, "Egypt—Next Step Recommendations for Affordable Housing Policy and the National Housing Program," 11.

94 The Ministry of Housing report had a different breakdown stating LE7.5 billion in cash subsidies, LE6.5 billion for land and infrastructure, and LE1 billion

to cover cost overruns. Ministry of Housing, Utilities, and Urban Development, "al-Mashru' al-qawmi," 4.

95 Ministry of Finance, "al-Bayan al-mali 'an mashru' al-muwazana al-'amma li-l-dawla li-l-sana al-maliya 2008/2009," 70.

96 All figures in this section, except where otherwise noted, are from Shawkat, "A Million Units for Whom?"

97 The World Bank has called them out as "inefficient and poorly targeted supply-side subsidies." Instead it supports what it calls "transparent, well-targeted and economically efficient demand-side" subsidies that are paid to buyers upon purchase of a unit. In any case, the units cost far more than they should. See World Bank, "Inclusive Housing Finance Program-for-Results Project—Project Appraisal Document," 5.

98 World Bank, "Projects: Inclusive Housing Finance Program." This follows on a $300 million loan in 2009 for a similar, though simpler, project implemented during the tail end of the NHP. See World Bank, "Projects: Affordable Mortgage Finance DPL."

99 Social Housing Law 33/2014.

100 Social Housing and Mortgage Subsidy Law 93/2018.

101 IMF, "Arab Republic of Egypt First Review Under the Extended Arrangement," 8.

102 *al-Masri al-yawm*, "Mai 'Abd al-Hamid ra'is sanduq al-iskan al-ijtima'i wa-l-tamwil al-'aqari: 120 alf 'amil yatasallamun wihdatihim fi 2019."

103 This calculation makes the assumption of the rule-of-thumb of twenty units per feddan. *Al-Mal*, "Bani Sueif al-Jadida turafiq aradi al-iskan al-ijtima'i bi-qimat 52 million jinih."

104 Ministry of Finance, "al-Bayan al-mali 'an mashru' al-muwazana al-'amma li-l-dawla li-l-sana al-maliya 2017/2018," 76.

105 Riad, "Alexandria."

106 Hanna, *al-Iskan wa-l-siyasa*, 80.

107 While the Tender Law 89/1998 stipulates that all government agencies should put procurement contracts to public tender (Article 1). Article 1 allows for exceptions where limited tenders, negotiated bids, and direct agreements would be acceptable. In a recently updated form, the Public Agency Contracts Law 182/2018 allows for the same (Article 7).

108 *al-Ahram*, "La ahad fawq al-qanun."

109 *Egypt Independent*, "Sisi Inaugurates the 'Bashayer al-Khair-2' Project in Alexandria."

110 Mohie, "Asmarat: The State's Model Housing for Former 'Slum' Residents."

111 Mounir, "How State Luxury Housing Projects Affect Egypt's Real Estate Market."

112 Presidential Decree 57/2016 established the New Administrative Capital City and the company that runs it.

113 *Egypt Independent*, "More Housing Units Available in New Administrative Capital."

114 *Invest-Gate*, "City Edge to Invest EGP 1 Bn in Sheikh Zayed's Etapa in 2019."

115 Units in the North Edge Towers in New Alamein were advertised for an average of LE35,000 per square meter. Al-Aees, "City Edge Developments Completes 40% of Commercial Area of North Edge Towers in New Alamein City." In 2015, average income was LE44,200 per year. CAPMAS, "Aham mu'ashirat bahth al-dakhl wa-l-infaq wa-l-istihlak li 'am 2015," 30.

116 The treasury did not benefit from NUCA's projected revenue of LE76.1 billion and LE95.9 billion for FYs 2017/18 and 2018/19 respectively, as a budget stipulation to do so for those years was waived. See NUCA Budget Enactment Laws 177/2017 and 133/2018.

Chapter 7

1 Sejourne, "Inhabitants' Daily Practices to Obtain Legal Status for Their Homes and Security of Tenure: Egypt."

2 Between 1997 and 2013, urban development plans have resulted in the eviction and supposed resettlement of 24,126 families outside of the city, as well as the rehousing of 17,113 families in newly built housing in or close to their original place of residence. Shawkat, *al-'Adala al-ijtima'iya wa-l-'umran—kharitat Misr*, 83.

3 Shawkat, *al-'Adala al-ijtima'iya wa-l-'umran—kharitat Misr*.

4 Human Rights Watch, "Look for Another Homeland: Forced Evictions in Egypt's Rafah."

5 It is customary practice to pay an Old Rent tenant half of a unit's value to end the contract in a practice known as *khiliw rigl* (key money), covered in chapter 3. It has also been used an upfront payment to acquire an Old Rent apartment from the landlord. Since 2011, a growing practice has emerged whereby owners partner with contractors to demolish the old buildings, and build higher ones on the same plot, and then sell the new extra units. They rehouse the tenants in homes that may be smaller, of lower quality than the originals, or delivered unfinished. Interview, A.S., an Old Rent tenant in Alexandria, July 19, 2016.

6 The latter involve deliberate damage to a building, from the outside or the inside. Shadow Ministry of Housing, EIPR, and TTC, "Why Do Buildings Collapse in Egypt?"

7 See Law 10/1990 Expropriation for Public Benefit. It has many caveats, chief of which is allowing for compensation well below market rates, in addition to the lack of any meaningful means for negotiation or the ability to appeal the expropriation. Other laws also allow or amount to expropriation of private property for various purposes including urban renewal *(i'adit takhtit)* and street widening *(tanzim)* as per the Unified Building

Law 119/2008 or urban development as per the New Communities Law 59/1979.

8 IPRI, "IPRI 2018—Egypt."

9 World Justice Project, "Rule of Law Index 2017–2018: Egypt."

10 Rasmussen, "Some Live It Up."

11 Trading Economics, "Egypt Government Budget—2019."

12 See Prime Ministerial Decree 2589/2015, outlining the committee's role as "building a database of unused assets belonging to ministries, local government, and the agencies affiliated with them, and establishing a plan to utilize them in a manner that would realize the highest possible return."

13 The concept of the rent gap was developed in the 1980s by the geographer Neil Smith. Smith, "Gentrification and the Rent Gap."

14 Common Law 131/1948, Articles 968 and 969.

15 For more detail, see some of the related bylaws in Prime Ministerial Decrees 2041/2006 and 2843/2009, Minister of Agriculture Decree 1317/2010, and Giza Governor Decree 14325/2006.

16 Interview, M.E., a resident of al-Salamoni village, Suhag, November 19, 2013.

17 Presidential Decree 75/2016.

18 Presidential Decree 378/2016, Law 144/2017 Managing State Private Property, and Prime Ministerial Decree 18/2017, Executive Bylaws.

19 Committee to Recover State Land, "al-Dawla tastarid milyun faddan wa 132 million mitr muraba' fi 18 shahr."

20 Committee to Recover State Land, "al-Muhandis Sharif Isma'il: al-awlawiya li-inha ijra'at taqnin aradi al-dawla khilal al-fatra al-qadima."

21 *al-Bawaba News*, "Ra'is majlis idarat Jam'iyyat Rijal Amn al-Mustaqbal yatahaddath li-l-Bawaba News."

22 CRSL Committee to Recover State Land, "Ihalat malaf 215 faddan bi-Misr al-Iskandiriya li-l-amwal al-'amma."

23 Interview, G.U., a resident of Ramlit Bulaq, Cairo, December 17, 2013.

24 According to Cairo Governor Galal Sa'id, a land plot sold in 2005 for LE8,000 per square meter was valued at LE40,000 per square meter in 2014. See *al-Bursa*, "al-Qahira tukhattit li-i'adat hikr Abu Duma li-l-kharita al-istithmariya li-l-muhafaza."

25 Cairo Governor Decree 7901/2009.

26 Egypt News, "Wazir: lijan li-hasr al-'aqarat al-lati tushakil khutura 'ala Bulaq Abu al-'Ila."

27 *al-Bursa*, "Sanduk tatwir al-'ashwa'iyat yabda' tatwir Ramlit Bulaq."

28 Shadow Ministry of Housing, *Badal Matshiluna, Tawaruna!*

29 *Egypt Independent*, "EIPR Accuses Police Officer of Murder in Nile City Incident."

30 Egypt State Council ruling 55949/66. August 21, 2013.

31 EIPR was already representing thirty of the fifty young men arrested from Ramlit Bulaq, so Ahmed Hossam was already familiar with the community when he noticed the expropriation decree and brought it to the attention of the residents there. They were able to lodge an appeal, which they won. EIPR, "'Ala al-hukuma al-mirsiya daman huquq al-muwatinin fi maskan mula'ma qabl hadm masakinhum."

32 Egypt State Council ruling 55949/66.

33 For more on the project see Khalil, al-Marsafi, and Hegazy, "Ramlit Bulaq."

34 Egypt State Council ruling 55949/66.

35 *al-Ahram*, "Mas'ul bi-l-iskan: hunak 3 malayin 'aqar mukhalif fi-Misr."

36 *al-Yawm al-sabi'*, "Iskan al-barlaman: qanun al-tasaluh fi mukhalafat al-bina' yuwaffir li-l-dawla 300 milyar jinih."

37 *al-Masri al-yawm*, "Abaza yuqaddim taqriran li-Nazif hawl mukhalafat al-sharikat wa-l-afrad 'ala al-tariq al-sahrawi."

38 Sims, *Egypt's Desert Dreams: Development or Disaster*, 158–62.

39 According to the head of the General Agency for Reclamation Projects and Development (GARPAD), the fines were raised to LE357 per square meter, or roughly LE1.5 million per acre, while there were 87,809 acres under its jurisdiction where land use was illegally changed to urban. *Al-Ahram*, "Ba'd al-ta'addi 'ala alaf al-afdina min al-ruq'a al-zira'iya."

40 Committee to Recover State Land, "Ihalat malaf 215 faddan bi Misr al-Iskandiriya li-l-amwal al-'amma."

41 New Urban Communities Authority, "Fath bab al-taqadum li-man sabaq al-ta'amul bi-mujab 'uqud bi' aw mustanadat milkiyat al-aradi alati taqa' dakhil hudud al-qarar al-jumhuri li-madinat Sphinx al-Jadida." This also happened in a number of areas including the Cairo–Ismailiya highway.

42 NUCA has a range of options depending on whether the land is owned, rented, or adversely possessed. For more see New Urban Communities Authority, "Qarar majlis al-idara bi-jalsatih raqam 112 bi-tarikh 12/9/2018."

43 Almoghazy, "Forced Informality: When Housing Rights and Building Laws Collide."

44 Cases of bribery of municipal authority new city administrators are not rare with the Administrative Control Authority that monitors civil servants. ACA, "Dabtiyat hay'at al-riqaba al-idariya khilal usbu'"; *al-Masri al-yawm*, "al-Sijn 3 sanawat li-na'ib ra'is al-Qahira al-Jadida wa akahrin fi rashwat al-narjis."

45 A 2015 article in *al-Watan* newspaper mentions 100,000 unimplemented decrees for 27,500 buildings or parts of buildings in Alexandria alone. *Al-Watan*, "al-Iskandiriya . . . 27 alf wa 500 'aqar. Wa 100 alf qarar izala dun tanfiz."

46 In 1981, the agriculture census counted 925,142 land tenancies, while assuming each tenancy meant one family, and contemporary demographics calculated six individuals per rural family. Springborg estimated that six million people, representing 12 percent of the population, could be affected.

Springborg, "State-Society Relations in Egypt: The Debate over Owner-Tenant Relations."
47 Law 96/1992, Joint Parliamentary Committee Report.
48 Land Center for Human Rights, "Fuqd al-ard al-zira'iya wa-l-'unf fi al-rif."
49 Land Center for Human Rights, "Fuqd al-ard al-zira'iya wa-l-'unf fi al-rif."
50 About fifty families sought legal support against eviction from a rights NGO in 2004. See Land Center for Human Rights, "Markaz al-ard yuqaddim balagh ila al-na'ib al-'am. Inqidhu fallahin Basyun min al-tasharud."
51 Land Center for Human Rights, "Markaz al-ard yuqaddim balagh ila al-na'ib al-'am. Inqidhu fallahin Basyun min al-tasharud."
52 The government gave priority to evictees, though only 16,727 families were resettled there by 2003. See Adriansen, "Land Reclamation in Egypt: A Study of Life in the New Lands."
53 Interview, A.Z., an heir of a *'izba*, Sharqiya, July 4, 2017.
54 As the share of one heir was all rented out to the fellahin, she made a deal, transferring a third of the tenancy to each fellah, in exchange for the remaining two-thirds. Abaza, *The Cotton Plantation Remembered: An Egyptian Family Story*, 403 and 428. It is not clear if the exchange included titles for the houses or the land they were built on.
55 A very small proportion of the inhabitants of 'Izbit Tunis in Fayoum have bought their houses from the ARA, while the rest pay an annual land tax without a dated contract. Interview, M.S., a resident of a 'Izbet Tunis, Fayoum, June 30, 2017.
56 Agrarian Reform Law 178/1952 and Laws 152/1957 about general waqfs and 44/1962 about private waqfs.
57 EIPR, "'Izbet al-'Arab/ Muthalath al-Montazah Evictions."
58 EIPR, "'Izbet al-'Arab/ Muthalath al-Montazah Evictions."
59 *Al-Ahram*, "Ra'is hay'at al-awqaf fi-hiwar ma' *al-Ahram*: la tasluh ma' al-tuta'adi 'ala mal al-waqf."
60 Wazarat al-Awqaf—Muhafazat al-Iskandiriya, Protocol Ta'awun 3/696, Ministry of Awqaf Internal document, January 31, 2008. EIPR, "'Izbet al-'Arab/ Muthalath al-Montazah Evictions."
61 The Awqaf claimed the parcel was valued at more than LE9 billion in a half page ad it put out on the front page of a state-owned newspaper urging the Egyptian president to implement eviction orders on the Muthalath al-Montazah land parcel because the Alexandria governorate was slow to act. Al-Awqaf Authority, "Istighatha thalitha."
62 *al-Mal*, "al-Awqaf tabi'a usul bi-qimat 1.2 milyar jinih fi mazad 'alani."
63 EIPR, "'Izbet al-'Arab/ Muthalath al-Montazah Evictions."
64 EIPR, "'Izbet al-'Arab/ Muthalath al-Montazah Evictions."
65 *al-Yawm al-sabi'*, "Maqtal za'im al-fallahin al-rafidin li-bi'a aradihum bi-l-Muntazah."

66 EIPR, "'Izbet al-'Arab/ Muthalath al-Montazah Evictions."
67 *al-Shuruk*, "1,200 Usra bi-l-Iskandiriya tuhadid bi-l-idrab 'an al-ta'am wa-l-i'tisam fi al-shawari' i'tiradan 'ala hadm manazilhum."
68 Presidential Decree 300/2016.
69 De Soto, "Dead Capital and the Poor in Egypt."
70 Interview, Muhammad Wafiq, a lawyer, Cairo, February 15, 2016.
71 Sims, *Understanding Cairo: The Logic of a City Out of Control*, 153.
72 Court of Cassation ruling 680/64. October 12, 2003.
73 Law 180/1952.
74 Claimants of two hundred properties set up a Facebook group to promote their cause, Facebook, "Rabitat Mustahiqi al-Awqaf al-Misriya." (Guild of the Entitled to Egyptian Awqaf). For an estimated scale of the issue see *al-Ahram al-'arabi*, "Mufaja'a madwiya yukshifuha al-liwa' Ahmad al-Galbi ra'is jama'iyat mustahaqi al-waqf."
75 Interview, U.I., resident of a *tikiya*, al-Gumruk, Alexandria, April 22, 2016.
76 One of these blocks resulted in one of the most disastrous building collapses in recent history and over twenty-two people were killed. See Shadow Ministry of Housing, "Taqrir 'an karithat 'umarat hayy al-Gumruk bi-l-Iskandariya 1/2."
77 Interview, A.K., heir of a *tikiya*, al-Gumruk, Alexandria, April 22, 2016.
78 Sims, Kamal, and Solomon, "Housing Study for Urban Egypt," 42.
79 Social Housing and Mortgage Subsidy Law 93/2018 restricts the resale or rent of units for five years, unless approved by the Social Housing Fund. Failure to comply may result in the sequestration of the home, as well as payment of a fine between LE20,000 and LE100,000 and a jail term of no less than a year, or either of the two.
80 Abotawila, "Understanding Egyptian Social Housing Squatting Phenomenon Post January 2011: The Production of Space in Elmouhtalla," 59–62.
81 The de Soto study cited here erroneously puts the number at 800,000 units, based itself on an erroneous CAPMAS report. For clarification, see the section on methodology in chapter 1.
82 A group of tenants in Kafr al-Sheikh had rented out middle units of four bedrooms for LE6 and three bedrooms for LE5 in 1960 and 1961. Ensuing rent reductions brought them down to LE3.5 and LE2.3 respectively by 1965. The Court of Cassation overruled an earlier ruling upholding the tenants' application to buy, stating that both the original and reduced rents were less than the stipulated LE1.5 per room. See Court of Cassation Appeal 526/53. In Tanta, Gharbiya, a three-bedroom economic unit was originally rented for LE9.2 in 1971 (LE2.3 per room), and reduced to LE6.25 (LE1.6 per room) and then to LE3 (LE0.75 per room). The court only accepted the second reduction as it was upheld by an earlier rent reduction ruling, and stated it was higher than the stipulated LE1 per room, blocking its sale, exactly ten years after the case

was first lodged. See Court of Cassation Appeal 7214/64.

83 *Ahwal Misr*, "Ahwal Misr tarsud mu'anat sukkan mantiqat al-Amin bi-Bur Sa'id."

84 Port Said governorate, "Duf'a min natijat halat izalat al-masakin al-hukumiya."

85 Volait, "Réforme Sociale et Habitat Populaire: Acteurs et Formes (1848–1964)."

86 Law 111/1961 amending Investment Company Law 26/1954. See also interview with M.W., head of the worker's pension fund, in EIPR, "Mosta'maret al-Mahalla Workers' 'Evictions.'"

87 Beinin and el-Hamalawy, "Egyptian Textile Workers Confront the New Economic Order."

88 *Daily News Egypt*, "Cotton Spinning and Weaving to Pump EGP 150m Investments into 8 Subsidiaries."

89 *al-Ahram*, "Mufaja'a bi-l-mustanadat: masakin madinat al-'ummal bi-l-Mahalla al-Kubra. Amlak dawla!"

90 Interview with Muhammad Wadi, head of the pensioners' union fighting the evictions. EIPR, "Mosta'maret al-Mahalla Workers' 'Evictions.'"

91 Interview with EIPR lawyer, Samuel Tharwat, who represented thirty-three of the families challenging eviction rulings.

92 For excellent overviews of local administration in Egypt see Néfissa, "Cairo's City Government: The Crisis of Local Administration and the Refusal of Urban Citizenship"; Tadamun, "The Right to Democratic Local Government in the Egyptian Constitution."

93 10 Tooba, "Built Environment Deprivation Index." Affordability.

94 NUCA has been servicing and selling urban land at an average rate of 4,000 feddans per year, while informal urbanization of agricultural land has been happening at a rate of 16,000 feddans per year. Shawkat, *al-'Adala al-ijtima'iya wa-l-'umran—kharitat Misr*.

95 TIMEP, "Legislation Tracker Report."

Epilogue

1 10 Tooba, "Built Environment Deprivation Index." Affordability.

2 10 Tooba. Crowding, and Durable Housing.

3 10 Tooba. Secure Tenure.

4 Madden and Marcuse, *In Defense of Housing: The Politics of Crisis*, 191.

5 Ministry of Planning, Monitoring, and Administrative Reform, "Sustainable Development Strategy: Egypt Vision 2030—Urban Development Pillar."

6 Farha, "Visit of Leilani Farha, the Special Rapporteur on The Right to Adequate Housing to Egypt: End of Mission Statement."

7 In 2015 the two biggest banks, that are also state-owned, Misr and al-Ahly, owned assets worth LE14 billion that they were seeking to sell off because they are required by law to do so within five years of acquiring them. *Al-Shuruk*,

"al-Bunuk tukhattit li-l-isti'ana bi-sharikat khalijiya li-taswiq usuluha al-'aqariya khilal al-mu'tamar al-iqtisadi." Not to mention the real estate taxes they start racking up, pushing them to seek an exemption.

8 It is very likely that in an uneven market where formal homes have far greater value than informal homes, that investor/speculators move in to quickly buy the regularized homes, while the owners, who are generally poor and in need for cash to cover other basic costs succumb to capitalizing on this newfound surge in value. Payne, Durand-Lasserve, and Rakodi, "The Limits of Land Titling and Home Ownership."

9 Madden and Marcuse, *In Defense of Housing: The Politics of Crisis*, 218.

BIBLIOGRAPHY

10 Tooba. "Built Environment Deprivation Index," *10Tooba website*, September 2016.

Abaza, Mona. *The Cotton Plantation Remembered: An Egyptian Family Story*. Cairo: The American University in Cairo Press, 2013.

'Abd al-Gawwad, Tawfiq Ahmad. "al-Maskan al-sihhi li-l-fallah." *Majallat al-'imara* 7, no. 5 and 6 (1947): 44–57.

'Abd al-Gawwad, Tawfiq Ahmad. "al-Mu'tamar al-handasi al-thalith." *Majallat al-'imara* 7, no. 5 and 6 (1947): 4–16.

'Abd al-Gawwad, Tawfiq Ahmad. "Mushkilat al-masakin fi Misr wa 'ilajiha." *Majallat al-'imara* 9, no. 6, 7 and 8 (1949): 71–84.

'Abd al-Tawwab, Isma'il. "Bila rutush: Sakin al-Hujra al-Safih yamshi kul yawm 3 kilu li-aqrab hanafiyat miyah." *al-Masa'*. Anwar Sadat Digital Archive/Bibliotheca Alexandrina, August 21, 1974.

Abdel-Mohsen, Ali. "Maadi Demolition Campaign Turns Fatal," *Mada Masr*, April 8, 2014.

Abdul Wahab, Mohamed Fikri. "Problems of Nubian Migration," In *Nubian Encounters*, 227–36. The Story of the Nubian Ethnological Survey 1961–1964. The American University in Cairo Press, 2010.

Abotawila, Amr. "Understanding Egyptian Social Housing Squatting Phenomenon Post January 2011: The Production of Space in Elmouhtalla." Master's thesis, Ain Shams University and University of Stuttgart, 2017.

Abouelnaga, Shereen. *Women in Revolutionary Egypt: Gender and the New Geographics of Identity*. Cairo New York: American University in Cairo Press, 2016.

Abuda, Mustafa. "Tatwir manzil al-fallah." *Majallat al-'imara* 8, no. 1 and 2 (1948): 13–17.

Abu-Lughod, Janet L. *Cairo: 1001 Years of the City Victorious*. Princeton: Princeton University Press, 1971.

Administrative Control Authority. "Dabtiyat hay'at al-raqaba al-idariya khilal usbu'," November 23, 2017.

Adriansen, Hanne Kirstine. "Land Reclamation in Egypt: A Study of Life in the New Lands," *Geoforum* 40 (2009): 664–74.
Al-Aees, Shaimaa. "Bedouin Protection Money Raises Average Cost of Real Estate Projects by 15–20%," *Daily News Egypt*, October 13, 2018.
Afify, Heba. "Battle over the Nile," *Mada Masr*, July 16, 2017.
Aga Khan Award for Architecture. "Ismaïliyya Development Projects." Aga Khan Award for Architecture, 1986.
al-Ahaly. "Madinat al-ahlam yahjurha al-shabab wa mi'at al-usar ta'jaz 'an al-daf'," Egyptian Press Archive of CEDEJ/Bibliotheca Alexandrina, October 23, 1991.
al-Ahram. "35 million jinih li-da'm al-iskan al –'ummali." May 5, 1978.
al-Ahram. "Ra'is jihaz madinat 6 Uktubur al-jadida: al-initiha' min 'adad kabir min mashru'at al-marafiq bi-mantiqat Ibni Baytak." September 12, 2018.
al-Ahram. "Mas'ul bi-l-iskan: hunak 3 malayin 'aqar mukhalif fi Misr." August 31, 2018.
al-Ahram. "Wazir al-iskan fi nadwat *al-Ahram*: infiraj azamat al-iskan khilal 4 sanawat." September 13, 2017.
al-Ahram. "Qaryata Musa wa-l-Khidr kharij nitaq al-khidma." July 28, 2016.
al-Ahram."Bi-sabab al-baltaja wa-l-sariqat. Shabab al-kharijin yuhajirun qaryat Siddiq al-Minshawi bi-Suhag." June 12, 2016.
al-Ahram. "La ahad fawq al-qanun." May 13, 2016.
al-Ahram. "Ba'd al-ta'addi 'ala alaf al-afdina min al-ruq'a al-zira'iya." March 6, 2016.
al-Ahram. "*al-Ahram* yahsul 'ala nass qanun al-tasaluh fi ba'd mukhalafat al-bina'." February 21, 2015.
al-Ahram. "al-Sisi yakshif li-l-*Ahram* 'an al-khutut al-'arida li-l-barnamij al-intikhabi." May 16, 2014.
al-Ahram. "al-Sisi yutliq mubadarat al-milyun wihda sakaniya li-l-shabab." March 10, 2014.
al-Ahram. "Taqadam laha 5.5 million muwatin. Al-Iskan tatarah 35 alf wihda sakaniya jadida fi 19 muhafza." April 1, 2013.
al-Ahram. "Ra'is hay'at al-awqaf fi hiwar ma' *al-Ahram*: la tasaluh ma' al-muta'adi 'ala mal al-waqf." June 10, 2011.
al-Ahram. "al-Ashbah taskun qaryat al-Zahir al-Sahrawi bi-l-Mahamid." May 19, 2011.
al-Ahram. "12 da'wa qada'iya did muhafiz Kafr al-Sheikh." June 24, 2010.
al-Ahram. "Mufaja'a bi-l-mustanadat: masakin madinat al-'ummal bi-l-Mahalla al-Kubra. Amlak dawla!" November 23, 2009.
al-Ahram. "Qura Sahl al-Husayniya hajarha 80% min al-shabab!" March 15, 2008.
al-Ahram. "Ra'i *al-Ahram*: tatwir al-manatiq al-'ashwa'iya awlawiya muhimma." October 16, 2005.
al-Ahram. "Suzanne Mubarak khilal ziyaratiha li-mashru' al-tanmaiya al-mujtama'iya bi-l-Dweiqa." September 1, 2005.

al-Ahram. "Suzanne Mubarak tu'akkid fi hafl taslim 'uqud takhsis shiqaq iskan al-mustaqbal." December 2, 1999.
al-Ahram. "Mubarak haris 'ala tawfir al-khadamat li-l-muwatinin wa hal mushkilat iskan mahdudi al-dakhl," Egyptian Press Archive of CEDEJ/Bibliotheca Alexandrina, December 15, 1998.
al-Ahram. "Wazir al-ta'mir wa-l-iskan: 22 al-hali . . . bad' al-hajz fi iskan al-mustaqbal." Egyptian Press Archive of CEDEJ/Bibliotheca Alexandrina, August 7, 1998.
al-Ahram. "600 sadad muqaddam al-hajz fi mashru' Mubarak li-iskan al-shabab." Egyptian Press Archive of CEDEJ/Bibliotheca Alexandrina, October 12, 1996.
al-Ahram. "Mahragan Hub Wa Wafa' Wa Asala Fi Mit Abul Kom." Egyptian Press Archive of CEDEJ/Bibliotheca Alexandrina, December 25, 1980.
al-Ahram. "Tarh 3,000 shiqqa li-l-tamlik fi madinat al-'Ashir min Ramadan." May 4, 1979.
al-Ahram. "Dhahabt ila za'im al-mu'arada fi Shirbin mu'akkidan 'ala mafhum jadid li-l-hayat al-hizbiya." December 26, 1978.
al-Ahram. "al-Sakan al-nadir!" September 14, 1977.
al-Ahram. "al-Sadat a'ta isharat al-bad' li-awwal mugamma' zira'i sina'i fi al-sahara'." Egyptian Press Archive of CEDEJ/Bibliotheca Alexandrina, June 10, 1977.
al-Ahram. "Tawqi' 'aqd ta'sis sharikat al-Ismailiya-Misr li-l-Tanmiya al-Zira'iya." April 20, 1977.
al-Ahram. "Shakawi khiliw al-rigl: ihalatiha ila al-mudda'i al-ishtiraki." March 21, 1973.
al-Ahram. "Qurud bi fayda 3% li-tarmim al-manazil al-qadima." March 1, 1975.
al-Ahram. "Maza Tam Ba`d Khamas Asabi` Min Bid' Tanfiz Mashru` Nasser Lil-Iskan?" December 10, 1965.
al-Ahram al-'arabi. "Mufaja'a mudawwiya yakshifha al-liwa' Ahmad al-Galbi ra'is jam'iyat mustahaqi al-waqf." March 18, 2014.
al-Ahram al-masa'i. "Mashru' jadid li-bina' million wihda." February 4, 2018.
al-Ahram al-masa'i. "al-Sallab yarfa' al-raya al-bayda'." May 24, 2010.
al-Ahram al-masa'i. "al-Damin yaghtal hilm al-shabab fi shiqqa." April 7, 2010.
al-Akhbar. "Taftish al-iskan: 2 million wa 900 alf 'aqar mukhalif fi Misr." February 26, 2018.
Akhbar al-Wadi al-Jadid. "Musalsal jadid min al-ihmal wa istighlal al-atfal: wafat al-tifl Mubarak athna' jam'i al-batatis bi-l-'Uwaynat." May 16, 2017.
Akhbar al-Wadi al-Jadid. "*Akhbar al-Wadi al-Jadid* takshif ma'sat 'amalat al-atfal fi sharq al-'Uwaynat." September 24, 2013.
Almoghazy, Ali. "A Tied Life: The Rise and Fall of Company Town Housing in Egypt," *Built Environment Observatory*, January 30, 2018.
Almoghazy, Ali. "Forced Informality: When Housing Rights and Building Laws Collide," *Built Environment Observatory*, April 2018.

Alterman, Jon B. *Egypt and American Foreign Assistance 1952–1956: Hopes Dashed.* New York: Palgrave Macmillan, 2002.
Amin, Galal. *Egypt's Economic Predicament: A Study in the Interaction of External Pressure, Political Folly, and Social Tension in Egypt, 1960-1990.* Leiden: E.J. Brill, 1995.
Amwal al-ghad. "Saudi Al Rajhi Co. to Pump $135mn in Egypt's Toshka until 2020," September 4, 2016.
Antar, Elias. "Suez Reborn." In *Saudi Aramco World*, 28:26–32. 5. *Saudi Aramco*, 1977.
Anwar Sadat Digital Archive. "Mashakilna mashakil ta'mir wa taqaddum," Bibliotheca Alexandrina, June 8, 1977.
Anwar Sadat Digital Archive. "al-Sadat adda salat al-'id ma' abna' al-Suways wa salat al-jum'a fi-al-Isma'iliya," Bibliotheca Alexandrina, September 25, 1976.
Arab Socialist Union. "al-Jalsa al-hadiya wa-l-'ushrun li-l-lajna al-markaziya li-ittihad al-ishtiraki al-'arabi." Gamal Abd al-Nasser Digital Archive/Bibliotheca Alexandrina, April 21, 1970.
Arab Television. "Hadith al-ra'is Muhammad Anwar al-Sadat ila al-tilifisyun al-'arabi fi 24 Yulyu 1977," Anwar Sadat Digital Archive/Bibliotheca Alexandrina, July 24, 1977.
Arabtec Holding. "Arabtec Signs Historic Agreement with Egypt's Defence Ministry to Develop and Construct One Million Housing Units in Egypt—Official Press Release," March 9, 2014.
Arafat, Nada, and Sakr El Nour. "How Egypt's Water Feeds the Gulf." Mada Masr, May 15, 2019.
Ashour, Shaimaa. *al-Mi'mariyin al-misriyin al-ruwwad khilal al-fatra al-libiraliya bayn thawratay 1919 wa 1952*. Cairo: Maktabat Madbuli, 2012.
al-Asmar, Khalid. "Ahwal Misr tarsud mu'anat sukkan mantiqat al-Amin bi Bur Said." *Ahwal Misr*, October 12, 2014.
Aulas, Marie-Christine. "Sadat's Egypt: A Balance Sheet." *MER 107—Egypt in the New Middle East* 12 (August 1982).
al-Awqaf Authority. "al-Istithmar al-zira'i." al-Awqaf Authority, n.d. http://www.hyatelawqaf-eg.org/z-s-v/index.php?page=6 (Accessed October 28, 2019).
Ayrout, Henry Habib. *The Egyptian Peasant*. Cairo: The American University in Cairo Press, 2005.
Azzam, Omar. "The Development of Urban and Rural Housing in Egypt." PhD diss., ETH Zürich, 1960.
el-Bahrawy, Amr. "A House of No Importance: The Rise and Fall of Nasr City's Middle-Class Extended Family Houses." Master's thesis, UWSpace, 2015.
al-Banna, Ragab. "Laysa bi-l-qanun wahdahuh." *al-Ahram*. February 4, 1996.
Barlamani. "Na'ib al-Marg Ahmad 'Ali: tadbir al-i'timad al-mali li-naql 'ishash al-Andalus wa tir'at Birlant bi-mantiqat al-'Assara." *Barlamani*, May 15, 2017.
Barnard, Lucy. "Arabtec's Egypt Housing Deal Still Under Discussion, Says Chairman." *The National*, November 16, 2015.

Barrada, Abdel Mohsen, William C. Wheaton, and Phillipe Annez. "Public Policy and the Economics of Housing. Appendix A: Public Policy and the 'Shortage' of Housing in Egypt." In *The Housing and Construction Industry in Egypt: Interim Report Working Papers 1979/80*, by Joint Research Team on the Housing and Construction Industry Cairo University/MIT, 5–14. USAID, 1980.

Barrada, Abdel Mohsen. "Public Policy and the Economics of Housing. Appendix B: A Proposal for Improving the Legal Relationship Between Tenant and Landlord in Egypt." In *The Housing and Construction Industry in Egypt: Interim Report Working Papers 1979/80*, by Joint Research Team on the Housing and Construction Industry Cairo University/MIT, 15–21. USAID, 1980.

Bavelaar, Rahma Esther. "Waqi' al-bahth 'an maskan mula'im." In *al-'Adala al-ijtima'iya wa-l-'umran—kharitat Misr*, edited by Yahia Shawkat, 142–44. 2013.

Bayat, Asef. *Life as Politics: How Ordinary People Change the Middle East*. Cairo: The American University in Cairo Press, 2009.

Bayat, Asef, and Eric Denis. "Who is Afraid of Ashwaiyyat? Urban Change and Politics in Egypt." *Environment and Urbanization* 12, no. 2 (October 1, 2000): 185–99.

al-Bawaba News. "Ra'is majlis idarat Jam'iyyat Rijal Amn al-Mustaqbal yatahad-dath li-l-Bawaba News." March 20, 2016.

al-Bawaba News. "Ra'is sunduq al-tamwil al-'aqari tatahaddath li-l-*Bawaba News*." *al-Bawaba News*, February 14, 2018.

Beinin, Joel. *Workers and Peasants in the Modern Middle East*. Cambridge: Cambridge University Press, 2001.

Beinin, Joel, and Hossam el-Hamalawy. "Egyptian Textile Workers Confront the New Economic Order." *Middle East Report Online*, March 25, 2007.

Bishop, Elizabeth Anona. "Talking Shop: Egyptian Engineers and Soviet Specialists at the Aswan High Dam." PhD diss., University of Chicago, 1997.

Buna, "al-Mashru' al-fa'iz bi-l-musabaqa al-qawmiya li-l-iskan," August 9, 2011.

Boughton, John. *Municipal Dreams: The Rise and Fall of Council Housing*. London: Verso, 2018.

Brown, Nathan J. *The Rule of Law in the Arab World Courts in Egypt and the Gulf*. Cambridge: Cambridge University Press, 1997.

Burchardt, Jeremy. *Paradise Lost: Rural Idyll and Social Change Since 1800*. London: I.B.Tauris, 2002.

al-Bursa. "al-Qahira tukhattit li-i'adat hikr Abu Duma li-l-kharita al-istithmariya li-l-muhafaza." August 26, 2014.

al-Bursa. "Sunduq tatwir al-'ashwa'iyat yabda' tatwir Ramlit Bulaq." March 6, 2013.

al-Bursa. "al-Iskandiriya tatrah 2,500 faddan li-iqamat mashru' istithmari mutakamil." September 25, 2012.

CAPMAS. "Annual Bulletin of Labour Force 2017." Cairo: Central Agency for Public Mobilization and Statistics, 2018.

CAPMAS. "al-Nata'ij al-niha'iya li-l-ti'dad al-'am li-l-sukkan wa-l-iskan wa-l-munsha'at li-'am 2017: al-sukkan wa-l-zuruf al-sakaniya." Cairo: Central Agency for Public Mobilization and Statistics, December 2017.

CAPMAS. "Egypt in Figures 2016." Cairo: Central Agency for Public Mobilization and Statistics, 2016.

CAPMAS. "Aham mu'ashirat bahth al-dakhl wa-l-infaq wa-l-istihlak li-'am 2015." Central Agency for Public Mobilization and Statistics, July 2015.

CAPMAS. "Dirasat al-manatiq al-'ashwa'iya fi Misr." Cairo: Central Agency for Public Mobilization and Statistics, 2008.

CAPMAS. "al-Ti'dad al-'am li-l-sukkan wa-l-iskan wa-l-munsha'at 2006: al-nata'ij al-niha'iya li-ti'dad al-mabani 2006 li-ijmali al-jumhuriya." Cairo: Central Agency for Public Mobilization and Statistics, November 2008.

CAPMAS. "al-Ti'dad al-'am li-l-sukkan wa-l-iskan wa-l-munsha'at 'am 1996: al-nata'ij al-niha'iya li-ti'dad al-mabani li-ijmali al-jumhuriya." Cairo: Central Agency for Public Mobilization and Statistics, September 1998.

CAPMAS. "al-Ti'dad al-'am 1986 al-mujallad al-awwal—al-juz' al-thani: khasa'is al-sukkan wa-l-zuruf al-sakaniya." Cairo: Central Agency for Public Mobilization and Statistics, January 1990.

CAPMAS. "al-Ti'dad al-'am li-l-mabani 1976: al-natai'j al-tafsiliya li-ijmali al-jumhuriya." Cairo: Central Agency for Public Mobilization and Statistics, December 1984.

CAPMAS. "al-Kitab al-ihsa'i al-sanawi li-jumhuriyat Misr al-'arabiya 1952–1980." Cairo: Central Agency for Public Mobilization and Statistics, July 1981.

CAPMAS. "al-Kitab al-ihsa'i al-sanawi li-jumhuriyat Misr al-'arabiya 1952–1976." Cairo: Central Agency for Public Mobilization and Statistics, October 1977.

CAPMAS. "al-Kitab al-ihsa'i al-sanawi li-jumhuriyat Misr al-'arabiya 1952–1973." Cairo: Central Agency for Public Mobilization and Statistics, October 1974.

CAPMAS. "al-Zimam wa-l-masahat al-munzari'a fi jumhuriyat Misr al-'arabiya 'am 1970." Cairo: Central Agency for Public Mobilization and Statistics, 1973.

Central Bank of Egypt. "Circular Dated October 8, 2017 Regarding Raising Mortgage Fund and Casualties and Families of Martyrs of Army and Police." Cairo: Central Bank of Egypt, October 8, 2017.

Charbel, Jano. "What Fate Awaits Ezbet El-Haggana?" *Egypt Independent*, December 27, 2009.

Committee to Recover State Land. "al-Dawla tastarid milyun faddan wa 132 milyun mitr muraba' fi 18 shahr." November 4, 2018.

Committee to Recover State Land. "al-Muhandis Sharif Isma'il: al-awlawiya li-inha ijra'at taqnin aradi al-dawla khilal al-fatra al-qadima." October 18, 2018.

Committee to Recover State Land. "Ihalat malaf 215 faddan bi-Misr al-Iskandiriya li-l-amwal al-'amma." August 10, 2016.

Cooper, Artemis. *Cairo in the War: 1939-45*. Second. London: John Murray, 2013.

Croese, Sylvia. "State-Led Housing Delivery as an Instrument of Developmental Patrimonialism: The Case of Post-War Angola." *African Affairs* 116, no. 462 (January 1, 2017): 80–100.
Al-Dahra Egypt. "Al-Dahra Holding." Al-Dahra Holding, n.d.
Daily News Egypt. "Cotton Spinning and Weaving to Pump EGP 150m Investments into 8 Subsidiaries." September 13, 2015.
Daily News Egypt. "City Edge Developments Completes 40% of Commercial Area of North Edge Towers in New Alamein City." July 16, 2018.
Dawud, Mahir. "al-Kafrawi: hal mushkilat al-iskan ba'd 3 sanawat." Egyptian Press Archive of CEDEJ/Bibliotheca Alexandrina, May 15, 1990.
de Soto, Hernando. "Dead Capital and the Poor in Egypt." ECES/ILD, January 1998.
Deboulet, Agnès. "The Dictatorship of the Straight Line and the Myth of Social Disorder: Revisiting Informality in Cairo." In *Cairo Contested: Governance, Urban Space, and Global Modernity*, 199–234. Cairo: The American University in Cairo Press, 2009.
Deputy, Emmarie Kathleen. "Designed to Deceive: President Hosni Mubarak's Toshka Project." Master's thesis, University of Austin, 2011.
Dorman, William J. "The Politics of Neglect: The Egyptian State in Cairo, 1974–98." PhD diss., School of Oriental and African Studies, UCL, 2007.
Downs, Bill. "Revolutionary Egypt Reclaims the Land, November 27, 1954." *Bill Downs CBS*, May 2017.
al-Dustur al-asli. "Sukkan al-Iwa': min wa'd bi-l-iqama fi masakin mu'aqatta ila al-nisyan li-akthar min 30 sana." *al-Dustur al-asli*, September 23, 2010.
al-Dustur al-asli. "al-Na'ib al-'am yahzar tarh al-wihdat al-sakaniya bi-l-iskan al-qawmi fi mazad 'alani." *al-Dustur al-asli*, June 7, 2010.
Egypt Countryside Development Company. "al-Mashru' al-qawmi li-tanmaiyat al-milyun wa nisf faddan: al-tarh al-awwal, da'wa li-l-mustathmirin li-l-taqaddum li-l-ta'hil."
Egypt Countryside Development Company. "al-Mashru' al-qawmi li-tanmiyat al-milyun wa nisf faddan: al-tarh al-awwal li-sighar al-muzari'in wa-l-shabab."
Egypt Independent. "EIPR Accuses Police Officer of Murder in Nile City Incident." August 16, 2012.
Egypt Independent. "More Housing Units Available in New Administrative Capital." August 9, 2018.
Egypt Independent. "Sisi Inaugurates the 'Bashayer Al-Khair-2' Project in Alexandria." December 26, 2018.
Egypt News. "Kalimat ra'is al-Sisi fi mu'tamar Misr al-tanmaiya al-mustadama," 2016.
Egypt News. "Madbuli yu'akkid hal mushkilat al-iskan jadhriyyan khilal 3 sanawat." February 23, 2017.
Egypt News. "Wazir: ligan li-hasr al-'aqarat al-lati tushakkil khutura 'ala Bulaq Abu al-'Ila." January 2, 2011.

Egyptian Businessmen's Association. "Egyptian Businessmen's Association Website—Home Page."
Egyptian Initiative for Personal Rights. "'Ala al-hukuma al-mirsiya daman huquq al-muwatinin fi masakin mula'ima qabl hadm masakinuhum." October 4, 2014.
Egyptian Initiative for Personal Rights. "'Izbet Al-'Arab/ Muthalath Al-Montazah Evictions." Internal report. 2014.
Egyptian Initiative for Personal Rights. "Mosta'maret Al-Mahalla Workers' 'Evictions.'" Internal report. 2014.
Egyptian Press Archive of CEDEJ. "Hal mushkilat al-iskan yabda' hadha al-'am," Bibliotheca Alexandrina, May 19, 1986.
Egyptian Press Archive of CEDEJ. "Mubarak yatlub hallan jadhriyyan wa 'ajilan li-mushkilat al-iskan," Bibliotheca Alexandrina, February 28, 1982.
Essam El-Din, Gamal. "'Amendment of Egypt's Old Rent Law Not Expected Soon,' Says Senior MP." *Ahram Online*, January 7, 2019.
Ettouney, Sayed. "Low Income Family Housing: Notes on Egypt's Experience." In *Notes on Housing and Physical Planning: Selected Papers from International Conferences*, by Sayed Ettouney and Nasamat Abdel-Kader, 142–52. Cairo: al-'Arabi li-l-Nashr wa-l-Tawzi', 1992.
Ettouney, Sayed, and Nasamat Abdel-Kader. "Users' Participation in Low Cost Housing Projects: Post Occupancy Evaluation." In *Housing Process and Product*. Montreal, Canada, 2003.
Fahmy, Khaled. *All the Pasha's Men: Mehmed Ali, His Army, and the Making of Modern Egypt*. Cambridge: Cambridge University Press, 1997.
Fanon, Frantz. *The Wretched of the Earth*. Translated by Richard Philox. New York: Grove Press, 2004.
Farag, Fuad. "Mantiqat qanat al-Suways." *Majallat al-'imara* 3, no. 7 and 8 (1941): 263–73.
Farha, Leilani. "Visit of Leilani Farha, the Special Rapporteur on The Right to Adequate Housing to Egypt: End of Mission Statement." OHCHR, October 3, 2018.
Fawzy, Mahmud. "Wazir al-iskan fi hadith sakhin." Egyptian Press Archive of CEDEJ—Bibliotheca Alexandrina, December 17, 1995.
Foucault, Michel. *Security, Territory, Population: Lectures at the College de France 1977–78*. Edited by Michel Senellart. Hampshire: Palgrave Macmillan, 2009.
Arab Socialist Union. "Central Committee Meeting Reports dated March 26, February 19, February 12, February 5, 1969, and December 12, 1968," Gamal Abd al-Nasser Digital Archive - Bibliotheca Alexandrina.
Ghallab, Mahmud, and Gihad 'Abd al-Mun'im. "Maglis al-sha'b yuwafiq 'ala tahrir al-ijar fi al-maskin al-jadida wa-l-khaliya." *al-Wafd*. January 31, 1996.
Ghannam, Farha. *Remaking the Modern: Space, Relocation, and the Politics of Identity in a Global Cairo*. 1st ed. Berkeley: University of California Press, 2002.

Gorman, Anthony. *Historians, State and Politics in Twentieth Century Egypt: Contesting the Nation*. London: Routledge Curzon, 2003.

Hall, Thomas, and Sonja Vidén. "The Million Homes Programme: A Review of the Great Swedish Planning Project." *Planning Perspectives* 20, no. 3 (January 1, 2005): 301–28.

Hammad, Hanan. *Industrial Sexuality: Gender, Urbanization, and Social Transformation in Egypt*. Austin: University of Texas Press, 2016.

Hanna, Milad. *al-Iskan wa-l-masyada: al-mushkila wa-l-hal*. Cairo: al-Mustaqbal al-'Arabi, 1988.

Hanna, Milad. *al-Iskan wa-l-siyasa*. Cairo: al-Hay'a al-Misriya al-'Amma li-l-Kitab, 1996.

Hanna, Milad. *Le logement en Égypte: Essai Critique*. Recherches et Témoignages. Cairo: CEDEJ, 1992.

Hanna, Milad. "Real Estate Rights in Urban Egypt: The Changing Sociopolitical Winds." In *Property, Social Structure, and Law in the Modern Middle East*, edited by Ann Elizabeth Mayer, 189–211. New York: State University of New York Press, 1985.

Harlow, Alvin Fay. *Paper Chase: The Amenities of Stamp Collecting*. New York: Henry Holt and Company, 1940.

Hawas, Mohamed Zaki. "The Industrial Centres: Factories and Workers' Housing." PhD diss., ETH Zürich, 1963.

Herleth, Mason J. "The Good Life: Reshaping Society and Social Values through Public Housing in Red Vienna." *Vanderbilt Historical Review* (blog), April 16, 2018.

Hoeven, Frank van der. "Woonschool." *Project Baikal*, no. 57 (September 21, 2018): 100–104.

Hopkins, Nicholas S., Abderrahim el-Hadart, Salah el-Zoghby, Hanaa Singer, Hanan Sabea, Hania Sholkamy, Reem Saad, and Ziad Bahaa el-Din. *Participation and Community in the Egyptian New Lands: The Case of South Tahrir*. Cairo Papers in Social Science. Cairo: The American University in Cairo Press, 1988.

Human Rights Watch. "Look for Another Homeland: Forced Evictions in Egypt's Rafah." Human Rights Watch, September 22, 2015.

Ibrahim, Bedour. "Infirad: al-Raqaba al-idariya tuhaqiq fi waqa'i' al-hadm bi-qura al-sahil al-shamali." *al-Mal*, August 2, 2018.

Ibrahim, Ishak. "Whose Customs? The Role of Customary Reconciliation in Sectarian Disputes and State Responsibility." Egyptian Initiative for Personal Rights, 2015.

Ibrahim, Nagwa. "Hikayat barlamaniya. Inqilab al-dubbat al-ahrar taht qubbat al-barlaman." *al-Tahrir*, February 21, 2015.

"Id wahda li-l-qada' 'ala al-balatjiya fi Ibni Baytak." Facebook, n.d. https://tinyurl.com/yy3lybck (Accessed May 5, 2018).

Ilbert, Robert. "Heliopolis: Colonial Enterprise and Town Planning Success." In *The Expanding Metropolis: Coping with the Urban Growth of Cairo*, edited by Ahmed Evin. Singapore: Concept Media/Aga Khan Award for Architecture, 1985.

Information Decision and Support Center. "Dalil al-taqsim al-idari li-l-muhafzat hatta mustawa al-shiyakha wa-l-qarya." Information Decision and Support Center, 2012.

International Monetary Fund. "Arab Republic of Egypt First Review Under the Extended Arrangement." IMF Country Report No. 17/290. Washington D.C. September 2017.

International Property Rights Index. "IPRI 2018—Egypt." International Property Rights Index (IPRI).

Invest-Gate. "City Edge to Invest EGP 1 Bn in Sheikh Zayed's Etapa in 2019." *Invest-Gate*, December 25, 2018.

Japan International Cooperation Agency. "The Feasibility Study on the North Sinai Integrated Rural Development Project (Phase II) in the Arab Republic of Egypt—Final Report." Japan International Cooperation Agency, 1997.

el-Jesri, Manal. "The Other Side of the Tracks: Ezbet Arab Abu Regeila." In *Cairo's Informal Areas between Urban Challenges and Hidden Potentials*, edited by Regina Kipper and Marion Fischer, 96–101. Cairo: GTZ Egypt Participatory Development Programme in Urban Areas (PDP), 2009.

Joint Housing and Community Upgrading Team. "Housing and Community Upgrading for Low-Income Egyptians." USAID, August 1977. pdf.usaid.gov/pdf_docs/PNAAG049.pdf (Accessed October 28, 2019).

Joint Housing Team. "Immediate Action Proposals for Housing in Egypt." USAID, June 1976. pdf.usaid.gov/pdf_docs/PNAAC825.pdf (Accessed October 28, 2019).

Joint Housing Team. "Immediate Action Proposals for Housing in Egypt—Statistical Appendix." USAID, June 1976. http://pdf.usaid.gov/pdf_docs/PNAAC826.pdf (Accessed October 28, 2019).

al-Jumhuriya. "Istighatha thalitha." *al-Jumhuriya*, November 11, 2014.

Kadi, Galila El. *L'urbanisation Spontanée Au Caire*. Paris: Tours, 1987.

Karim, Sayyed. "Madinat Faruq al-Awwal bi-wadi Kom Ombo." *Majallat al-ʿimara* 9, nos. 6–8 (1949): 23–26.

Karim, Sayyed. "Islah al-qarya, bayn al-qarya al-namuzajiya wa-qaryat al-intiqal." *Majallat al-ʿimara* 3, no. 2 (1941): 51–64.

Kaul, Vivek. "Why Are More than 10 Million Homes Vacant in India?" BBC, May 21, 2015.

Khalifa, Marwa A. "Redefining Slums in Egypt: Unplanned versus Unsafe Areas." *Habitat International* 35, no. 1 (January 1, 2011): 40–49.

Khalil, Omnia, Nouran El-Marsafy, and Abdelrahman Hegazy. "al-Nashatat, al-tahmish, wa ʻilaqat al-quwwa fi Ramlit Bulaq." 10 Tooba, 2016.

Kingdom Agricultural Development Company. "KADCO Egypt."
Kipper, Regina, and Marion Fischer, eds. *Cairo's Informal Areas between Urban Challenges and Hidden Potentials*. Cairo: GTZ Egypt Participatory Development Programme in Urban Areas (PDP), 2009.
Kohn, George C. *Encyclopedia of Plague and Pestilence: From Ancient Times to the Present*. Infobase Publishing, 2007.
Kuwait Fund. "Completion of Development Of 400,000 Faddan In North Sinai." Kuwait Fund, August 11, 2001.
Lakeland Ledger. "Building Collapses Kill 26 in Egypt," August 22, 1983.
Land Center for Human Rights. "Faqd al-ard al-zira'iya wa-l-'unf fi al-rif." Arab Network for Human Rights, August 19, 2004.
Land Center for Human Rights. "Markaz al-ard yuqaddim balagh ila al-na'ib al-'am. Anqidhu fallahin Basyun min al-tasharud." Arab Network for Human Rights, August 7, 2004.
Lippman, Thomas W. "Pyramids Loom Off the 18th Green." *Washington Post*, May 1, 1978.
Madd. "Maspero Parallel Participatory Project." Madd, 2015.
Madden, David, and Peter Marcuse. *In Defense of Housing: The Politics of Crisis*. London: Verso, 2016.
El Maghraby, Ahmed. "H.E. Ahmed El Maghraby, Minister of Housing, Utilities, and Urban Development—Speech at the AmCham Egypt Conference: Real Estate: Where Is It Heading?" AmCham Egypt, video, November 3, 2008.
El-Mahdawy, Hadeer. "'Nobody Is Leaving Their Homes': Government Decision to Reclaim Land Fuels Anger in Warraq Island." *Mada Masr*, November 29, 2018.
El-Mahdi, Rabab. "Against Marginalization: Youth, Class, and Revolution." In *Marginality and Exclusion in Egypt and the Middle East*, by Ray Bush and Habib Ayeb, 133–47. Cairo and New York: The American University in Cairo Press, 2012.
Mahdy, Dina Samir Ahmad. "Dynamics of Development in Rural Egypt to New Desert Communities: The Case of the Basaisa." Master's thesis, Ain Shams University, University of Stuttgart, 2015.
Makkar, Sahil. "4 Years of Modi Govt: NDA's 'Housing for All' Project Falls Short of Target." Business Standard, May 18, 2018.
al-Mal. "al-Sisi: mafish dawla bi-l-'alam tiqdar ta'mil zayyina 'adad wihdat iskan." *al-Mal*, December 15, 2018.
al-Mal. "Bani Sweif al-Jadida turafiq aradi al-iskan al-ijtima'i bi-qimat 52 million jinih." *al-Mal*, June 18, 2018.
al-Mal. "al-Awqaf tabi' usul bi qimat 1.2 milyar jinih fi mazad 'alani." *al-Mal*, November 11, 2013.
Masrawy. "Dabt 227 alf qadiyat sariqat tayyar kahraba'i 'abr al-tawsilat al-ghayr al-qanuniya." *Masrawy*, June 8, 2017.

al-Masri al-yawm. "Mai Abd al-Hamid ra'is sanduq al-iskan al-ijtima'i wa-l-tamwil al-'aqari: 120 alf 'amil yatasallamun wihdatihim fi 2019." December 29, 2018.

al-Masri al-yawm. "al-Sijn 3 sanawat li-na'ib ra'is al-Qahira al-Jadida wa akahrin fi rashwat al-Narjis." August 15, 2018.

al-Masri al-yawm. "Mushajaratan bi-l-Qalubiya bi-sabab al-khilaf 'ala shiqqatayn." March 28, 2018.

al-Masri al-yawm. "Ra'is sanduqay al-tamwil al-'aqari wa-l-iskan al-ijtima'i: ziyadat as'ar al-i'lanat al-jadida." March 20, 2017.

al-Masri al-yawm. "588 wihda sakaniya li-l-mutadaririn min al-suyul bi-Ras Gharib." November 1, 2016.

al-Masri al-yawm. "Qura al-Minya al-namuzajiya. Buyut ashbah." July 13, 2016.

al-Masri al-yawm. "al-Muhasabat: ihdar 500 milyun jinih fi al-Zahir al-Sahrawi." March 23, 2015.

al-Masri al-yawm. "Mihlib: 21 alf wihda sakaniya munaffadha bi-l-muhafazat bi-l-mashru' al-qawmi al-sabiq dun marafiq." December 4, 2013.

al-Masri al-yawm. "al-Qabd 'ala ra'is majlis madina fi al-Daqahliya taqada rashwa li-tashil al-istila' 'ala shiqaq iskan Mubarak." May 27, 2010.

al-Masri al-yawm. "Gaddafi Met with Tribal Representatives in Sinai and Visits Beheira Today." July 3, 2009.

al-Masri al-yawm. "al-Iskan tukhassis mashru' bayt al-'a'ila li-l-naqabat wa-l-hay'at al-hukumiya hifazan 'ala al-mustawa al-ijtima'i." September 16, 2007.

al-Masri al-yawm. "Abaza yuqaddim taqriran li-Nazif hawl mukhalafat al-sharikat wa-l-afrad 'ala al-tariq al-sahrawi." January 21, 2007.

al-Masri al-yawm. "Mad hajz wihdat al-mashru' al-qawmi li-l-iskan ila Ughustus al-muqbil." April 24, 2006.

Mas'ud, Ali al-Miligi. "al-Maskan al-sihhi min al-nahiya al-takhtitiya wa-l-iqtisadiya." *Majallat al-'imara* 7, no. 5 and 6 (1947): 17–35.

Mas'ud, Ali al-Miligi. "al-Muwatin al-namuzaji." *Majallat al-'imara* 3, no. 2 (1941): 76–79.

Matteucci, Claudio. "Long-Term Evaluation of an Urban Development Project: The Case of Hai El Salam." In *7th N-Aerus Conference*. Darmstadt: N-Aerus, 2006.

Mayo, Stephen K., Harry Garnett, and Mohamed Ramez. "Informal Housing in Egypt." Cambridge, Mass.: Abt Associates, Dames and Moore, GOBHR, USAID, January 1982. http://pdf.usaid.gov/pdf_docs/PNAAS449.pdf (Accessed October 28, 2019).

Ministry of Defense and Military Production. "al-Sharika al-wataniya li-istislah wa-zira'at al-aradi al-sahrawiya bi-sharq al-'Uwaynat."

Ministry of Electricity and Energy. "Egypt Electricity Holding Company Annual Report 2011/2012." 2012.

Ministry of Electricity and Energy. "Egypt Electricity Holding Company Annual Report 2010/2011." 2011.

Ministry of Electricity and Energy. "Egypt Electricity Holding Company Annual Report 2006/2007." 2007.
Ministry of Finance. "al-Bayan al-mali 'an mashru' al-muwazana al-'amma li-l-dawla li-l-sana al-maliya 2017/2018." Cairo, June 2017.
Ministry of Finance. "al-Bayan al-mali 'an mashru' al-muwazana al-'amma li-l-dawla li-l-sana al-maliya 2008/2009." Cairo, June 2008.
Ministry of Foreign Affairs. "Letter from the Ministry of Foreign Affairs to Al-Shark Insurance Company." Unpublished personal documents, 1967.
Ministry of Housing and Urban Communities. "al-Wathiqa al-marji'iya li-istiratijiyat wa-siyasat al-iskan fi Misr 2012–2027 (Unpublished Report)." April 2013.
Ministry of Housing, Communities, and Local Government. "Housing Supply: Net Additional Dwellings, England: 2017 to 2018." November 15, 2018.
Ministry of Housing, Utilities and Urban Communities. "State of the Built Environment and Housing Indicators in Seven Egyptian Cities—Comprehensive Report." Cairo, 2011.
Ministry of Housing, Utilities, and Urban Development. "al-Mashru' al-qawmi li-l-iskan." 2012.
Ministry of Housing, Utilities, and Urban Development. "Mashru' qura al-Zahir al-Sahrawi." 2010.
Ministry of Housing, Utilities, and Urban Development. "al-Mashru' al-qawmi." 2009.
Ministry of Housing, Utilities, and Urban Development. "Kurasat Shurut Musabaqat I`dad Alnamazig Al-Mi`mariya Wal-Tasmim al-`omrani Li Mawaqi` al-Iskan Dumn Birnamig al-Dawla Lil-Iskan al-Ijtima`i." June 2011.
Ministry of Interior. "Musdarat al-qita'." Civil Status Organization.
Ministry of Planning, Monitoring, and Administrative Reform. "Sustainable Development Strategy: Egypt Vision 2030—Urban Development Pillar." Cairo, May 17, 2016.
al-Misriyun. "740 usra tataqaddam bi-shakwa did muhafiz al-Gharbiya li-'adam tasallumihim al-shiqaq." *al-Misriyun*, November 18, 2012.
Mitchell, Timothy. "No Factories, No Problems: The Logic of Neo-liberalism in Egypt." *Review of African Political Economy*, February 24, 2007.
Mitchell, Timothy. *Rule of Experts: Egypt, Techno-Politics, Modernity*. London: University of California Press, 2002.
Mohie, Mostafa. "Asmarat: The State's Model Housing for Former 'Slum' Residents." *Mada Masr*, June 18, 2018.
Al-Monitor. "Following Deadly Clashes, Nile Island Residents Keep Up Fight Against Evictions." *Al-Monitor*, July 27, 2017.
Mossallam, Alia. "Hikayat Sha'b—Stories of Peoplehood: Nasserism, Popular Politics and Songs in Egypt, 1956-1973." PhD diss., London School of Economics and Political Science, 2012.

Mostafa, Ahmed Abd al-Rahim. *'Asr Hekekyan.*. Cairo: al-Hay'a al-Misriya al-'amma lil-kitab, 1990.

Mounir, Safeya. "How State Luxury Housing Projects Affect Egypt's Real Estate Market." *Ahram Online*, July 12, 2018.

Mu'assasat Mudiriyat al-Tahrir. *Muzakkira marfu'a ila majlis al-wuzara' 'an al-hisab al-khitami fi 30 junyu 1954 li mu'assasat mudiriyat al-tahrir min majlis idarat al-mu'assasa.* In *Ri'asat majlis al-wuzara'—masa'il wa-jadwal a'mal jalsat 12 Yanayir 1955*, by Egyptian Cabinet, 173–80. Gamal 'Abd al-Nasser Digital Archive—Bibliotheca Alexandrina, 1955.

Mubarak, Ali. *al-Khitat al-tawfiqiya al-jadida li-Misr al-Qahira wa-muduniha wa-biladiha al-qadima wa-l-shahira (20 Volumes).* Bulaq: al-Matba'a al-Kubra al-Amiriya, 1887.

Mubarak, Muhammad Hosni. "Mubarak's Speech in the Final Session of the Fourth Congress of the National Democratic Party (Official Translation)." Egypt State Information Service (SIS), September 21, 2006.

Mubarak, Muhammad Hosni. "Kalimat al-ra'is Muhammad Husni Mubarak fi al-liqa' al-sha'bi bi-khitam al-hamla al-intikhabiya." Egypt State Information Service (SIS), September 4, 2005.

Mubarak, Muhammad Hosni. "Khitab al-ra'is Muhammad Husni Mubarak fi iftitah al-dawra al-barlamaniya al-jadida." Egypt State Information Service (SIS), December 18, 2000.

Mubarak, Muhammad Hosni. "Khitab al-ra'is Mubarak fi al-ihtifal bi 'id al-'ummal." Egypt State Information Service (SIS), May 1, 1993.

Mubarak, Muhammad Hosni. "Nas kalimat al-ra'is Muhammad Husni Mubarak fi iftitah mu'tamar Misr sanat 2000." Egypt State Information Service (SIS), December 27, 1984.

Mubarak, Muhammad Hosni. "Khitab al-ra'is Muhammad Husni Mubarak fi al-ijtima' al-mushtarak li-majlisay al-sha'b wa-l-shura." Egypt State Information Service (SIS), November 8, 1981.

al-Naba'. "Manshur bi-Facebook yakshif sulukan khatiran min muwazzaf istilam shiqaq al-iskan al-ijtima'i." *al-Naba'*, April 15, 2018.

Naguib, Muhammad. *Kalimati li-l-tarikh*. Cairo: al-Maktab al-Misri al-Hadith, 2011.

Nasser, Gamal Abd al-. "Mufakkira bi qalam al-ra'is 'an takwin majlis a'la li-l-difa' wa khitta li tahrir Filastin wa-l-sukkan wa-l-'ilaj wa-l-ta'min al-sihhi wa-l-sina'a." In *Gamal 'Abd al-Nasser al-awraq al-khassa—al-juz' al-rabi': al-wihda al-misriya al-suriya*, edited by Huda Gamal 'Abd al-Nasser, 747–50. Cairo: al-Hay'a al-Misriya al-'Amma li-l-Kitab, 2016.

Nasser, Gamal Abd al-. "Kalimat al-ra'is Gamal 'Abd al-Nasser amam al-hay'a al-barlamaniya li-l-Ittihad al-Ishtiraki 16/5/1965." In *al-Majmu'a al-kamila li-khutab wa tasrihat al-ra'is Gamal 'Abd al-Nasser—al-mujallad al-rabi'*, edited by Huda Gamal 'Abd al-Nasser, 681–721. Cairo: al-Maktaba al-Akadimiya, 2007.

Nasser, Gamal Abd al-. "Munaqashat al-ra'is Gamal 'Abd al-Nasser min jami'at Iskandiriya ma' al-mab'uthin—al-yawm al-thani." Gamal 'Abd al-Nasser Digital Archive/Bibliotheca Alexandrina, July 8, 1966.
Nasser, Gamal Abd al-. "Munaqashat al-ra'is Gamal 'Abd al-Nasser min Gam'at Iskandiriya ma' al-mab'uthin." Gamal 'Abd al-Nasser Digital Archive/Bibliotheca Alexandrina, June 8, 1966.
Nasser, Gamal Abd al-. "Kalimat al-ra'is Gamal 'Abd al-Nasser fi jami'at al-Qahira bi-munasabat 'id al-wihda." Gamal 'Abd al-Nasser Digital Archive/Bibliotheca Alexandrina, February 22, 1964.
Nasser, Gamal Abd al-. "Kalimat al-ra'is Gamal 'Abd al-Nasser wa-ta'qibatuh fi munaqashat al-lajna al-tahdiriya li-l-mu'tamar al-watani li-l-quwwa al-sha'biya—al-jalsa al-thaniya." Gamal 'Abd al-Nasser Digital Archive/Bibliotheca Alexandrina, November 27, 1961.
Nasser, Gamal Abd al-. "Kalimat al-ra'is Gamal 'Abd al-Nasser fi al-ihtifal bi-tawzi' al-masakin al-sha'biya fi Hallab." Gamal 'Abd al-Nasser Digital Archive/Bibliotheca Alexandrina, February 19, 1960.
Nasser, Gamal Abd al-. "Kalimat al-ra'is Gamal 'Abd al-Nasser fi Bur Sa'id fi dhikra yawm al-nasr." Gamal 'Abd al-Nasser Digital Archive/Bibliotheca Alexandrina, December 23, 1958.
Nasser, Gamal Abd al-. "Kalimat al-ra'is Gamal 'Abd al-Nasser fi iftitah majlis al-umma." Gamal 'Abd al-Nasser Digital Archive/Bibliotheca Alexandrina, July 22, 1957.
Nasser, Gamal Abd al-. "Kalimat al-ra'is Gamal 'Abd al-Nasser fi al-ihtifal bi-tawzi' al-masakin al-sha'biya fi Hilmiyat al-Zaytun." Gamal 'Abd al-Nasser Digital Archive/Bibliotheca Alexandrina, July 24, 1955.
Nasser, Gamal Abd al-. "Kalimat al-ra'is Gamal 'Abd al-Nasser fi al-mu'tamar al-sha'bi bi-midan al-Jumhuriya bi-l-Qahira ma' al-ra'is Sukarno bi-munasabat al-'id al-thalith li-thawrat Yulyu." Gamal 'Abd al-Nasser Digital Archive/Bibliotheca Alexandrina, July 22, 1955.
Nathan Associates. "Mortgage Market Reform in Egypt—Final Report." USAID, December 1999.
Nazmi, Nimat. "Ru'ya taqyimiya li-mashru' Ibni Baytak." In *al-Ard wa-l-sakan fi Misr*, edited by Ala' al-Din 'Arafat, 269–328. PID, 2012.
National Bureau of Statistics of China. "National Real Estate Development and Sales in the First Nine Months of 2018." National Bureau of Statistics of China, October 19, 2018.
Néfissa, Sarah Ben. "Cairo's City Government: The Crisis of Local Administration and the Refusal of Urban Citizenship." In *Cairo Contested: Governance, Urban Space, and Global Modernity*, 177–98. Cairo: The American University in Cairo Press, 2009.
New Urban Communities Authority. "Qarar majlis al-idara bi-jalsatih raqam 112 bi-tarikh 12/9/2018." September 12, 2018.

New Urban Communities Authority. "Kurrasat al-shurut al-khassa bi-hajz al-wihdat al-sakaniya bi-l-marhala al-ula bi-mashru' sakan Misr." September 2017.
New Urban Communities Authority. "Wazir al-iskan wa-muhafiz janub Sina' yuwaqqi'an brutukulan li-bay' 3 alaf wihda sakaniya bi-l-iskan al-ijtima'i li-l-muhafaza li-tawzi'iha 'ala muwatiniha." March 18, 2017.
New Urban Communities Authority. "Fath bab al-taqaddum li-man sabaq al-ta'amul bi-mujab 'uqud bi' aw mustanadat milkiyat al-aradi al-lati taqa' dakhil hudud al-qarar al-jumhuri li-madinat Sphinx al-Jadida." October 1, 2010.
New Urban Communities Authority. "Iskan al-shabab wa-l-mustaqbal."
New Urban Communities Authority. "Madinat Toshka al-Jadida."
The New York Times. "Sadat's Half Brother Is Sentenced to Jail." February 13, 1983, sec. World.
Nur, Kamal. "Islah al-qarya al-misriya." *Majallat al-'imara* 7, no. 7 and 8 (1941): 29–30.
OLX. "Rental Ad—Furnished Apartment for Foreigners Only in St.85 Sarayat." October 31, 2018. http://archive.is/i7JoO (Accessed October 28,2019)
ONA. "Tawaqquf harakat Qattarat al-Sa'id bi-Bani Sweif bi-sabab al-ihtijaj 'ala 'adam taslim shiqaq al-iskan." December 18, 2012.
Pallini, Cristina, and Annalisa Riccarda Scaccabarozzi. "British Planning Schemes for Alexandria and Its Region, 1834–1958." In *Urban Planning in North Africa*, by Carlos Nunes Silva. Routledge, 2016.
Payne, Geoffrey, Alain Durand-Lasserve, and Carole Rakodi. "The Limits of Land Titling and Home Ownership." *Environment and Urbanization* 21, no. 2 (October 1, 2009): 443–62.
Permanent Committee for Public Services. "Majlis al-khadamat fi 'am: taqrir 'an al-majlis fi 'amahu al-awwal." In *Ri'asat majlis al-wuzara'—masa'il wa-jadwal a'mal jalsat 12 Yanayir 1955*, by Egyptian Cabinet, 119–22. Gamal 'Abd al-Nasser Digital Archive/Bibliotheca Alexandrina, 1955.
Piaton, Claudine. "Architecture Patronale Dans l'Isthme de Suez (1859–1956)." *Annales Islamologiques* 50 (2016): 11–53.
Port Said governorate. "Duf'a min natijat halat izalat al-masakin al-hukumiya." Port Said governorate, April 4, 2013. http://web.archive.org/web/20181212102333/http://www.portsaid.gov.eg/eskan/Lists/List72/AllItems.aspx (Accessed October 28, 2019).
Raafat, Samir. "The Zamalek Legend 1860-1940." Egy.com, December 15, 2000.
"Rabitat mustahiqi al-awqaf al-misriya." Facebook, n.d. http://archive.is/UQe61 (Accessed December 12, 2018).
Rafe'i, Abdelrahman al-. *Muqadimat Thawrat 23 Yulyu Sanat 1952*. Cairo: Dar al-Ma'aref, 1987.
Rageh, Abouzeid. *al-'Umran al-misri*. Vol. 2. Cairo: al-Maktaba al-Akadmiya, 2008.
Rasmussen, Will. "Some Live It Up: Life on Cairo Rooftops." *Reuters*, October 1, 2007.

Reuters. "China Plans Two Million New Units of Public Housing for 2017: Xinhua." April 18, 2017.
Riad, Mahmud. "Tahdid al-manatiq al-sina'iya wa-insha' masakin al-'ummal." *Majallat al-'imara* 5, nos. 2 and 3 (1945): 13–18.
Riad, Mahmud. "Alexandria: Its Town Planning Development." *The Town Planning Review* 15, no. 4 (1933): 233–48.
Ruz al-yusuf. "Rihlat 'adhab min jahannam ila qura al-anbiya' bi-l-Fayyum." September 16, 2013.
Ruz al-yusuf. "I'fa 17 alf muta'aththir fi al-qawm li-l-iskan min fawa'id al-ta'khir." June 8, 2010.
Ruz al-yusuf. "Tajaddud al-sira' bayn rijal al-a'mal wa-l-mashahir wa-muhafiz al-Qahira 'ala ard al-Haggana." January 14, 2011.
Saad, Reem. "Peasants' Perceptions of Recent Egyptian History." DPhil diss., University of Oxford, 1994.
Sada al-balad. "*Sada al-balad* yanfarid bi-nashr tafasil mashru' al-3 alaf wihda sakaniya al-khasa bi-mashru' al-quwwat al-musallaha bi-Dahshur." December 26, 2012.
Sadat, Anwar. "Kalimat al-ra'is Muhammad Anwar al-Sadat fi al-'id al-thani li-l-thawra al-khadra' fi 29 Yanayir 1981." Anwar Sadat Digital Archive/Bibliotheca Alexandrina, January 29, 1981.
Sadat, Anwar. "Kalimat al-ra'is Muhammad Anwar al-Sadat ila rijal al-sahafa wa-l-i'lam fi 26 Yunyu 1977." Anwar Sadat Digital Archive/Bibliotheca Alexandrina, June 26, 1977.
Sadat, Anwar. "Kalimat al-ra'is Muhammad Anwar al-Sadat ila 'ummal al-naql fi 18 Yunyu 1977." Anwar Sadat Digital Archive/Bibliotheca Alexandrina, June 18, 1977.
Sadat, Anwar. "Kalimat al-ra'is Muhammad Anwar al-Sadat ila al-sha'b fi munasabat irsa' hajar asas madinat 10 Ramadan fi 29 Mayu 1977." Anwar Sadat Digital Archive/Bibliotheca Alexandrina, May 29, 1977.
Sadat, Anwar. "Message by President Anwar El Sadat to the Habitat Conference in the City of Vancouver, June 6th, 1976." Anwar Sadat Chair for Peace and Development, 1976.
al-Said, Rifa'at. *Tarikh al-haraka al-shuyu'iya al-misriya min 1940–50—al-mujallad al-thalith: tarikh al-munazzamat al-yasariya al-misriya*. Cairo: Dar al-Thaqafa al-Jadida, 1987.
al-Salamoni, Hisham. *al-Jil al-ladhi wajah 'Abd al-Nasser wa-l-Sadat*. Cairo: Dar Qiba'a, 1999.
el-Sanga, Magda. "Egypt Demolishes Vacation Homes." *Gettysburg Times*, December 16, 1981.
al-Saqqar, Waguih. "Ba'd tatbiquh bi-saba' sanawat: al-ikhla. Mushkilat qanun al-ijarat al-jadid!" *al-Ahram*, April 28, 2003.
Sawt al-umma. "Qari' yurwi tajribatih ma' mabahith al-kahraba'." May 25, 2009.

Scott, James C. *Seeing Like a State: How Certain Schemes to Improve the Human Condition Have Failed*. New Haven: Yale University Press, 1998.

Scudder, Thayer. "Evaluative Research on Human Settlements." *Workshop on Human Settlements in New Lands*, 1971.

Sejourne, Marion. "Inhabitants' Daily Practices to Obtain Legal Status for Their Homes and Security of Tenure: Egypt." In *Popular Housing and Urban Land Tenure in the Middle East: Case Studies from Egypt, Syria, Jordan, Lebanon, and Turkey*, edited by Myriam Ababsa, Baudouin Dupret, and Eric Denis, 91–110. Cairo: The American University in Cairo Press, 2012.

Selim, Gehan. *Unfinished Places: The Politics of (Re)Making Cairo's Old Quarters*. 1st ed. New York: Routledge, 2016.

al-Sisi, Abd al-Fattah. "Kalimat al-ra'is 'Abd al-Fattah al-Sisi khilal al-ihtifaliya bi-murur 60 'aman 'ala ta'mim qanat al-Suways wa murur 'am 'ala iftitah al-qanat al-jadida." Egypt State Information Service (SIS), August 6, 2016. http://web.archive.org/web/20181214084416/http://www.sis.gov.eg/Story/126118?lang=ar (Accessed October 28, 2019).

Shadow Ministry of Housing. *Badal matshiluna, tawwaruna!*, Youtube Video, 2013. https://www.youtube.com/watch?v=qrIAReY7XUI

Shadow Ministry of Housing. *Qissat mantiqat 'Izbit al-Haggana/al-Kilu Arba'a wa-Nus, al-Qahira*, Youtube Video, 2013. https://www.youtube.com/watch?v=LCUzkgS1_A0.

Shadow Ministry of Housing. "Taqrir 'an karithat 'imarat hayy al-Gumruk bi-l-Iskandariya 1/2." *Shadow Ministry of Housing* (blog). July 23, 2017. http://blog.shadowministryofhousing.org/2012/07/blog-post.html.

Shadow Ministry of Housing, EIPR, and Tactical Technology Collective. "Why are houses collapsing in Egypt?" https://egyptbuildingcollapses.org (Accessed April 16, 2018).

el Shakry, Omnia. "Cairo as Capital of Socialist Revolution?" In *Cairo Cosmopolitan: Politics, Culture, and Urban Space in the New Globalized Middle East*, 73-98. Cairo: American University in Cairo Press, 2006.

Shakur, Mohamed Abdel, Sohair Mehanna, and Nicholas S. Hopkins. "War and Forced Migration in Egypt: The Experience of Evacuation from the Suez Canal Cities (1967–1976)." *Arab Studies Quarterly* 27, no. 3 (2005): 21–39.

al-Sharq al-Awsat. "Mubarak ya'id fi jawla intikhabiya bi-l-Nubariya bi-istislah milyun faddan wa manh qurud 100 alf jinih li-kul usra." August 23, 2005.

al-Sharqawi, Hassan. "Madha yatlub al-mullak wa-l-musta'jirun wa-rijal al-qanun min al-qanun al-jadid li-l-iskan . . . ?" *al-Ahram*, January 5, 1977.

Shawkat, Yahia. "The Duweika Disaster Ten Years On – Part 1: Disaster and Aftermath." Built Environment Observatory, September 7, 2018.

Shawkat, Yahia. "A Million Units for Whom? Six Facts about the Social Housing Project." Built Environment Observatory, May 28, 2018.

Shawkat, Yahia. "Egypt State of Rent 2017." Built Environment Observatory, February 2018.
Shawkat, Yahia. "Property Market Deregulation and Informal Tenure in Egypt: A Diabolical Threat to Millions." *Architecture_MPS*, June 1, 2016.
Shawkat, Yahia. "Mubarak's Promise. Social Justice and the National Housing Programme: Affordable Homes or Political Gain?" *Egypte Monde Arabe* Troisième série, no 11, 2014, no. Ville et révolution en Égypte (2014).
Shawkat, Yahia. *"al-'Adala al-ijtima'iya wa-l-'umran—kharitat Misr,"* Shadow Ministry of Housing, 2013.
Shawkat, Yahia, and MennatuAllah Hendawy. "Myths and Facts of Urban Planning in Egypt." Built Environment Observatory, November 2016.
Shehayeb, Dina. "Advantages of Living in Informal Areas." In *Cairo's Informal Areas between Urban Challenges and Hidden Potentials*, edited by Regina Kipper and Marion Fischer, 35–43. Cairo: GTZ Egypt Participatory Development Programme in Urban Areas (PDP), 2009.
Shehayeb Consult. "Housing Relocation in Cairo." GTZ, 2010.
el-Shimi, Rowan. "10 Nabrawy Street, in Danger Again, Points to Web of Interests behind Demolitions." *Mada Masr*, July 14, 2016.
Shukrallah, Salma. "Despite Cost, 'New Rent' Leaves Tenants Wanting." Built Environment Observatory, February 26, 2018.
Shukrallah, Salma, and Yahia Shawkat. "Analysis: Government Policy Commodifies Housing." Built Environment Observatory, November 17, 2017.
al-Shuruk. "al-Bunuk tukhattit li-l-isti'ana bi-sharikat khalijiya li-taswiq usuliha al-'aqariya khilal al-mu'tamar al-iqtisadi." March 8, 2015.
al-Shuruk. "1,200 usra bi-l-Iskandiriya tuhaddid bi-l-idrab 'an al-ta'am wa-l-i'tisam fi al-shawari' i'tiradan 'ala hadm manazilihum." *al-Shuruk*. December 16, 2014.
al-Shuruk. "Shafiq: taqnin awda' al-mu'tadin 'ala al-aradi al-zira'iya (bas di akhir marra)." *al-Shuruk*. May 13, 2012.
al-Shuruk. "Nazif yusdir qararan fawriyan bi-waqf qararat izalat amlak 'a'ilat al-Sallab." *al-Shuruk*. February 17, 2010.
Simcik Arese, Nicholas. "Urbanism as Craft: Practicing Informality and Property in Cairo's Gated Suburbs, from Theft to Virtue." Annals of the American Association of Geographers 108, no. 3 (May 4, 2018): 620–37.
Sims, David. *Egypt's Desert Dreams: Development or Disaster*. Cairo: The American University in Cairo Press, 2014.
Sims, David. *Understanding Cairo: The Logic of a City Out of Control.* Cairo: The American University in Cairo Press, 2010.
Sims, David, Hazem Kamal, and Doris Solomon. "Housing Study for Urban Egypt." United States Agency for International Development (USAID), December 2008.
Sims, David, Marion Sejourne, and Monika El Shorbagi. "The Case of Cairo, Egypt." Understanding Urban Slums: Case Studies for the Global Report on Human Settlements. University College London, 2003.

Singerman, Diane. "The Siege of Imbaba, Egypt's Internal 'Other,' and the Criminalization of Politics." In *Cairo Contested: Governance, Urban Space, and Global Modernity*, 111–44. Cairo: The American University in Cairo Press, 2009.

Smith, Neil. "Gentrification and the Rent Gap." *Annals of the Association of American Geographers* 77, no. 3 (1987): 462–65.

Social Housing Fund. "Egyptians Abroad SHP Advertisment," January 18, 2018.

Social Housing Fund. "Ninth SHP Advertisment." New Urban Communities Authority (NUCA), July 24, 2017.

Social Housing Fund. "Rental SHP Advertisment." New Urban Communities Authority (NUCA), September 7, 2016.

Social Housing and Mortgage Finance Fund. "Performance Report Fiscal Year 2017/2018." Cairo: Social Housing and Mortgage Finance Fund (SHMFF), 2018.

Social Housing Fund, Guarantee and Subsidy Fund. "Taqrir al-ada' 'an nash'at sanduq al-tamwil al-'aqari wa-l-iskan al-ijtima'i hatta tarikh 30 Yunyu 2017." Cairo: Social Housing Fund, Guarantee and Subsidy Fund (GSF,SHF), 2017.

Soliman, Ahmed M. *A Possible Way Out: Formalizing Housing Informality in Egyptian Cities*. Dallas: University Press of America, 2004.

Sonbol, Amira el-Azhary. *The New Mamluks: Egyptian Society and Modern Feudalism*. Syracuse: Syracuse University Press, 2000.

South Valley Development Company. "Nubdha 'an mashru'at sharikat Janub al-Wadi." South Valley Development Company, n.d. Accessed July 17, 2018. http://archive.is/jFBMI.

Springborg, Robert. "Patrimonialism and Policy Making in Egypt: Nasser and Sadat and the Tenure Policy for Reclaimed Lands." *Middle Eastern Studies* 15, no. 1 (1979).

Springborg, Robert. "State-Society Relations in Egypt: The Debate over Owner-Tenant Relations." *Middle East Journal* 45, no. 2 (1991): 232–49.

State Information Service. "Sisi: Nobody Above Right & Law." Egypt State Information Service (SIS), May 24, 2017.

State Information Service. "1.5 Million Feddan Project." Egypt State Information Service (SIS), n.d. Accessed July 7, 2018. https://web.archive.org/web/20170614034220/http://www.sis.gov.eg/section/352/4996?lang=en-us.

Tadamun. "'Izbit Awlad 'Allam." Tadamun: Cairo Urban Solidarity Initiative, August 24, 2014.

Tadamun. "'Izbit Khayrallah and the Struggle for Land: Security of Land Tenure." Tadamun: Cairo Urban Solidarity Initiative, December 25, 2013.

Tadamun. "The Right to Democratic Local Government in the Egyptian Constitution." Tadamun: Cairo Urban Solidarity Initiative, December 5, 2013.

Tadros, Helmi. "The Human Aspects of Rural Resettlement Schemes in Egypt." In *Anthropology and Social Change in Rural Areas*, edited by Bernardo Berdichewsky, 121–48. The Hague: Mouton, 1979.

Taher, Nadia Adel. “Foreign Aid and Power Relations: The Government of Egypt, USAID and Housing in Helwan.” PhD diss. London School of Economics and Political Science, 1997.
Tawakol, Donia. “Speculative Informal Housing Provision and Its Sociospatial Impacts on Greater Cairo Areas: A Case Study on ‘El-Matareya.’” Master’s thesis, IHS, Erasmus University Rotterdam, 2015.
Tignor, Robert L. *State, Private Enterprise and Economic Change in Egypt, 1918–1952*. Princeton, New Jersey: Princeton University Press, 2017.
TIMEP. “Legislation Tracker Report.” TIMEP, September 1, 2016.
Tipple, A. Graham. “Transforming Government-Built Housing: Lessons from Developing Countries.” *Journal of Urban Technology* 6, no. 3 (1999): 17–35.
el-Tohamy, Olfat M. “Mubarak Builds Power Base on Favorable Public Opinion . . . and Vows to Put Muzzle on Egypt’s Corrupt ‘Fat Cats.’” *Christian Science Monitor*, February 17, 1982.
Trading Economics. “Egypt Government Budget—2019.” Accessed February 1, 2019.
Trading Economics. “Building Permits: Countries—List.”
Turner, John F.C. *Housing by People: Towards Autonomy in Building Environments*. 3rd ed. London: Marion Boyars, 1991.
United Nations Department of Humanitarian Affairs. “Egypt—Earthquake Oct 1992 UN DHA Situation Reports 1–9.” ReliefWeb, December 29, 1992.
United Nations Development Programme. “Egypt’s Progress Towards Millennium Development Goals.” United Nations Development Programme (UNDP) and the Ministry of Planning, Monitoring and Administrative Reform, 2015.
United Nations Educational, Scientific, and Cultural Organization. “Safeguarding Project of Hassan Fathy’s New Gourna Village, Preliminary Phase Document.” UNESCO, 2011.
United States Agency for International Development. “Egypt Affordable Home Production Program (AHPP).” Egypt Financial Services Project Technical Report. United States Agency for International Development (USAID), February 2006.
United States Agency for International Development. “A.I.D. Project Impact Evaluation Report No. 43, The Egyptian American Rural Improvement Service, A Point Four Project, 1952–63.” United States Agency for International Development (USAID), 1983.
United States Census Bureau. “Building Permits Survey—United States, 2017.
United States National Archives. “Record Group 59, Department of State, Central Files, Egypt.” University Publictaions of America, 1985.
Volait, Mercedes. *Egypt (1914–2014): Global Architecture Before Globalization*, 2014.
Volait, Mercedes. “Town Planning Schemes for Cairo Conceived by Egyptian Planners in the ‘Liberal Experiment’ Period.” *Middle Eastern Cities 1900–1950: Public Spaces and Public Spheres in Transformation* I (2000): 44–71.

Volait, Mercedes. "Réforme Sociale et Habitat Populaire: Acteurs et Formes (1848–1964)." In *Entre Réforme Sociale et Mouvement National: Identité et Modernisation En Égypte (1882–1962)*, edited by Alain Roussillon, 379–409. Cairo: CEDEJ, 1995.

Voll, Sarah P. "Egyptian Land Reclamation since the Revolution." *Middle East Journal* 34, no. 2 (1980): 127–48.

al-Wafd. "35 alf muwatin sajjalu bayanatihim khata' fi al-i'lan al-tasi' li-l-iskan al-ijtima'i." April 25, 2018.

al-Wafd. "Mumarasat al-kahraba' tuhadid nisf sukkan Shubra Khayma bi-l-habs." December 20, 2015.

Wahdan, Dalia. *Planning Egypt's New Settlements: The Politics of Spatial Inequities*. Cairo Papers. Cairo New York: The American University in Cairo Press, 2013.

al-Watan. "al-Iskandiriya. 27 alf wa 500 'aqar. Wa 100 alf qarar izala dun tanfiz." November 30, 2015.

Waterbury, John. *The Egypt of Nasser and Sadat: The Political Economy of Two Regimes*. Princeton, New Jersey: Princeton University Press, 1983.

World Bank. "Projects: Inclusive Housing Finance Program." World Bank Website, 2015. Accessed February 5, 2016.

World Bank. "Inclusive Housing Finance Program-for-Results Project—Project Appraisal Document." Washington, D.C., April 2015.

World Bank. "Projects: Affordable Mortgage Finance DPL." World Bank Website, 2009. Accessed April 4, 2018.

World Bank. "Egypt—A Framework for Housing Policy Reform in Urban Areas in Egypt." Washington D.C. June 30, 2008.

World Bank. "Egypt—Next Step Recommendations for Affordable Housing Policy and the National Housing Program: Mortgaged-Linked Subsidies And Housing Supply Considerations." June 30, 2008.

World Bank. "Egypt—Analysis of Housing Supply Mechanisms: Final Note." February 1, 2007.

World Bank. "New Land Development Project (West Nubariya)." Washington D.C., October 1980.

World Justice Project. "Rule of Law Index 2017–2018: Egypt." WJP Rule of Law Index 2017–2018, 2018.

al-Yawm al-sabi'. "Iskan al-barlaman: qanun al-tasaluh fi mukhalafat al-bina' yuwaffir li-l-dawla 300 milyar jinih." Yuwafir Lil-Dawla 300 Milyar Genieh." January 26, 2019.

al-Yawm al-sabi'. "Maqtal za'im al-fallahin al-rafidin li-bay' aradihim bi-l-Muntazah." September 23, 2009.

al-Yawm al-sabi. "Habs 14 shakhsan tashajaru bi-l-asliha al-nariya bi-sabab al-ijar al-qadim fi al-Marg." March 14, 2018.

al-Yawm al-sabi. "al-Tamwil al-'aqari: yatim istib'ad sharikat al-isti'lam hal tikrar shakawa al-muwatinin." February 26, 2018.

al-Yawm al-sabi. "al-Quwwat al-musallahha tahtal al-markaz al-awwal fi istislah aradi Sharq al-'Uwaynat." August 16, 2014.
al-Yawm al-sabi. "Muhafiz al-Wadi al-Jadid yujri i'adat qur'at shiqaq al-Awqaf ghadan." December 22, 2013.
al-Yawm al-sabi. "Bi-l-suwar, tajamhur al-alaf amam al-iskan li-hajz wihdat sakaniya." February 14, 2011.
al-Yawm al-sabi. "Musa wa-l-Khidr. Qaryatan mansiyyatan bila khadamat bi-l-Fayyum." August 9, 2010.
Yunis, Sherif. *Nida' sha'b, tarikh naqdi li-l-idiyulujiya al-nasiriya*. Cairo: Dar al-Shorouk, 2012.
Zabbal, Selim. "al-Qahira tujaddid shababha: al-ta'mir fiha 'ala qadamin wa-saq." *al-'Arabi 12* (November 1, 1959): 74–91.

INDEX

Page numbers in *italics* refer to illustrations and tables.